TURKISH

A ROUGH GUIDE DICTIONARY PHRASEBOOK

Compiled by

LEXUS

D0035517

Credits

Compiled by Lexus with Memduha Tee
Lexus Series Editor: Sally Davies
Rough Guides Phrase Book Editor: Jonathan Buckley
Rough Guides Series Editor: Mark Ellingham

First edition published in 1996 by Rough Guides Ltd,
62–70 Shorts Gardens, London WC2H 9AB.
Revised in 2000.

Distributed by the Penguin Group.

Penguin Books Ltd, 27 Wrights Lane, London W8 5TZ
Penguin Books USA Inc., 375 Hudson Street, New York 10014, USA
Penguin Books Australia Ltd, 487 Maroondah Highway,
PO Box 257, Ringwood, Victoria 3134, Australia
Penguin Books Canada Ltd, Alcorn Avenue,
Toronto, Ontario, Canada M4V 1E4
Penguin Books (NZ) Ltd, 182–190 Wairau Road,
Auckland 10, New Zealand

Typeset in Bembo and Helvetica to an original design by Henry Iles.
Printed in Spain by Graphy Cems.

British Library Cataloguing in Publication Data
A catalogue for this book is available from the British Library.

ISBN 1-85828-751-0

HELP US GET IT RIGHT

Lexus and Rough Guides have made great efforts to be accurate and
informative in this Rough Guide Turkish phrasebook. However, if you feel
we have overlooked a useful word or phrase, or have any other
comments to make about the book, please let us know. All contributors
will be acknowledged and the best letters will be rewarded with a free
Rough Guide phrasebook of your choice. Please write to 'Turkish
Phrasebook Update', at either Shorts Gardens (London) or Hudson Street
(New York) – for full addresses see above. Alternatively you can email us at
mail@roughguides.co.uk

Online information about Rough Guides can be found at our website
www.roughguides.com

CONTENTS

Introduction   5

Basics

Pronunciation 9

Abbreviations 10

The Turkish Alphabet 10

Suffixes 11

Vowel Harmony 11

Articles 12

Nouns 13

Cases 14

Adjectives 18

Possessive Suffixes 20

Demonstratives; Pronouns 23

Verbs 26

Questions; Also, Too 39

Can, to be able 40

Dates 41

Days; Months; Time 42

Numbers 43

Basic Phrases 44

Conversion Tables 46

English - Turkish   49

Turkish - English   158

Menu Reader

Food 240

Drink 258

Introduction

The Rough Guide Turkish dictionary phrasebook is a highly practical introduction to the contemporary language. Laid out in clear A-Z style, it uses key-word referencing to lead you straight to the words and phrases you want – so if you need to book a room, just look up 'room'. The Rough Guide gets straight to the point in every situation, in bars and shops, on trains and buses, and in hotels and banks.

The main part of the Rough Guide is a double dictionary: English-Turkish then Turkish-English. Before that, there's a section called Basics, which sets out the fundamental rules of the language, with plenty of practical examples. You'll also find here other essentials like numbers, dates, telling the time and basic phrases.

Forming the heart of the guide, the English-Turkish section gives easy-to-use transliterations of the Spanish words wherever pronunciation might be a problem, and to get you involved quickly in two-way communication, the Rough Guide includes dialogues featuring typical responses on key topics – such as renting a car and asking directions. Feature boxes fill you in on cultural pitfalls as well as the simple mechanics of how to make a phone call, what to do in an emergency, where to change money, and more. Throughout this section, cross-references enable you to pinpoint key facts and phrases, while asterisked words indicate where further information can be found in the Basics.

In the Turkish-English dictionary, we've given not just the phrases you're likely to hear (starting with a selection of slang and colloquialisms), but also many of the signs, labels, instructions and other basic words you may come across in print or in public places.

Finally the Rough Guide rounds off with an extensive Menu Reader. Consisting of food and drink sections (each starting with a list of essential terms), it's indispensable whether you're eating out, stopping for a quick drink, or browsing through a local food market.

iyi yolculuklar!
have a good trip!

Basics

Pronunciation

In this phrasebook, the Turkish has been written in a system of imitated pronunciation so that it can be read as though it were English, bearing in mind the notes on pronunciation given below:

a	as in f**a**r
ay	as in m**ay**
e/eh	as in g**e**t
ew	as in f**ew**
g	always hard as in **g**oat
H	a harsh 'ch' as in the Scottish way of pronouncing lo**ch**
ī	'i' as in m**i**ght
J	's' as in mea**s**ure
o	as in h**o**t
oh	'o' as in **o**pen
s	always 's' as in dre**ss** (never 'z')
uh	'u' as in b**u**t
y	as in **y**es

Letters given in bold type indicate the part of the word to be stressed (although the stress is not heavy). In most cases, the stress is on the end of a word.

As i and u are always pronounced 'ee' and 'oo' in Turkish, pronunciation has not been given for words containing these letters unless they present other problems for the learner.

Turkish Pronunciation

a	as in f**a**r
â	as in L**a**tin
ay	'i' as in m**i**ght
c	'j' as in **j**elly
ç	'ch' as in **ch**at
e	as in 'g**e**t'

ey	'ay' as in m**ay**
g	always hard as in '**g**oat'
ğ	generally silent, but lengthens the preceding vowel
h	sometimes pronounced 'h' as in **h**en; occasionally pronounced 'ch' as in the Scottish pronunciation of lo**ch**
ı	'u' as in b**u**t
i	'ee' as in 'n**ee**d'
j	's' as in 'mea**s**ure'
o	as in 'h**o**t'; sometimes 'o' as in **o**pen (usually when followed by **g***)
ö	'ur' as in b**u**rn (like German 'ö')
öy	'uh-i' run together quickly as one sound
s	's' as in dre**ss** (never 'z')
ş	'sh' as in **sh**ape
u	'u' as in p**u**ll, transcribed as 'oo' in the pronunciation
ü	'ew' as in f**ew** (like French 'u' and German 'ü')

When e occurs at the end of a Turkish word, it is always pronounced, for example bile (already) is pronounced [beel**eh**].

Abbreviations

abl	ablative		loc	locative
acc	accusative		nom	nominative
adj	adjective		pl	plural
dat	dative		pol	polite
fam	familiar		sing	singular
gen	genitive			

The Turkish alphabet

The Turkish-English section and Menu Reader are in Turkish alphabetical order which is as follows:

a, b, c, ç, d, e, f, g, ğ, h, ı, i, j, k, l, m, n, o, ö, p, r, s, ş, t, u, ü, v, y, z

Suffixes

One very special feature of Turkish is that endings or suffixes are added to words where in the equivalent English separate words would be used. In Turkish, for example, all prepositions and possessive adjectives are suffixes and some verbal structures are made up of a stem and suffixes. In the Turkish-English section of this book, suffixes have been listed as separate entries, for example: **-da** (in).

> **oda-m-da**
> oda**md**a
> in my room
> (literally: room-my-in)

> **şehir-de**
> sheh-heerd**eh**
> in the city
> (literally: city-in)

Vowel harmony

Vowels in Turkish fall into two categories: hard vowels (**a**, **ı**, **o**, **u**) and soft vowels (**e**, **i**, **ö** and **ü**). Vowel harmony simply means that if the final vowel of a word is a hard vowel, any suffix added to the word will also contain hard vowels, and if the final vowel is a soft vowel, any suffix will contain only soft vowels:

final vowel in a word	can only be followed by
a or **ı**	**a** or **ı**
o or **u**	**a** or **u**
e or **i**	**e** or **i**
ö or **ü**	**e** or **ü**

For example:

dükkan dewkk**a**n shop	**İngiltere** eengeelt**e**reh England
dükkana dewkkan**a** to the shop	**İngiltere'den** eengeelt**e**reh-den from England
kapı kap**uh** door	**gemi** gem**ee** ship
kapıya kapuh-y**a** to the door	**gemiye** gemee-y**eh** to the ship
havuz hav**oo**z pool	**otobüs** otob**ew**s bus
havuzda havoozd**a** in the pool	**otobüste** otobewst**eh** in the bus

Articles

The indefinite article (a, an) is the same as the word for 'one' **bir**:

bir bardak çay beer bard**a**k ch**ī** a glass of tea	**bir otel odası** beer ot**e**l odas**uh** a hotel room
balkonlu bir oda balkonl**oo** beer od**a** a room with a balcony	**Türkiye hakkında bir film** t**ew**rkee-yeh hakkuhnd**a** beer feelm a film about Turkey

In phrases with an adjective, **bir** usually comes between the adjective and the noun:

büyük bir başarı
bewy**ewk** beer bashar**uh**
a great success

bize başka bir oda verebilir misiniz?
beez**eh** bashk**a** beer od**a** verebeel**eer** meeseen**eez**
can we have another room?

In Turkish, there is no separate word for the definite article (the):

yönetici	**yemek listesi**
yurneteej**ee**	yem**ek** leestes**ee**
manager/the manager	menu/the menu

The context will indicate whether 'the' is meant in English:

yöneticiyi görebilir miyim?
yurneteejee-y**ee** gurebeel**eer** mee-y**ee**m
can I see the manager?

yemek listesini görebilir miyim?
yem**ek** leesteseen**ee** gurebeel**eer** mee-y**ee**m
may I see the menu?

Nouns

Gender

Turkish nouns do not have genders.

Plural Nouns

To make a noun plural, add the ending **-ler** or **-lar** depending on whether the final vowel of the noun is a soft or a hard vowel:

	after hard vowels	after soft vowels
	a, ı, o, u	e, i, ö, ü
add	-lar	-ler

müze	**müzeler**	**minare**	**minareler**
mewz**eh**	mewzel**er**	meenar**eh**	meenarel**er**
museum	museums	minaret	minarets

tren	**trenler**
train	trains

çarşı	**çarşılar**	**çocuk**	**çocuklar**
charsh**uh**	charshuhl**ar**	choj**ook**	chojookl**ar**
market	markets	child	children

numara	**numaralar**
number	numbers

As a rule, plurals are used in Turkish only if there is no other indication of plurality such as a number or a word like 'a few', 'a lot' etc:

köpek	**iki köpek**
kurp**ek**	eek**ee** kurp**ek**
(the) dog	two dogs

birkaç köpek	**köpekler havlıyor**
beerk**ach** kurp**ek**	kurpekl**er** havl**uh**-yor
some dogs,	the dogs are barking
a couple of dogs	

In greetings and expressions of good wishes a plural is used in Turkish when the singular is used in English:

iyi akşamlar	**iyi geceler**
ee-y**ee** akshaml**ar**	ee-y**ee** gejel**er**
good evening	good night
(literally: good evenings)	(literally: good nights)

Cases

Turkish has six cases: nominative, accusative, genitive, dative, locative and ablative. These are all formed using suffixes. The

table on page 17 shows the endings for each case, examples
of which are given below.

Nominative Case

The nominative is the case of the subject of the sentence.
The nominative is the case in which nouns are given in the
English-Turkish section of this book. In the following
examples **dükkan** and **Ahmed** are in the nominative:

dükkan şimdi açık
dewkkan sheemdee achuhk
the shop is open now

Ahmed bugün geldi
aнmed bewgewn geldee
Ahmed arrived today

Accusative Case

The object of most verbs takes the accusative. In the following examples the object (e.g. Topkapi Palace) is in the
accusative:

Topkapı Sarayı'nı görmeye gittik
topkapuh sarī-**uh** gurmay**eh** geett**eek**
we went to see the Topkapi Palace

bavulumu gördünüz mü?
bavooloom**oo** gurdewn**ewz** mew
did you see my suitcase?

telefonu kullanabilir miyim?
may I use the phone?

Genitive Case

The genitive is used to indicate possession:

babamın evi
babam**uhn** ev**ee**
my father's house

Mustafa'nın annesi
moostafa-n**uhn** annes**ee**
Mustafa's mother

pilotun üniformaş
peelot**oon** ewneeformas**uh**
the pilot's uniform

There is no one word for 'of' in Turkish. The genitive suffix is used to translate 'of':

otelin adı
oteleen aduh
the name of the hotel

biletin fiyatı
beeleteen fee-yatuh
the price of the ticket

Dative Case

The dative is used for indirect objects with verbs like 'to give' and 'to send'. It often corresponds to 'to' (as in 'to me') in English:

anneme biraz lokum aldım
annemeh beeraz lokoom alduhm
I've bought my mother some Turkish delight

kitabı ona verdim
keetabuh ona verdeem
I gave the book to him

Locative Case

The locative is used to express position:

odada
odada
in the room

Türkiye'de
tewrkee-yeh-deh
in Turkey

Ablative Case

The ablative is used to indicate a point of origin in space or time and corresponds to the English 'from':

evden
from the house

istasyondan
from the station

dokuzdan beşe
dokoozdan besheh
from nine to five

The following table shows the endings for each case. The endings are regular apart from some consonant changes (see page 18). The rules of vowel harmony (see page 11) apply:

words ending in a consonant

final vowel	e or i	a or ı	o or u	ö or ü
nom	bez cloth	bar bar	koy cove	göz eye
acc	bez-i	bar-ı	koy-u	göz-ü
	bezee	baruh	koy-oo	gurzew
gen	bez-in	bar-ın	koy-un	göz-ün
	bezeen	baruhn	koy-oon	gurzewn
dat	bez-e	bar-a	koy-a	göz-e
	bezeh	bara	koy-a	gurzeh
loc	bez-de	bar-da	koy-da	göz-de
	bezdeh	barda	koyda	gurzdeh
abl	bez-den	bar-dan	koy-dan	göz-den
	bezden	bardan	koydan	gurzden

words ending in a vowel

final vowel	e or i	a or ı	o or u	ö or ü
nom	ülke country	masa table	boru pipe	ütü iron
acc	ülke-yi	masa-yı	boru-yu	ütü-yü
	ewlkeh-yee	masī-uh	boroo-yoo	ewtewyew
gen	ülke-nin	masa-nın	boru-nun	ütü-nün
	ewlkeneen	masanuhn	boroonoon	ewtewnewn
dat	ülke-ye	masa-ya	boru-ya	ütü-ye
	ewlkeh-yeh	masī-a	boroo-ya	ewtew-yeh
loc	ülke-de	masa-da	boru-da	ütü-de
	ewlkedeh	masada	borooda	ewtewdeh
abl	ülke-den	masa-dan	boru-dan	ütü-den
	ewlkeden	masadan	boroodan	ewtewden

nom **banka yakın mı?**
banka yakuhn muh
is the bank nearby?

acc **bankayı arıyorum**
bankī-uh aruh-yoroom
I am looking for the bank

gen **bankanın kapış**
bankanuhn kapuhsuh
the door of the bank

dat **karım bankaya gitti**
karuhm bankī-a geettee
my wife went to the bank

loc **bankada**
bankada
in the bank

abl **bankadan aldım**
bankadan alduhm
I got it from the bank

consonant changes

	k → ğ	p → b	ç → c	k → g	t → d
nom	köpek	dolap	amaç	kepenk	kurt
	dog	cupboard	purpose	shutter	wolf
acc	köpeğ-i	dolab-ı	amac-ı	kepeng-i	kurd-u
	kurpeh-**ee**	dolab**uh**	amaj**uh**	kepeng**ee**	koord**oo**
gen	köpeğ-in	dolab-ın	amac-ın	kepeng-in	kurd-un
	kurpeh-**een**	dolab**uhn**	amaj**uhn**	kepeng**een**	koord**oon**
dat	köpeğ-e	dolab-a	amac-a	kepeng-e	kurd-a
	kurpeh-**eh**	dolab**a**	amaj**a**	kepeng**eh**	koord**a**
loc	köpek-te	dolap-ta	amaç-ta	kepenk-te	kurt-ta
	kurpek**teh**	dolap**ta**	amach**ta**	kepenk**teh**	koort**ta**
abl	köpek-ten	dolap-tan	amaç-tan	kepenk-ten	kurt-tan
	kurpek**ten**	dolap**tan**	amach**tan**	kepenk**ten**	koort**tan**

However, if the final letter of a word is ç, f, h, k, p, d, ş, or t, the locative and ablative case endings will take **t** instead of **d**:

mutfakta	Sinop'tan	New York'tan
in the kitchen	from Sinop	from New York

Plural endings **-lar** and **-ler** are added to the word before case endings:

odalarda	çıkış kapılarına
in the rooms	to the exits

pencerelerden	yolcuların
from the windows	of the passengers

Adjectives

Adjectives do not change according to case:

kırmızı otobüs dışarıda
kurmuhz**uh** otob**ew**s duhsharuhd**a**
the red bus is outside

kırmızı otobüsü gördün mü?
kuhrmuhz**uh** otobews**ew** gurd**ew**n mew
did you see the red bus?

kırmızı otobüsten indi
kurmuhz**uh** otobews**ten** eend**ee**
he got out of the red bus

The indefinite article **bir** usually comes between the adjective and noun:

pahalı bir otel	**güzel bir kadın**	**uslu bir çocuk**
pahal**uh** b**ee**r otel	gewz**el** beer kad**uhn**	oosl**oo** beer choj**oo**k
an expensive hotel	a beautiful woman	a well-behaved child

It is also acceptable for **bir** to precede the adjective, but this form is much less common:

bir uzun ağaç
beer ooz**oo**n a-**a**ch
a tall tree

Comparatives

To form the comparative, place **daha** 'more' before the adjective:

daha pahalı	**daha yüksek**
dah**a** pahal**uh**	dah**a** yewks**ek**
more expensive	higher

To translate 'more... than' or '...-er than', add the ablative case suffixes (**-den** or **-dan**) to the noun (**daha** is optional):

İngiltere'den şıcak	**babamdan daha uzun**
eengeelt**ereh-den** suhj**ak**	babamd**an** dah**a** ooz**oo**n
warmer than England	taller than my father

Superlatives

To translate the superlative, use the word **en**:

bu en ilginç	en ucuz oda
boo en eelge**een**ch	en oo**joo**z o**da**
this is the most interesting	the cheapest room, the least expensive room

Adverbs

Most Turkish adjectives can be used as adverbs:

kötü	iyi	iyi uyudunuz mu?
kur**tew**	ee-y**ee**	ee-y**ee** oo-yoodoon**ooz** moo
bad/badly	good/well	did you sleep well?

Possessive Suffixes

Instead of possessive adjectives, Turkish uses suffixes or endings which are added to nouns to indicate possession. There are also possessive adjectives (i.e. as separate words) in Turkish, but these are generally used for special emphasis. The possessive suffixes must also follow the rules of vowel harmony (see page 11).

words ending in a consonant

final vowel

e or i	a or ı	o or u	ö or ü	
el hand	**baş** head	**boy** height	**göz** eye	
el-im	baş-ım	boy-um	göz-üm	my
el**eem**	bash**uhm**	boy-**oom**	gurz**ewm**	
el-in	baş-ın	boy-un	göz-ün	your (sing, fam)
el**een**	bash**uhn**	boy-**oon**	gurz**ewn**	
el-i	baş-ı	boy-u	göz-ü	his/her/its
el**ee**	bash**uh**	boy-**oo**	gurz**ew**	
el-imiz	baş-ımız	boy-umuz	göz-ümüz	our
el**eemeez**	bashuhm**uhz**	boy-oom**ooz**	gurzewm**ewz**	
el-iniz	baş-ınız	boy-unuz	göz-ünüz	your (pl or pol)
el**eeneez**	bashuhn**uhz**	boy-oon**ooz**	gurzewn**ewz**	
el-leri	baş-ları	boy-ları	göz-leri	their
el**leree**	bashlar**uh**	boylar**uh**	gurzler**ee**	

words ending in a vowel

final vowel

e or i	a or ı	o or u	ö or ü	
dede	araba	soru	ütü	
grandfather	car	question	iron	
dede-m	araba-m	soru-m	ütü-m	my
dedem	arabam	soroom	ewtewm	
dede-n	araba-n	soru-n	ütü-n	your (sing, fam)
deden	araban	soroon	ewtewn	
dede-si	araba-şı	soru-su	ütü-sü	his/her/its
dedesee	arabasuh	soroosoo	ewtewsew	
dede-miz	araba-mız	soru-muz	ütü-müz	our
dedemeez	arabamuhz	soroomooz	ewtewmewz	
dede-niz	araba-nız	soru-nuz	ütü-nüz	your (pl or pol)
dedeneez	arabanuhz	soroonooz	ewtewnewz	
dede-leri	araba-ları	soru-ları	ütü-leri	their
dedeleree	arabalaruh	soroolaruh	ewtewleree	

consonant changes

k → ğ	p → b	ç → c	
köpek dog	dolap cupboard	amaç purpose	
köpeğ-im	dolab-ım	amac-ım	my
kurpeh-eem	dolabuhm	amajuhm	
köpeğ-in	dolab-ın	amac-ın	your (sing, fam)
kurpeh-een	dolabuhn	amajuhn	
köpeğ-i	dolab-ı	amac-ı	his/her/its
kurpeh-ee	dolabuh	amajuh	
köpeğ-imiz	dolab-ımız	amac-ımız	our
kurpeh-eemeez	dolabuhmuhz	amajuhmuhz	
köpeğ-iniz	dolab-ınız	amac-ınız	your (pl or pol)
kurpeh-eeneez	dolabuhnuhz	amajuhnuhz	
köpek-leri	dolapları	amaçları	their
kurpekleree	dolaplaruh	amachlaruh	

k → g	t → d	
kepenk shutter	**kurt** wolf	
kepeng-im	**kurd-um**	my
kepengeem	koordoom	
kepeng-in	**kurd-un**	your (sing, fam)
kepengeen	koordoon	
kepeng-i	**kurd-u**	his/her/its
kepengee	koordoo	
kepeng-imiz	**kurd-umuz**	our
kepengeemeez	koordoomooz	
kepeng-iniz	**kurd-unuz**	your (pl or pol)
kepengeeneez	koordoonooz	
kepenk-leri	**kurt-ları**	their
kepenkleree	koortlaruh	

sırt çantam	**kız arkadaşım**	**odanız**
suhrt chantam	kuhz arkadashuhm	odanuhz
my backpack	my girlfriend	your room

defterim ve kalemim
deftereem veh kalemeem
my notebook and my pen

The possessive adjectives as follows are used for special emphasis:

benim	[beneem]	my
senin	[seneen]	your (sing, fam)
onun	[onoon]	his/her/its
bizim	[beezeem]	our
sizin	[seezeen]	your (pl or pol)
onların	[onlaruhn]	their

benim biletim ucuzdu	**senin odan rahat**
MY ticket was cheap	YOUR room is comfortable

The plural suffixes **-ler** and **-lar** precede the possessive suffix:

oda-lar-ınız bu katta
odalaruhn**uh**z boo k**a**tta
your rooms are on this floor

bilet-ler-imiz
beeletlereem**eez**
our tickets

All other suffixes are added after the possessive suffixes:

otel-im-de
oteleemd**eh**
in my hotel

ad-ı-nı bilmiyorum
aduhn**uh** b**ee**lmee-yoroom
I don't know his name

çanta-nız-a koyabilirsiniz
chantanuhz**a** koy-abeeleerseen**eez**
you can put it in your bag

Demonstratives

Demonstrative adjectives and pronouns are as follows:

bu	[boo]	this (near the speaker)
şu	[shoo]	that (just over there)
o	[o]	that (over there, out of sight)

Pronouns

Personal Pronouns

nom	ben	[ben]	I
	sen	[sen]	you (sing, fam)
	o	[o]	he/she/it
	biz	[beez]	we
	siz	[seez]	you (pl or pol)
	onlar	[onlar]	they
acc	beni	[ben**ee**]	me
	seni	[sen**ee**]	you (sing, fam)
	onu	[on**oo**]	him/her/it
	bizi	[beez**ee**]	us
	sizi	[seez**ee**]	you (pl or pol)
	onları	[onlar**uh**]	them

23

gen	benim	[beneem]	of me
	senin	[seneen]	of you (sing, fam)
	onun	[onoon]	of him/her/it
	bizim	[beezeem]	of us
	sizin	[seezeen]	of you (pl or pol)
	onların	[onlaruhn]	of them

dat	bana	[bana]	to me
	sana	[sana]	to you (sing, fam)
	ona	[ona]	to him/her/it
	bize	[beezeh]	to us
	size	[seezeh]	to you (pl or pol)
	onlara	[onlara]	to them

loc	bende	[bendeh]	in me
	sende	[sendeh]	in you (sing, fam)
	onda	[onda]	in him/her/it
	bizde	[beezdeh]	in us
	sizde	[seezdeh]	in you (pl or pol)
	onlarda	[onlarda]	in them

abl	benden	[benden]	from me
	senden	[senden]	from you (sing, fam)
	ondan	[ondan]	from him/her/it
	bizden	[beezden]	from us
	sizden	[seezden]	from you (pl or pol)
	onlardan	[onlardan]	from them

Personal pronouns are usually omitted as verb endings make it clear who is being referred to:

çok meşgul	**Ankara'ya gidiyorum**
chok meshgool	ankara-ya geedee-yoroom
he/she is very busy	I am going to Ankara

However, they can be retained for emphasis:

ben oradaydım, ama o yoktu
ben oradīduhm ama o yoktoo
I was there, but HE/SHE wasn't

o haklı, sen haksızsın

o hakl**uh** sen haksuhzs**uh**n

HE/SHE is in the right, YOU are in the wrong

'You'

There are two ways of saying 'you' in Turkish. **Sen** is the singular, familiar form and it is used to address a relative, a close friend or a child; it is also used among young people, even if they don't know each other well. **Siz** is the singular, polite or plural form, and it is used to address someone the speaker doesn't know well or to address more than one person.

Emphatic Pronouns

kendim	myself
kendin	yourself (sing, fam)
kendi	himself/herself/itself
kendimiz	ourselves
kendiniz	yourselves (pl or pol)
kendileri	themselves

bavulumu kendim taşıyabilirim

bavooloom**oo** kend**eem** tashuh-yabeeleer**eem**

I can carry my suitcase myself

kendimiz yaptık

kendeem**eez** yapt**uhk**

we made it ourselves

Possessive Pronouns

benimki	[beneemk**ee**]	mine
seninki	[seneenk**ee**]	yours (sing, fam)
onunki	[onoonk**ee**]	his/hers/its
bizimki	[beezeemk**ee**]	ours
sizinki	[seezeenk**ee**]	yours (pl or pol)
onlarınki	[onlaruhnk**ee**]	theirs

onunki benimkinden iyi

onoonk**ee** beneemkeend**en** ee-y**ee**

his is better than mine

oteliniz pahalı mı? Bizimki değil

oteleen**eez** pahal**uh** muh? beezeemk**ee** deh-**eel**

is your hotel expensive? Ours isn't

In English, questions like 'Does this belong to me/you etc?' can be reformulated as 'Is this mine/yours etc?', using possessive pronouns. In Turkish, however, possessive adjectives (without the suffix **ki**) are used in these cases:

bu bavul sizin mi?	hayır, onun
boo bav**oo**l seez**ee**n mee	hī-**uhr** on**oo**n
is this suitcase yours?	no, it's his

Verbs

Verbs are always at the end of a sentence. All Turkish verbs are regular, except for the consonant change **d → t** (see page 29).

Present Progressive Tense

The present progressive tense corresponds to 'I am leaving' in English. To form the present progressive tense, remove the last three letters of the verb and add the appropriate endings.

The present progressive tense has four endings. First person singular endings are:

after verb stems with the final vowel

e or i	-iyorum	o or u	-uyorum
a or ı	-ıyorum	ö or ü	-üyorum

final vowel in stem

e or i	a or ı	o or u	ö or ü
gel-mek	kal-mak	koy-mak	düşün-mek
to come	to stay	to put	to think
gel-iyorum	kal-ıyorum	koy-uyorum	düşün-üyorum
gel-iyorsun	kal-ıyorsun	koy-uyorsun	düşün-üyorsun
gel-iyor	kal-ıyor	koy-uyor	düşün-üyor
gel-iyoruz	kal-ıyoruz	koy-uyoruz	düşün-üyoruz
gel-iyorsunuz	kal-ıyorsunuz	koy-uyorsunuz	düşün-üyorsunuz
gel-iyorlar	kal-ıyorlar	koy-uyorlar	düşün-üyorlar

verb stem ends in a vowel

e or i	a or ı	o or u	ö or ü
elle-mek	atla-mak	oku-mak	yürü-mek
to touch	to jump	to read	to walk
ell-iyorum	atl-ıyorum	oku-yorum	yürü-yorum
ell-iyorsun	atl-ıyorsun	oku-yorsun	yürü-yorsun
ell-iyor	atl-ıyor	oku-yor	yürü-yor
ell-iyoruz	atl-ıyoruz	oku-yoruz	yürü-yoruz
ell-iyorsunuz	atl-ıyorsunuz	oku-yorsunuz	yürü-yorsunuz
ell-iyorlar	atl-ıyorlar	oku-yorlar	yürü-yorlar

Since two vowels together sound awkward in Turkish, in the case of stems ending in **e** or **a** the final vowel of the stem is omitted. In the case of stems ending in **u** or **ü** the first vowel of the ending is omitted.

In Turkish, the present progressive is also used for mental functions and emotions which in English are expressed in the simple present:

> **cevabı biliyorum**
> jevab**uh** beel**ee**-yoroom
> I know the answer

> **Tanrı'ya inanıyorum**
> tanruh-y**a** eenan**uh**-yoroom
> I believe in God

> **seni seviyorum**
> sen**ee** sev**ee**-yoroom
> I love you

Simple Present Tense

The simple present tense corresponds to 'I leave'. It is used to describe actions carried out habitually and regularly as well as for general statements, requests and promises.

The simple present tense has six endings. First person singular endings are:

after verb stems with the final vowel

e or i	-irim or -erim	o or u	-arım or -urum
a or ı	-ırım or -arım	ö or ü	-erim or -ürüm

27

If the verb stem ends in a vowel, the first vowel of the ending is omitted.

final vowel in stem

e or i	a or ı	o or u	ö or ü
gel-mek	kal-mak	koy-mak	düşün-mek
to come	to stay	to put	to think
gel-irim	kal-ırım	koy-arım	düşün-ürüm
gel-irsin	kal-ırsın	koy-arsın	düşün-ürsün
gel-ir	kal-ır	koy-ar	düşün-ür
gel-iriz	kal-ırız	koy-arız	düşün-ürüz
gel-irsiniz	kal-ırsınız	koy-arsınız	düşün-ürsünüz
gel-irler	kal-ırlar	koy-arlar	düşün-ürler

verb stem ends in a vowel

e or i	a or ı	o or u	ö or ü
dene-mek	atla-mak	koru-mak	yürü-mek
to try	to jump	to protect	to walk
dene-rim	atla-rım	koru-rum	yürü-rüm
dene-rsin	atla-rsın	koru-rsun	yürü-rsün
dene-r	atla-r	koru-r	yürü-r
dene-riz	atla-rız	koru-ruz	yürü-rüz
dene-rsiniz	atla-rsınız	koru-rsunuz	yürü-rsünüz
dene-rler	atla-rlar	koru-rlar	yürü-rler

babam çok okur
babam chok okoor
my father reads a lot

biraz daha alır mısınız?
beeraz daha aluhr muhsuhnuhz
would you like some more?

sonra öderim
sonra urdereem
I'll pay later

Past Tense

The past tense has four endings. First person singular endings are:

after verb stems with the final vowel

e or i	-dim		o or u	-dum
a or ı	-dım		ö or ü	-düm

final vowel in verb stem

e or i	a or ı	o or u	ö or ü
gel-mek	kal-mak	oku-mak	düşün-mek
to come	to stay	to read	to think
gel-dim	kal-dım	oku-dum	düşün-düm
gel-din	kal-dın	oku-dun	düşün-dün
gel-di	kal-dı	oku-du	düşün-dü
gel-dik	kal-dık	oku-duk	düşün-dük
gel-diniz	kal-dınız	oku-dunuz	düşün-dünüz
gel-diler	kal-dılar	oku-dular	düşün-düler

Consonant Changes: Verbs

If the final consonant in the verb stem is **ç, f, h, k, p, s, ş** or **t**, then the **d** in the past tense changes to a **t**:

aç-tım	[ach**tuh**m]	I opened or I have opened
çık-tı	[chuhk**tuh**]	he went out or he has gone out
it-tim	[itt**eem**]	I pushed or I have pushed

Imperfect Tense

This tense is used to describe an action that was taking place in the past or something that went on over a period of time (e.g. 'at that time I was living in Turkey'). To form the imperfect, take the verb stem and add the following endings:

iç-iyor-dum	I was drinking
iç-iyor-dun	you were drinking
iç-iyor-du	he/she/it was drinking
iç-iyor-duk	we were drinking
iç-iyor-dunuz	you were drinking
iç-iyor-lardı	they were drinking

Future Tense

The future tense has four endings. First person singular endings are:

after verb stems with the final vowel

e or i, ö or ü   -yeceğim or -eceğim
a or ı, o or u   -acağım or -yacağım

final vowel in verb stem

ending in a consonant		ending in a vowel	
e, i, ö or ü	a, ı, o or u	e, i, ö or ü	a, ı, o or u
içmek	kalmak	denemek	okumak
to drink	to stay	to try	to read
iç-eceğim	kal-acağım	dene-yeceğim	oku-yacağım
iç-eceksin	kal-acaksın	dene-yeceksin	oku-yacaksın
iç-ecek	kal-acak	dene-yecek	oku-yacak
iç-eceğiz	kal-acağız	dene-yeceğiz	oku-yacağız
iç-eceksiniz	kal-acaksınız	dene-yeceksiniz	oku-yacaksınız
iç-ecekler	kal-acaklar	dene-yecekler	oku-yacaklar

If the final vowel of the verb stem is **e** it is sometimes changed into **i**:

> **de-mek** to say
> **di-yecek** he will say

Present Tense of 'To Be'

The Turkish equivalent of the present tense of the verb 'to be' is formed by using suffixes which are attached to the adjective or noun and which follow the rules of vowel harmony:

final vowel if word ends in a consonant

e or i	a or ı	o or u	ö or ü	
Ingiliz	Fransız	uzun	üzgün	
English	French	tall	sad/sorry	
-im	-ım	-um	-üm	I am
-sin	-sın	-sun	-sün	you are (sing, fam)
-dir*	-dır*	-dur*	-dür*	he/she/it is
-iz	-ız	-uz	-üz	we are
-siniz	-sınız	-sunuz	-sünüz	you are (pl or pol)
-ler	-lar	-lar	-ler	they are

* These endings are omitted in spoken Turkish.

final vowel if word ends in a vowel

e or i	a or ı	o or u	ö or ü	
iyi	kısa	kuru	örtülü	
well	short	dry	covered	
-yim	-yım	-yum	-yüm	I am
-sin	-sın	-sun	-sün	you are (sing, fam)
-dir*	-dır*	-dur*	-dür*	he/she/it is
-yiz	-yız	-yuz	-yüz	we are
-siniz	-sınız	-sunuz	-sünüz	you are (pl or pol)
-ler	-lar	-lar	-ler	they are

* These endings are omitted in spoken Turkish.

Ingilizim	çok naziksiniz	kırmızı
eengeel**ee**zeem	chok naz**ee**kseeneez	kuhrmuhz**uh**
I am English	you are very kind	(it's) red

The following consonant changes take place when a suffix beginning with a vowel is added:

words ending in	change to
k	ğ
p	b
ç	c
t	d

Past Tense of 'To Be'

The past tense of 'to be' is formed by adding one of the suffixes below to the adjective or noun, following the rules of vowel harmony:

final vowel if word ends in a consonant

e or i	a or ı	o or u	ö or ü	
bitkin	kızgın	yorgun	üzgün	
exhausted	angry	tired	sad/sorry	
-dim	-dım	-dum	-düm	I was
-din	-dın	-dun	-dün	you were (sing, fam)
-di	-dı	-du	-dü	he/she/it was
-dik	-dık	-duk	-dük	we were
-diniz	-dınız	-dunuz	-dünüz	you were (pl or pol)
-diler	-dılar	-dular	-düler	they were

final vowel if word ends in a vowel

e or i	a or ı	o or u	ö or ü	
iyi	hasta	mutlu	açgözlü	
well	unwell	happy	greedy	
-ydim	-ydım	-ydum	-ydüm	I was
-ydin	-ydın	-ydun	-ydün	you were (sing, fam)
-ydi	-ydı	-ydu	-ydü	he/she/it was
-ydik	-ydık	-yduk	-ydük	we were
-ydiniz	-ydınız	-ydunuz	-ydünüz	you were (pl or pol)
-ydiler	-ydılar	-ydular	-ydüler	they were

kızgın-dım
kuhzguhnd**uh**m
I was angry

çekici-ydi
chekeej**ee**-idee
she was attractive

yeşil-di
yesh**ee**ldee
it was green

heyecanlıydık
hayejanluh-id**uh**k
we were excited

If the final letter of an adjective is ç, f, h, k, p, s, ş or t, then the d of the past tense changes to t:

aç-tım
achtuhm
I was hungry

boş-tu
boshtoo
it was empty

Present Tense of 'To Have'

The Turkish equivalent of the present tense of the verb 'to have' is formed by attaching possessive suffixes to the noun and adding **var** to the end of the sentence to mean 'have' and **yok** to mean 'have not':

(benim) biletim var
beneem beeleteem var
I have a ticket

(onun) parası yok
onoon parasuh yok
he has no money

(bizim) vaktimiz yok
beezeem vakteemeez yok
we don't have time

(sizin) rezervasyonunuz var mı?
seezeen reservas-yonoonooz var muh
do you have a reservation?

Past Tense of 'To Have'

This is formed in the same way as the present except that the past tense ending -dı is added to **var** and -tu is added to **yok**:

(benim) biletim vardı
beneem beeleteem varduh
I had a ticket

(onun) parası yoktu
onoon parasuh yoktoo
he had no money

(bizim) vaktimiz yoktu
beezeem vakteemeez yoktoo
we didn't have time

In questions, -ydı is added to the question particle, in this case **mı** (see **Questions** page 39):

(sizin) rezervasyonunuz var mıydı?
seezeen rezervas-yonoonooz muh-iduh
did you have a reservation?

Regular Verbs

The following list shows some common verbs conjugated in the first person:

infinitive	present progressive	simple present	past	future
almak to take	alıyorum	alırım	aldım	alacağım
bakmak to look	bakıyorum	bakarım	baktım	bakacağım
başlamak to begin	başlıyorum	başlarım	başladım	başlayacağım
beklemek to wait	bekliyorum	beklerim	bekledim	bekleyeceğim
bırakmak to leave	bırakıyorum	bırakırım	bıraktım	bırakacağım
bilmek to know	biliyorum	bilirim	bildim	bileceğim
bulmak to find	buluyorum	bulurum	buldum	bulacağım
çalışmak to work	çalışıyorum	çalışırım	çalıştım	çalışacağım
çıkmak to go out	çıkıyorum	çıkarım	çıktım	çıkacağım
demek to say	diyorum	derim	dedim	diyeceğim
etmek to do	ediyorum	ederim	ettim	edeceğim
gelmek to come	geliyorum	gelirim	geldim	geleceğim
getirmek to bring	getiriyorum	getiririm	getirdim	getireceğim
girmek to enter	giriyorum	girerim	girdim	gireceğim
gitmek to go	gidiyorum	giderim	gittim	gideceğim

infinitive	present progressive	simple present	past	future
göndermek to send	gönderiyorum	gönderirim	gönderdim	göndereceğim
görmek to see	görüyorum	görürüm	gördüm	göreceğim
içmek to drink	içiyorum	içerim	içtim	içeceğim
istemek to want	istiyorum	isterim	istedim	isteyeceğim
kalmak to stay	kalıyorum	kalırım	kaldım	kalacağım
kaybetmek to lose	kaybediyorum	kaybederim	kaybettim	kaybedeceğim
koymak to put	koyuyorum	koyarım	koydum	koyacağım
konuşmak to speak	konuşuyorum	konuşurum	konuştum	konuşacağım
okumak to read	okuyorum	okurum	okudum	okuyacağım
oturmak to live, to sit	oturuyorum	otururum	oturdum	oturacağım
sevmek to love	seviyorum	severim	sevdim	seveceğim
sormak to ask	soruyorum	sorarım	sordum	soracağım
söylemek to say, to tell	söylüyorum	söylerim	söyledim	söyleyeceğim
taşımak to carry	taşıyorum	taşırım	taşıdım	taşıyacağım
unutmak to forget	unutuyorum	unuturum	unuttum	unutacağım
uyumak to sleep	uyuyorum	uyurum	uyudum	uyuyacağım
varmak to arrive	varıyorum	varırım	vardım	varacağım

infinitive	present progressive	simple present	past	future
vermek to give	veriyorum	veririm	verdim	vereceğim
yapmak to make, to do	yapıyorum	yaparım	yaptım	yapacağım
yazmak to write	yazıyorum	yazarım	yazdım	yazacağım
yemek to eat	yiyorum	yerim	yedim	yiyeceğim

Negatives

To form the negative of a verb, add the negative particle -me- or -ma- after the verb stem and before the other endings. If the tense ending starts with a vowel, the negative particle changes to -mi-, -mı-, -mü- or -mu- according to the rules of vowel harmony (see page 11) and a **y** is inserted after the particle to separate the two vowels.

The tables below show how to form the negative of the verb in the first person:

	final vowel in verb stem	
	e or i gelmek to come	a or ı kalmak to stay
present progressive	gel-mi-yorum gelmee-yoroom	kal-mı-yorum kalmuh-yoroom
past tense	gel-me-dim gelmedeem	kal-ma-dım kalmaduhm
imperfect tense	gel-mi-yordum gelmee-yordoom	kal-mı-yordum kalmuh-yordoom
future tense	gel-mi-yeceğim gelmee-yejeh-eem	kal-mı-yacağım kalmuh-yaja-uhm

	final vowel in verb stem	
	o or u	ö or ü
	sormak to ask	**düşünmek** to think
present progressive	**sor-mu-yorum**	**düşün-mü-yorum**
	sormoo-yoroom	dewshewnmew-yoroom
past tense	**sor-ma-dım**	**düşün-me-dim**
	sormaduhm	dewshewnmedeem
imperfect tense	**sor-mu-yordum**	**düşün-mü-yordum**
	sormoo-yordoom	dewshewnmew-yordoom
future tense	**sor-ma-yacağım**	**düşün-mi-yeceğim**
	sorma-yaja-uhm	dewshewnmee-yejeh-eem

The negative of the simple present tense is irregular:

	verb stems ending in	
	e, i, ö or ü	a, ı, o or u
	gelmek to come	**kalmak** to stay
	gel-me-m	**kal-mam**
	gelmem	kalmam
	gel-mez-sin	**kal-maz-sın**
	gelmezseen	kalmazsuhn
	gel-mez	**kal-maz**
	gelmez	kalmaz
	gel-me-yiz	**kal-mayız**
	gelmeh-yeez	kalmī-uhz
	gel-mez-siniz	**kal-maz-sınız**
	gelmezseeneez	kalmazsuhnuhz
	gel-mez-ler	**kal-maz-lar**
	gelmezler	kalmazlar

okuyorum	**kalıyorum**	**söylemem**
okoo-yoroom	kaluh-yoroom	suh-ilemem
I am reading	I am staying	I won't say
okumuyorum	**kalmıyorum**	**sormaz**
okoomoo-yoroom	kalmuh-yoroom	sormaz
I am not reading	I am not staying	he/she doesn't/ won't ask

Negative of 'To Be'

The negative of the verb 'to be' is formed by using the following words which are placed after the adjective

değil-im	[deh-eel**eem**]	I am not
değil-sin	[deh-eel**seen**]	you are not (sing, fam)
değil	[deh-**eel**]	he/she/it is not
değil-iz	[deh-eel**eez**]	we are not
değil-siniz	[deh-eel**seeneez**]	you are not (pol or pl)
değil-ler	[deh-eel**ler**]	they are not

emin değilim
em**een** deh-eel**eem**
I am not sure

Türk değil
tewrk deh-**eel**
he/she is not Turkish

orada rahat değilsiniz
orad**a** rah**a**t deh-eel**seeneez**
you are not comfortable there

evde değiller
evd**eh** deh-eel**ler**
they are not at home

Imperative

To form the polite form of the imperative, take the verb stem and add the following suffixes:

final vowel of verb stem if ending in a consonant

e or i	a or ı	o or u	ö or ü
-in	-ın	-un	-ün

final vowel of verb stem if ending in a vowel

-yin	-yın	-yun	-yün

gelin!	**durun!**	**dinleyin!**
ge**leen**	d**oo**roon	deenl**ay**een
come!	stop!	listen!

The negative imperative is formed by taking the verb stem and adding **-me-** or **-ma-** according to the rules of vowel harmony; then onto this are added the endings as in the table above:

gelmeyin!	**durmayın!**	**dinlemeyin!**
ge**l**mayeen	d**oo**rmī-uhn	deenl**e**mayeen
don't come!	don't stop!	don't listen!

Questions

Questions are formed by using one of the particles mi-, mı-, mü- or mu-; the particle used depends on the preceding vowel and follows the rules of vowel harmony. To create a question, split the person ending of the verb as given in the tables earlier and add one of these particles as follows:

okumak to read

present progressive	**okuyor musunuz?**	are you reading?
	okoo-yor moosoonooz	
simple present	**okur musunuz?**	would you read?,
	okoor moosoonooz	do you read?
past tense	**okudunuz mu?**	did you read?
	okoodoonooz moo	
imperfect tense	**okuyor muydunuz?**	were you reading?
	okoo-yor moo-idoonooz	
future tense	**okuyacak mısınız?**	will you read?
	okoo-yajak muhsuhnuhz	

okuyorsunuz	**okuyor musunuz?**
okoo-yorsoonooz	okoo-yor moosoonooz
you are reading	are you reading?
okuyor	**okuyor mu?**
okoo-yor	okoo-yor moo
he/she is reading	is he/she reading?

Also, Too

Turkish has two words for 'also' and 'too': **de** and **da**. The one you use depends on the final vowel of the preceding word:

final vowel of preceding word

a, ı, o, u	e, i, ö, ü
da	de

Ahmed de	**ben de**	**onlar da**
Ahmed too	me too	they too

Da and de should not be confused with the suffixes -da and -de meaning 'at (the)', 'in (the)' or 'on (the)'.

Can, to be able

To translate this, take the stem of the relevant verb (e.g. kal- 'stay', gel- 'come'), add -a- or -e- according to the final vowel in the stem, then add the appropriate conjugation of bilmek 'to know':

final vowel in verb stem

a, ı, o, u	e, i, ö, ü
-a-	-e-

kal-a-bilmek	**gel-e-bilmek**
kalabeelmek	gelebeelmek
to be able to stay	to be able to come

girebilir miyim?
geerebeeleer mee-yeem
can I come in?

If the verb stem (e.g. taşı-) ends in a vowel, a y is inserted in front of the -a- or -e-:

bavulumu taşıyabilir misiniz?
bavooloomoo tashuh-yabeeleer meeseeneez
can you carry my suitcase?

Dates

The formation of dates is similar to English, except that, both in speech and writing, only cardinal numbers are used (e.g. 1 November, not 1st November) and years are also referred to by simple cardinal numbers (e.g. the year 1996 is referred to not as 'nineteen ninety-six' but 'one thousand nine hundred and ninety-six'):

1 Ocak (Bir Ocak)
beer ojak
1 January

10 Nisan 1996 (On Nisan bin dokuz yüz doksan altı)
on neesan been dokooz yewz doksan altuh
10 April 1996

1 Eylül, Cuma (Bir Eylül, Cuma)
beer aylewl jooma
Friday, 1 September

Days

Sunday Pazar
Monday Pazartesi
Tuesday Salı [sal**uh**]
Wednesday Çarşamba [char-shamba]
Thursday Perşembe [pershem-beh]
Friday Cuma [jooma]
Saturday Cumartesi [joomartesee]

Months

January Ocak [ojak]
February Şubat [shoobat]
March Mart
April Nisan
May Mayıs [mī-uhs]
June Haziran
July Temmuz
August Ağustos [a-oostos]
September Eylül [aylewl]
October Ekim
November Kasım [kasuhm]
December Aralık [araluhk]

Time

what time is it? saat kaç? [sa-at kach]
(it's) one o'clock saat bir
(it's) two o'clock saat iki
(it's) ten o'clock saat on
five past one biri beş geçiyor [besh gechee-yor]
ten past two ikiyi on geçiyor

quarter past one biri çeyrek geçiyor [chayrek]
quarter past two ikiyi çeyrek geçiyor
half past one bir buçuk [boochook]
half past ten on buçuk
twenty to ten ona yirmi var
quarter to one bire çeyrek var [beereh chayrek]
quarter to ten ona çeyrek var
at quarter to ten ona çeyrek kala
at quarter past one biri çeyrek geçe [gecheh]
at eight o'clock (saat) sekizde [sa-at sekeezdeh]
at half past four (saat) dört buçukta [durt boochookta]
2 a.m. gece iki [gejeh]
2 p.m. öğledensonra iki [ur-ledensonra]
6 a.m. sabah altı [sabaH altuh]
6 p.m. akşam altı [aksham]
10 a.m. sabah on [sabaH]
10 p.m. gece on [gejeh]
18.00 on sekiz
14.30 on dört otuz [durt]
noon öğle [urleh]
at noon öğleyin [urlayeen]
midnight gece yarısı [gejeh yaruhsuh]
hour saat [sa-at]
minute dakika
two minutes iki dakika
second saniye [sanee-yeh]
quarter of an hour çeyrek saat [chayrek sa-at]

42

half an hour yarım saat
[yar**uh**m]

three quarters of an hour
kırk beş dakika [**kuhrk** besh],
üç çeyrek saat [ewch chayrek
sa-**at**]

Numbers

0	sıfır [suhf**uhr**]	
1	bir	
2	iki	
3	üç [ewch]	
4	dört [durt]	
5	beş [besh]	
6	altı [alt**uh**]	
7	yedi	
8	sekiz	
9	dokuz	
10	on	
11	on bir	
12	on iki	
13	on üç [ewch]	
14	on dört [durt]	
15	on beş [besh]	
16	on altı [alt**uh**]	
17	on yedi	
18	on sekiz	
19	on dokuz	
20	yirmi	
21	yirmi bir	
22	yirmi iki	
30	otuz	
31	otuz bir	
32	otuz iki	
33	otuz üç [ewch]	
40	kırk [**kuhrk**]	
50	elli	
60	altmış [altm**uh**sh]	

70	yetmiş [yetm**ee**sh]
80	seksen
90	doksan
100	yüz [yewz]
101	yüz bir
102	yüz iki
200	iki yüz
300	üç yüz [ewch]
500	beş yüz [besh]
1,000	bin
2,000	iki bin
3,000	üç bin [ewch]
5,000	beş bin [besh]
10,000	on bin
1,000,000	bir milyon
1,000,000,000	bir milyar

Ordinals

1st	birinci	[beere**enjee**]
2nd	ikinci	[eeke**enjee**]
3rd	üçüncü	[ewchewn**jew**]
4th	dördüncü	[durdewn**jew**]
5th	beşinci	[beshe**enjee**]
6th	altıncı	[altuhn**juh**]
7th	yedinci	[yede**enjee**]
8th	sekizinci	[sekeeze**enjee**]
9th	dokuzuncu	[dokoozoonj**oo**]
10th	onuncu	[onoonj**oo**]

43

Basic Phrases

yes
evet

no
hayır
hī-**uhr**

OK
tamam

please
lütfen
le**w**tfen

thank you
teşekkür ederim
teshekk**ewr**

thanks
teşekkürler
teshekke**wr**l**er**

don't mention it
bir şey değil
shay deh-**eel**

yes, please
(evet) lütfen
le**w**tfen

no thank you
hayır, teşekkür ederim
hī-**uhr** teshekk**ewr**

hello
merhaba

good morning
günaydın
gewnïd**uhn**

good evening
iyi akşamlar
akshaml**ar**

good night
iyi geceler
gejel**er**

goodbye (general use)
hoşça kalın
hosh-ch**a** kal**uhn**

(said by person leaving)
Allahaısmarladık
al**a**ha-uhsmarladuhk

(said to person leaving)
güle güle
g**ewl**eh

hi! (hello)
merhaba!

see you!
görüşürüz!
g**u**rewshewrewz

see you later
görüşmek üzere
g**u**rewshmek ewzer**eh**

how are you?/how do you
do?
nasılsınız?
nasuhl-suhn**uhz**

44

I'm fine, thanks
iyiyim, teşekkür ederim
teshekk**ewr**

nice to meet you
memn**u**n old**u**m

excuse me (to get past)
pardon

(to get attention) affed**e**rsiniz

(to say sorry) özür dilerim
urz**ewr**

(I'm) sorry
özür dil**e**rim
urz**ewr**

sorry?/pardon (me)?
(didn't understand/hear)
ef**e**ndim?

what?
ne?
neh

what did you say?
ne dediniz?

I see/I understand
anlıyorum
anl**uh**-yoroom

I don't understand
anlamıyorum
anl**a**muh-yoroom

do you speak English?
İngilizce biliy**o**r musun**u**z?
eengeel**ee**zjeh

I don't speak Turkish
Türkçe bilmiyorum
tewrkch**eh**

could you speak more slowly?
lütfen dah**a** yavaş konuşur musun**u**z?
l**ew**tfen – yav**a**sh konoosh**oor**

could you repeat that?
tekrarl**a**r mısınız?
muhsuhn**uh**z

please write it down
lütfen yaz**a**r mısınız?
l**ew**tfen – muhsuhn**uh**z

I'd like ...
... istiyorum

can I have ...?
bana ... verebilir misiniz?

how much is it?
kaça?
kach**a**

(at) what time?
kaçta?
kach**ta**

cheers! (toast)
şerefe!
sheref**eh**

where is/are the ...?
... nerede?
neredeh

Conversion Tables

1 centimetre = 0.39 inches   1 inch = 2.54 cm

1 metre = 39.37 inches = 1.09 yards   1 foot = 30.48 cm

1 kilometre = 0.62 miles = 5/8 mile   1 yard = 0.91 m

1 mile = 1.61 km

km	1	2	3	4	5	10	20	30	40	50	100
miles	0.6	1.2	1.9	2.5	3.1	6.2	12.4	18.6	24.8	31.0	62.1

miles	1	2	3	4	5	10	20	30	40	50	100
km	1.6	3.2	4.8	6.4	8.0	16.1	32.2	48.3	64.4	80.5	161

1 gram = 0.035 ounces   1 kilo = 1000 g = 2.2 pounds

g	100	250	500
oz	3.5	8.75	17.5

1 oz = 28.35 g

1 lb = 0.45 kg

kg	0.5	1	2	3	4	5	6	7	8	9	10
lb	1.1	2.2	4.4	6.6	8.8	11.0	13.2	15.4	17.6	19.8	22.0

kg	20	30	40	50	60	70	80	90	100
lb	44	66	88	110	132	154	176	198	220

lb	0.5	1	2	3	4	5	6	7	8	9	10	20
kg	0.2	0.5	0.9	1.4	1.8	2.3	2.7	3.2	3.6	4.1	4.5	9.0

1 litre = 1.75 UK pints / 2.13 US pints

1 UK pint = 0.57 l   1 UK gallon = 4.55 l

1 US pint = 0.47 l   1 US gallon = 3.79 l

centigrade / Celsius $°C = (°F - 32) \times 5/9$

°C	-5	0	5	10	15	18	20	25	30	36.8	38
°F	23	32	41	50	59	64	68	77	86	98.4	100.4

Fahrenheit $°F = (°C \times 9/5) + 32$

°F	23	32	40	50	60	65	70	80	85	98.4	101
°C	-5	0	4	10	16	18	21	27	29	36.8	38.3

English

→

Turkish

A

a, an* bir

about: about 20 yirmi
civarında [**jee**varuhn**da**]
   at about 5 o'clock saat beş
civarında [sa-**at**]
   a film about Turkey Türkiye
hakkında bir film
[**tew**rkee-yeh hakk**uh**nda]

above: above the ... ...-in
üstünde [ewstewnd**eh**]

abroad yurt dışında
[duh-shuhn**da**]

absolutely! (I agree) kesinlikle!
[keseenl**ee**kleh]

absorbent cotton hidrofil
pamuk

accelerator gaz pedalı
[pedal**uh**]

accept kabul etmek

accident kaza
   there's been an accident bir
kaza old**u**

accommodation kalacak yer
[kala**jak**]
   see room, hotel and guesthouse

accurate doğru [doh-r**oo**]

ache ağrı [a-r**uh**]
   my back aches sırtım
ağrıyor [suhrt**uhm** a-r**uh**-yor]

across: across the ... (road
etc) ...-un karşı tarafında
[karsh**uh** tarafuhn**da**]

adapter adaptör [adapt**ur**]

address adres
   what's your address?
adresiniz nedir?

In Turkish addresses,
street names precede the
number; if the address is
on a minor alley, this will be
included after the main thoroughfare
it leads off. If you see a right-hand
slash between two numbers, the
first is the building number, the
second the apartment or office
number. A letter following a right-
hand slash can mean either the
shop or unit number, or be part of
the general building number. For
example:

Halil Güner
Kıbrıs Şehitleri Cad.
Poyraz Sok.
Ulus Apartmanı 36/2, Kat 1
Deliklıçınar
34800 Direkköy

which means that **Halil Güner** lives
on **Poyraz Sokak No. 36**, just off
Kıbrıs Şehitleri Caddesi, on the
first floor, Apartment 2, of the **Ulus**
apartments, in the **Deliklıçınar** area
of a larger postal district known as
Direkköy.

address book adres defteri

admission charge giriş ücreti
[geer**ee**sh ewjret**ee**]

adult yetişkin [yeteesh-k**een**]

advance: in advance önceden
[urnjed**en**]

Aegean Ege [eg**eh**]

aeroplane uçak [**oo**chak]

after: after the ... ...-den sonra
   after you siz buyrun
[**boo**-iroon]

after lunch öğle yemeğinden sonra
afternoon öğleden sonra [ur-leden]
in the afternoon öğleden sonra
this afternoon bugün öğleden sonra [boogewn]
aftershave tıraş losyonu [tuhrash]
aftersun cream güneş sonrası kremi [gewnesh sonrasuh]
afterwards sonra
again yine [yeeneh]
against: against the ... ...-e karşı [-eh karshuh]
age yaş [yash]
ago: a week ago bir hafta önce [urnjeh]
an hour ago bir saat önce
agree: I agree olur
Aids Aids
air hava
by air uçakla [oochakla]
air-conditioning klima, havalandırma [-duhrma]
airmail: by airmail uçak postasıyla [oochak postasuhla]
airmail envelope uçak zarfı [zarfuh]
airport havaalanı [hava-alanuh]
to the airport, please havaalanına, lütfen [-alanuhna lewtfen]
airport bus havaalanı otobüsü [otobewsew]
aisle seat koridor yanı [yanuh]
alarm clock çalar saat [chalar sa-at]

alcohol alkol
alcoholic alkollü [alkollew]
all: all the boys bütün oğlanlar [bewtewn]
all the girls bütün kızlar
all of it hepsi
all of them onların hepsi [onlaruhn]
that's all, thanks hepsi bu kadar, teşekkür ederim [teshekkewr]
allergic: I'm allergic to ... ...-a alerjim var [alerJeem]
allowed: is it allowed? serbest mi?
all right peki
I'm all right ben iyiyim
are you all right? iyi misin?
almond badem
almost neredeyse [neredayseh]
alone yalnız [yalnuhz]
alphabet alfabe [alfabeh]

a	a	m	meh
b	beh	n	neh
c	jeh	o	o
ç	cheh	ö	ur
d	deh	p	peh
e	eh	r	reh
f	feh	s	seh
g	geh	ş	sheh
ğ	yoomooshak geh	u	oo
h	ha	ü	ew
ı	uh	t	teh
i	ee	v	veh
j	Jeh	y	yeh
k	ka	z	zeh
l	leh		

already bile [beel**eh**]
 the film has already started
 film başladı bile [bashl**a**duh]
also de [deh], da
although halde [h**a**ldeh]
altogether tümüyle
 [tewm**ew**leh]
always hep
am*: I am ... (ben) ...-im
a.m. (from midnight to 4 a.m.)
 gece [gej**eh**]
 (from 4 a.m. to noon) sabah
 [saba**H**]
amazing (surprising) şaşılacak
 [shash**uh**laj**a**k]
 (very good) şahane [shah**a**neh]
ambulance cankurtaran
 [jankoortar**a**n]
 call an ambulance! bir
 cankurtaran çağırın!
 [cha-**uh**ruhn]

Dial 112 for an
ambulance. This call costs
one small **jeton** or one
phonecard unit.

America Amerika
American (adj) Amerikan
 I'm American Amerikalıyım
 [-luh-y**uh**m]
among: among the ... ...-in
 arasında [aras**uh**nda]
amount miktar
 (money) tutar
amp: a 13-amp fuse on üç
 amperlik sigorta
amphitheatre amfiteatr
Anatolia Anadolu

and ve [veh]
angry kızgın [kuhzg**uh**n]
animal hayvan [h**ī**van]
ankle ayak bileği [**ī**-ak
 beeleh-ee]
anniversary (wedding) evlenme
 yıldönümü [evlenm**eh**
 yuh**l**-durnewmew]
annoy: this man's annoying
 me bu adam beni rahatsız
 ediyor [rahats**uh**z]
annoying can sıkıcı [jan
 suhkuhj**uh**]
another başka bir [b**a**shka]
 can we have another room?
 bize başka bir oda verebilir
 misiniz? [beez**eh**]
 another beer, please bir bira
 daha, lütfen [l**ew**tfen]
antibiotics antibiyotik
antifreeze antifriz
antihistamine antihistamin
antique: is it an antique? bu
 antika mı? [muh]
antique shop antikacı
 [anteekaj**uh**]
antiseptic antiseptik
any: do you have any ...?
 sizde ... var mı? [seezd**eh** –
 muh]
 sorry, I don't have any
 üzgünüm, hiç yok
 [**ew**zgewnewm heech]
anybody kimse [k**ee**mseh]
 does anybody speak
 English? İngilizce bilen var
 mı? [**een**geeleezjeh – muh]
 there wasn't anybody there
 orada kimse yoktu [k**ee**mseh]

anything bir şey [shay]

dialogues

anything else? başka bir
şey? [bashka]
nothing else, thanks hepsi
bu kadar, teşekkür
ederim [teshekkewr]

would you like anything to
drink? bir şey içmek ister
misiniz? [eechmek]
I don't want anything,
thanks hiç bir şey
istemiyorum, teşekkür
ederim [heech]

apart from ... ...-den başka
[bashka]
apartment apartman dairesi
[da-eeresee], daire
da-eereh]
apartment block apartman
aperitif aperitif
aperitif aperitif
apology özür [urzewr]
appendicitis apandisit
appetizer ordövr [ordurvr],
meze [mezeh]
apple elma
appointment randevu

dialogue

good morning, how can I
help you? günaydın,
buyrun? [gewnīduhn
boo-iroon]
I'd like to make an

appointment randevu
almak istiyorum
what time would you like?
saat kaç için istersiniz?
[sa-at kach eecheen]
three o'clock üç için
I'm afraid that's not possible,
is four o'clock all right?
korkarım o mümkün değil,
saat dörtte olur mu?
[korkaruhm o mewmkewn deh-eel
sa-at durtteh]
yes, that will be fine evet, o
çok iyi [chok]
the name was? isim neydi?
[naydee]

apricot kayısı [kī-uhsuh]
April nisan
are*: we are ... biz ...-iz
you are ... siz ...-siniz
they are ... onlar ...-dırlar
[duhrlar]
area (place) semt
(space) alan
area code şehir kodu [sheh-
heer]
arm kol
Armenia Ermenistan
Armenian (adj, person) Ermeni
arrange: will you arrange it for
us? bunu bizim için ayarlar
mısınız? [icheen ī-arlar
muhsuhnuhz]
arrival varış [varuhsh]
arrive varmak
when do we arrive? ne
zaman varacağız? [neh –
varaja-uhz]

has my fax arrived yet?
faksım geldi mi?
we arrived today bugün
geldik
art sanat
art gallery sanat galerisi
artist sanatçı [sanatch**uh**]
as: as big/small as ... ... kadar
büyük/küçük
as soon as possible en kısa
zamanda [k**uh**sa]
ashtray kül tablası [kewl
tablas**uh**]
Asia Asya
ask (question etc) sormak
I didn't ask for this ben bunu
istemedim
could you ask him/her to ...?
ondan ...-mesini isteyebilir
misiniz?
asleep: he/she's asleep
uyuyor [oo-y**oo**-yor]
aspirin aspirin
asthma astım [ast**uh**m]
astonishing şaşırtıcı
[shashuhr-tuhj**uh**]
at: at the hotel otelde [oteld**eh**]
at the station istasyonda
at six o'clock saat altıda
[sa-at altuh**da**]
at Ali's Ali'de [alee-d**eh**]
Athens Atina
athletics atletizm
attractive çekici [chekeej**ee**]
aubergine patlıcan [patluhjan]
August ağustos [a-oost**os**]
aunt (maternal) teyze [tayz**eh**]
(paternal) hala
Australia Avustralya

Australian (adj) Avustralya
I'm Australian
Avustralyalıyım
[–yal**uh**-yuhm]
automatic otomatik
automatic teller bankamatik
autumn sonbahar
in the autumn sonbaharda
avenue cadde [jadd**eh**]
average (ordinary) sıradan
[suhradan]
(not good) orta
on average ortalama olarak
awake: is he/she awake?
uyanık mı? [oo-yan**uh**k muh]
away: go away! çekil git!
[chek**ee**l geet]
is it far away? uzakta mı?
[muh]
awful berbat
axle aks

B

baby bebek
baby food mama
baby's bottle biberon
baby sitter çocuk bakıcısı
[choj**ook** bakuhjuhs**uh**]
back (of body) sırt [s**uh**rt]
(back part) arka
at the back arkada
can I have my money back?
paramı geri alabilir miyim?
[param**uh**]
to come back geri gelmek
to go back dönmek
[durnm**ek**]

backache sırt ağrısı [suhrt a-ruh**suh**]
bacon beykın [**bay**kuhn]
bad kötü [kurt**ew**]
 not bad fena değil [deh-**eel**]
badly kötü [kurt**ew**]
bag çanta [chan**ta**]
 (handbag) el çantası chanta**suh**]
 (suitcase) bavul [bav**ul**]
baggage bagaj [baga**J**]
baggage check emanet
baggage claim bagaj alım
 [baga**J** al**uhm**]
bakery fırın [fuhr**uhn**]
balcony balk**on**
 a room with a balcony balkon**lu** bir oda
bald kel
ball top
ballet bale [bal**eh**]
ballpoint pen tükenmez kal**e**m [tewkenm**ez**]
banana muz
band (musical) ork**e**stra
bandage sargı [sarg**uh**]
Bandaids® flaster, yara bandı [band**uh**]
bank (money) banka

Banks are open Monday to Friday, 8.30 to noon and 1.30 to 5 p.m. Between April and October most coastal resorts between Çanakkale and Alanya have **nöbetçi** (duty banks) which are open at the weekend and in the evening; a list is posted in the window or door of each branch telling you who's open that week. Banks charge around three per cent commission; the PTT (post and telephone office) charges one per cent; and free transactions and the best rates are to be had at the new **döviz** or exchange houses all over western Turkey – though they rarely deal with travellers' cheques. Because of the Turkish lira's constant devaluation you should only change money every few days as you need it, unless you're going east.

bank account banka hesabı [hesab**uh**]
bar bar

Turkey is primarily a Muslim country and bars are not social places for most people. In large cities and resorts, Western-style bars are found in areas frequented by foreign visitors. You might also come across traditional drinking places called **meyhane** (literally: wine house), whose customers are usually regulars enjoying their drinks (**rakı** or wine) with the traditional accompaniment of various **mezes** (snacks). Women should avoid **meyhanes** and **birahanes** (beer halls) as they are exclusively male drinking preserves.

a bar of chocolate bir paket çikolata [cheeko**lata**]

barber's berber
bargain (verb) pazarlık etmek
[pazarl**uh**k]

bargaining
It is customary to bargain in Turkish bazaars. Begin at a figure rather lower than whatever you are prepared to pay, usually around half of your shopkeeper's starting price. Once a price has been agreed on, you are ethically committed to buy, so don't commence haggling unless you are reasonably sure you want the item. You can haggle for souvenir purchases, minor repair services, rural taxis, car rental, hotels out of season, and meals – especially seafood ones – at eateries where a menu is absent.

dialogue

how much do you want for this? bunun için ne kadar istiyorsunuz? [eech**een** neh]
30,000,000 lira otuz milyon lira
that's too much – I'll give you 20,000,000 lira o çok fazla – size yirmi milyon lira veririm [chok – see**zeh**]
I'll let you have it for 25,000,000 lira size yirmi beş milyon liraya bırakırım [besh – buhrakuhr**uhm**]
can't you make it

cheaper?/OK it's a deal daha ucuza olmaz mı?/tamam, anlaştık [oo**joo**za – muh/anlast**uh**k]

basket sepet
bath banyo
can I have a bath? banyo yapabilir miyim?
bathroom banyo
with a private bathroom banyolu oda
bath towel havlu
bathtub küvet [kewvet]
battery pil
bay koy
(large) körfez [kurfez]
bazaar çarşı [charsh**uh**], pazar

There are several kinds of bazaar in Turkey. Covered bazaars are found in large towns like İstanbul, Bursa and Kayseri. Surrounding these covered bazaars are large areas of small shops, essentially open-air extensions of the covered areas and governed by the same rules. Prices on the street are often a bit lower than in the covered areas, owing to lower rents. In addition there are weekly or twice-weekly street markets in most towns selling everyday household products.

be* olmak
beach plaj [plaJ]
on the beach plajda

Pollution and over-crowding are not yet as problematic as in the Western Mediterranean, though beaches close to big cities are often polluted. Look out for signs: **denize girmek tehlikeli ve yasaktır** (it is dangerous and prohibited to go in the sea) and **yüzmek tehlikelidir** (swimming is dangerous). While most beaches do not have lifeguards, a line of buoys indicate the safe distance from the shore. Most large hotels have their own beach facilities within an enclosed area: topless sunbathing and swimming should be confined to these areas.

beach mat plaj yaygısı [plaJ yiguhs**uh**]
beach umbrella plaj şemsiyesi [shemsee-yes**ee**]
beans fasulye [fahs**ool**-yeh]
  French beans ayşekadın fasulyesi [ishekaduhn]
  broad beans bakla
bear ayı [ı-**uh**]
beard sakal
beautiful güzel [gewz**el**]
because çünkü [**chew**nkew]
  because of ... ... nedeniyle [neden**ee**leh]
bed yatak
  I'm going to bed now ben artık yatıyorum [art**uh**k yatuh-y**o**room]
bed and breakfast pansiyon
  see guesthouse

bedroom yatak odası [odas**uh**]
beef sığır eti [suh-**uhr**]
beer bira
  two beers, please iki bira, lütfen [**lew**tfen]

Beer is sold principally in bottles but also in cans (expensive) and on draught (cheaper). There are three main brands, **Efes Pilsen**, **Tuborg**, and **Venus**, also produced by Tuborg. The **birahane**, an imitation-German beer hall, has cropped up in many tourist towns but often has a distinctly aggressive atmosphere.

before önce [**u**rnjeh]
begin başlamak [bashlamak]
  when does it begin? ne zaman başlıyor? [neh – bashluh-yor]
beginner acemi [ajemee]
beginning: at the beginning başlangıçta [bashlanguhchta]
behind: behind the ... ...-in arkasında [arkasuhnda]
  behind me arkamda
beige bej [beJ]
Belgian (adj) Belçika [belcheeka]
Belgium Belçika
believe inanmak
below: below the ... ...-in altında [altuhnda]
belt kemer
bend (in road) viraj [veeraJ]
berth (on ship) ranza, yatak
beside: beside the ... ...-in

yanında [yanuhnda]
best en iyi
better daha iyi
  are you feeling better?
  kendınızı daha ıyı
  hissediyor musunuz?
between: between the ... ...-
  lerin arasında [arasuhnda]
beyond: beyond the ...-in
  ötesinde [urteseendeh]
bicycle bisiklet
big büyük [bew-yewk]
  too big fazla büyük
  it's not big enough yeterince
  büyük değil [yetereenjeh –
  deh-eel]
bike bisiklet
  (motorbike) motosiklet
bikini bikini
bill hesap
  (US) kâğıt para [ka-uht]
  could I have the bill, please?
  hesap, lütfen [lewtfen]

Apart from self-service
cafés and cafeterias etc,
where you pay in
advance, you normally pay in cafés
and restaurants when you are ready
to leave. Turks enjoy treating their
friends and guests and often insist
on paying for your drink or meal
even if no special invitation was
made to take you out.

bin çöp kutusu [churp]
bin liners çöp torbası
  [torbasuh]
bird kuş [koosh]

birthday doğum günü
  [doh-oom gewnew]
  happy birthday! doğum
  gününüz kutlu olsun!
  [gewnewnewz]
biscuit bisküvi [beeskew-vee]
bit: a little bit birazcık
  [beerazjuhk]
  a big bit büyük bir parça
  [bew-yewk beer parcha]
  a bit of ... bir parça ...
  a bit expensive/small biraz
  pahalı/küçük
bite (by insect) sokma
  (by dog) ısırma [uhsuhrma]
bitter (taste etc) acı [ajuh]
black siyah [see-yaн], kara
Black Sea Karadeniz
blanket battanjye
  [battanee-yeh]
bleach (for toilet) tuvalet
  temizleyicisi [temeezlay-eejee-
  see]
bless you! çok yaşa! [chok
  yasha]
blind kör [kur]
blinds jaluzi [Jaloozee]
blister su toplaması
  [toplamasuh]
  I have a blister on my heel
  topuğum su topladı [topoo-
  oom soo topladuh]
blocked (road) kapalı [kapaluh]
  (sink, pipe) tıkalı [tuhkaluh]
blond (adj) sarışın [saruh-shuhn]
blood kan
  high blood pressure yüksek
  tansiyon [yewksek]
blouse bluz

blow-dry (noun) fön [furn]
  I'd like a cut and blow-dry
  lütfen kesip fönleyin [**lew**tfen
  – **fu**rnlayeen]
blue mavi
blusher allık [all**uh**k]
boarding house pansiyon
boarding pass biniş kartı
  [ben**ee**sh kart**uh**]
boat gemi
  (small) kayık [kī-**uh**k]
body vücut [vew**joo**t]
boiled egg haşlanmış
  yumurta [hashlanm**uh**sh]
boiler kazan
bone kemik
bonnet (of car) motor kapağı
  [kapa-**uh**], kaput
book (noun) kitap
  (verb: seat etc) ayırtmak
  [ī-**uh**rtmak]
  can I book a seat? bir yer
  ayırtabilir miyim?
  [ī-uhrtabeel**eer**]

dialogue

**I'd like to book a table for
two** iki kişilik bir masa
ayırtmak istiyorum
[keesheel**eek**]
**what time would you like it
booked for?** saat kaç için
ayırtmak istiyorsunuz?
[sa-**at** kach eech**en**]
half past seven yedi
buçuk
that's fine tamam, olur
and your name? isminiz?

bookshop, bookstore kitapçı
  [keetap-chuh]
boot (footwear) çizme
  [cheez**meh**]
  (of car) bagaj [baga**J**]
border (of country) sınır
  [suhn**uhr**]
bored: I'm bored canım
  sıkılıyor [jahn**uh**m suhkuhluh-
  y**or**]
boring sıkıcı [suhkuh-**juh**]
**born: I was born in
Manchester** Manchester'de
doğdum [–d**eh** doh-d**oom**]
  I was born in 1960 bin
  dok**u**z yüz altmış'da
  doğdum
borrow ödünç almak
  [urd**ew**nch]
  may I borrow ...? ...-i ödünç
  alabilir miyim?
Bosphorus İstanbul Boğazı
  [eestanbool bo-**az**uh]
both ikisi de [eekees**ee** deh]
bother: sorry to bother you
rahatsız ettiğim için özür
dilerim [rahats**uh**z ett**ee**-eem
eech**en** urz**ewr**]
bottle şişe [sheesh**eh**]
bottle-opener şişe açacağı
  [achaja-uh]
bottom (of person) popo
  at the bottom of the hill
  tepenin eteğinde
  [eteh-eend**eh**]
  at the bottom of the street
  yolun alt kısmında
  [kuhsm**uh**nda]
box kutu

(large) sandık [sand**uhk**]
box office bilet gişesi
[geeshe**see**]
boy oğlan [oh-**lan**]
boyfriend erkek arkadaş
[arkad**ash**]
bra sütyen [sewt-**yen**]
bracelet bilezik
brake fren
brandy konyak
brass pirinç [peer**eench**]
bread ekmek
white bread beyaz ekmek
[bay**az**]
brown bread kara ekmek
wholemeal bread kepekli
ekmek
break (verb) kırmak [kuhr**mak**]
I've broken the ... ...'i kırdım
[kuhrd**uhm**]
I think I've broken my wrist
sanırım bileğimi kırdım
[sanuh-r**uhm**]
break down arıza yapmak
[ar**uhza**]
I've broken down arabam
arıza yaptı [yapt**uh**]
breakdown (mechanical) arıza

The Turkish motoring
organization, the **TTOK**
(Turkish Touring and
Automobile Association) can advise
on Turkish insurance and related
matters, especially if you are
planning on staying several months.
They have branches in a number of
cities. You will have to pay for their
breakdown service unless you've

equipped yourself with vouchers or
an insurance policy prior to arrival.

breakdown service araç
kurtarma [ar**ach**]
breakfast kahvaltı
[kaнvalt**uh**]

The Turkish breakfast
served at hotels and
pansiyons is almost
invariably a pile of day-old bread
slices with a pat of margarine, a
slice of cheese, a dab of jam and a
couple of olives. Only tea is likely to
be available in quantity; seconds are
likely to be charged for.

break-in: I've had a break-in
evime hırsız girdi [eveem**eh**
huhrs**uhz**]
breast göğüs [gur-**ews**]
breathe nefes almak
breeze esinti
bridge köprü [kurpr**ew**]
brief kısa [kuhs**a**]
briefcase evrak çantası
[chantas**uh**]
bright (light etc) aydınlık
[iduhnl**uhk**]
(colour) canlı [janl**uh**]
bright red ateş kırmızısı
[at**esh** kuhrmuhzuhs**uh**]
brilliant (person) çok zeki
[ch**ok**]
(idea) parlak
bring getirmek
I'll bring it back later sonra
geri getiririm

Britain Büyük Britanya [bew-yewk]
British İngiliz [**een**geeleez]
brochure broşür [broshewr]
broken bozuk
  (leg etc) kırık [kuhr**uh**k]
bronchitis bronşit [bronsh**eet**]
brooch broş [brosh]
broom süpürge [sewrpewrg**eh**]
brother erkek kardeş [kardesh]
brother-in-law (husband's/wife's brother) kayınbirader [kı-uhn-beerader]
  (sister's husband) enişte [eneesht**eh**]
brown kahverengi [kaнverengee]
bruise çürük [chewr**ewk**]
brush (for cleaning) fırça [**fuh**rcha]
  (for hair) saç fırçası [sach fuhrchas**uh**]
  (artist's) resim fırçası
bucket kova
buffet car yemekli vagon
buggy (for child) puset
building bina
bulb (light bulb) ampul
Bulgaria Bulgaristan
Bulgarian (adj, person) Bulgar
bumper tampon
bunk ranza
bureau de change kambiyo
  see **bank**
burglary hırsızlık [huhrsuhzl**uh**k]
burn (noun) yanık [yan**uh**k]
  (verb) yanmak
burnt: this is burnt bu yanmış [yahnm**uh**sh]
burst: a burst pipe patlamış boru [patlam**uh**sh]
bus otobüs [otob**ews**]
  what number bus is it to ...? ...-'a kaç numaralı otobüs gidiyor? [kach noomaral**uh**]
  when is the next bus to ...? ...-'a bundan sonraki otobüs ne zaman? [neh]
  what time is the last bus? son otobüs saat kaçta? [sa-at kachta]

The Turkish long-distance bus is an immensely popular form of transport. There is no national bus company in Turkey. Most routes are covered by several firms, with ticket booths both at the **otogar** (bus terminal) from which they operate, and also in the city centre. When you buy your ticket at a **yazıhane**, or sales office in a town centre, you should ask about free service buses to the otogar, especially if it's located a few miles out. Most companies provide small minibuses even for a single passenger; the question to ask is '**servis arabası var mı?**'. In larger towns the main means of transport are the red and white city buses, which take pre-purchased tickets available from kiosks near the main terminals, newsagents, or from touts (at slightly inflated prices). The only exceptions are the orange buses in İstanbul, whose drivers have been known to take cash in place of tickets.

On public transport there is a tendency to act protectively towards women travelling on their own: when a lone woman buys a seat ticket, it is customary to arrange things so that she does not sit next to a man. The bus steward (**yardımcı** or **muavin**) may well intervene if you try to contravene the convention.

see **taxi**

dialogue

> **does this bus go to ...?**
> bu ... otobüsü mü? [boo – mew]
> **no, you need a number ...** hayır, onun için ... nolu otobüse binmeniz lazım [hī-**uhr** – eech**een** ... no**loo** otob**ew**seh – laz**uhm**]

business iş [eesh]
bus station otobüs garajı [otob**ews** gara**Juh**], otogar
bus stop otobus durağı [doora-**uh**]
bust göğüs [gur-**ews**]
bus terminal otogar
busy (restaurant etc) kalabalık [kalabal**uhk**]
  I'm busy tomorrow yarın meşgulüm [meshg**oo**lewm]
but ama
butcher's kasap

butter tereyağı [ter**a**ya-uh]
button düğme [dewm**eh**]
buy satın almak [sat**uhn**]
  where can I buy ...? nerede ... bulabilirim? [n**e**redeh]
by: by bus/car otobüs/ otomobil ile [eel**eh**]
  written by ... ... tarafından yazılan [tarafuhndan yazuhlan]
  by the window pencere yanında [yan**uh**nda]
  by the sea deniz kenarında [kenar**uh**nda]
  by Thursday Perşembeye kadar
bye (general use) hoşça kalın [hosh-cha kal**uhn**]
  (said by person leaving) hoşça kal [**hosh**-cha]
  (said to person leaving) güle güle [gewl**eh**]
Byzantine Bizans

C

cabbage lahana [la**H**ana]
cabin (on ship) kamara
cable car teleferik
café (for men) kahve [ka**H**v**eh**], kahvehane [ka**H**v**eh**-**H**aneh], çayhane [chī**H**aneh]
  (for families) pastane [p**a**staneh], cafe [kaf**eh**]

Cafés serve hot drinks, soft drinks, snacks, cakes and ice cream. Hot drinks include tea, coffee and salep, a hot sweetened milk drink. You can also get these at a **pastane** (pastry shop), where they make and sell cakes as well as serving them. Some cafés also serve alcoholic drinks but a pastane does not.

cagoule naylon yağmurluk
[**nilon** ya-moorl**ook**]
cake pasta
cake shop pastane [**pastaneh**]
call (verb) çağırmak
[cha-uhr**mak**]
(verb: to phone) telefon etmek
what's it called? ona ne
denir? [neh]
he/she is called ... adı ...
[ad**uh**]
please call the doctor lütfen
doktoru çağırın [**lewt**fen –
cha-uhr**uhn**]
please give me a call at 7.30
a.m. tomorrow lütfen yarın
sabah yedi buçukta bana bir
telefon edin
please ask him/her to call me
lütfen beni aramasını
söyleyin [aramasuhn**uh**
suh-ilay-**een**]
call back: I'll call back later
sonra tekrar uğrarım
[oo-rar**uhm**]
(phone back) sonra tekrar
ararım [arar**uhm**]
call round: I'll call round
tomorrow yarın uğrarım
[oo-rar**uhm**]
camcorder video kamera

camel deve [dev**eh**]
camera fotoğraf makinesi
[foto-raf]
camera shop fotoğrafçı
[foto-rafch**uh**]
camp (verb) kamp yapmak
can we camp here? burada
kamp yapabilir miyiz?
camping gas tüpgaz
[**tewp**gaz]

 Camping gas is mostly imported from Greece and impossible to find away from the west coast.

campsite kamping, kamp
yeri

 Wherever a **pansiyon** (guesthouse) is found, there will also be a campsite – often run by the same people, who in the absence of a proper site may simply allow you to crash out in the garden. Campsites often rent out tents or provide A-frame chalet accommodation, which can be anything from a stuffy garden hut with a bed inside to a fairly luxurious affair with a bathroom. Campsites are open from April or May until October. Camping rough is not illegal, but hardly anybody does it except when trekking in the mountains.

can teneke kutu [tenek**eh**]
a can of beer bir kutu bira

can*: can you ...? ...-ebilir misiniz?
can I have ...?
bana ... verebilir misiniz?
I can't ... ...-emem
Canada Kanada
Canadian (adj) Kanada
I'm Canadian Kanadalıyım [kanadaluh-yuhm]
canal kanal
cancel iptal etmek
candies şeker [sheker]
candle mum [moom]
canoe kano
canoeing kano kullanmak
can-opener konserve açacağı [konserveh achaja-uh]
cap (hat) kasket
(of bottle) kapak
car otomobil, araba
by car otomobil ile [eeleh]
carafe sürahi [sewrahee]
a carafe of house white, please bir sürahi beyaz şarabınızdan, lütfen [bayaz sharabuhnuhzdan lewtfen]
caravan karavan
caravan site kamping
carburettor karbüratör [karbewratur]
card (birthday etc) kart
here's my (business) card buyrun, kartvizitim [boo-iroon]
cardigan hırka [huhrka]
cardphone kartlı telefon [kartluh]
careful dikkatli
be careful! dikkatli olun!

caretaker kapıcı [kapuhjuh]
car ferry feribot
car hire kiralık otomobil [keeraluhk]
see car rental
carnival karnaval
car park otopark
car rental kiralık otomobil [keeraluhk]

 Car rental in Turkey is usually exorbitant, with rates equalling or exceeding any in Europe, but there's often considerable scope for bargaining. Unlimited mileage is invariably a better deal than any time-plus-distance rate.
To rent a car you need to be at least 21 years of age, with a driver's licence held for at least one year. An International Driving Permit, from the RAC or AA in Britain or the AAA in the US, is not essential but very helpful. You'll also need to flash a credit card or leave a substantial cash deposit to cover the estimated rental total.
see **bargaining** and **rent**

carpet halı [haluh]
carriage (of train) vagon
carrier bag naylon torba [nīlon]
carrot havuç [havooch]
carry taşımak [tashuhmak]
carry-cot portbebe [portbebeh]
carton kutu
carwash (place) otomobil

Ca

yıkama yeri [yuhkama]
case (suitcase) valiz, bavul
cash (noun) nakit para
(verb) paraya çevirmek
[parī-a cheveermek]
will you cash this cheque for me? benim için bu çeki bozar mısınız? [eecheen – muhsuhnuhz]

It's wise to carry a fair wad of overseas cash with you in Turkey as you can often pay for souvenirs or accommodation with foreign currency directly (prices for both are often quoted in dollars, sterling or Deutschmarks) and it allows you to take advantage of the **döviz** brokers' convenient service and excellent rates.

cash desk kasa
cash dispenser bankamatik
cashier kasiyer
cassette kaset
cassette recorder kasetli teyp [tayp]
castle kale [kaleh]
casualty department acil servis [ajeel]
cat kedi [kedee]
catacomb yeraltı mezarları [yeraltuh mezarlaruh]
catch (verb: ball etc) yakalamak
where do we catch the bus to İzmir? İzmir otobüsüne nereden binebiliriz? [eezmeer]

cathedral katedral
Catholic Katolik
cauliflower karnabahar
cave mağara [ma-ara]
ceiling tavan
celery sap kerevizi
cemetery mezarlık [mezarluhk]
centigrade* santigrat
centimetre* santimetre [santeemetreh]
central merkezi
central heating kalorifer
centre merkez
how do we get to the city centre? şehir merkezine nasıl gidilir? [sheh-heer merkezeeneh nasuhl]
certainly kesinlikle [keseenleekleh]
certainly not kesinlikle hayır [hī-uhr]
chair iskemle [eeskemleh]
champagne şampanya [shampanya]
change (noun: money) bozuk para
(verb: money) bozmak
can I change this for ...? bunu ... ile değiştirebilir miyim? [eeleh deh-eeshteereh-beeleer]
I don't have any change hiç bozuk param yok [heech]
can you give me change for a 1,000,000 lira note? bana bir milyon lira bozabilir misiniz?

dialogue

do we have to change (trains)? aktarma yapmamız lazım mı? [yapmam**uhz** laz**uhm** muh]

yes, change at Bursa/no, it's a direct train evet, Bursa'da değiştirin [**boors**ada deh-eeshteer**een**]/hayır, bu tren direkt gider [h**ī**-**uhr**]

changed: to get changed üstünü değiştirmek [**ewstewnew** deh-eeshteermek]

chapel kilise [keeless**eh**]

charge (noun) alınan para [al**uhnan**]
(verb) para almak

charge card kredi kartı [kart**uh**]
see **credit card**

cheap ucuz [ooj**ooz**]

do you have anything cheaper? daha ucuz bir şey var mı? [shay var muh]

check (verb) kontrol etmek
(US: noun) çek [chek]
see **cheque**
(US: bill) hesap
see **bill**

could you check the ..., please? ...-i kontrol eder misiniz, lütfen? [**lewt**fen]

checkbook çek defteri [chek]

check card çek kartı [kart**uh**]

check-in bagaj kayıt [baga**J** kī-**uht**], check-in

check in (at hotel) yerleşmek [yerleshmek]
(at airport) check-in yaptırmak [yapt**uhr**mak]

where do we have to check in? nerede check-in yaptırmamız lazım? [**ne**redeh – yaptuhrmam**uhz** laz**uhm**]

cheek yanak

cheerio! eyvallah! [ayvalla**н**]

cheers! (toast) şerefe! [sheref**eh**]

cheese peynir [payn**eer**]

chemist's eczane [ejzan**eh**]
see **pharmacy**

cheque çek [chek]

do you take cheques? çek kabul ediyor musunuz?

Traveller's cheques are not always accepted – most **döviz gişesi** won't take them at the moment, and the bank must have a specimen for the brand you carry, or they'll refuse to serve you. This is less of a problem with Thomas Cook and American Express cheques. For both cash and travellers' cheques transactions, sterling, Deutschmarks or US dollars are the preferred currencies.

cheque book çek defteri [chek]

cheque card çek kartı [kart**uh**]

cherry kiraz

chess satranç [satran**ch**]

chest göğüs [gur-**ews**]

chewing gum çiklet [cheeklet]

chicken tavuk

chickenpox suçiçeği
[soochech**eh**-ee]
child çocuk [choj**ook**]
children çocuklar [choj**ook**lar]

Children are adored in Turkey; childless couples will be asked when they plan to have some, and bringing children along guarantees red carpet treatment almost everywhere. Three- or four-bedded hotel rooms are easy to find, and airlines, ships and trains offer substantial discounts. Baby formulas are cheap and readily available; disposable nappies aren't.

child minder çocuk bakıcısı
[choj**ook** bakuhjuhs**uh**]
children's pool çocuk havuzu
children's portion çocuk porsiyonu
chin çene [chen**eh**]
china porselen
Chinese (adj) Çin [cheen]
chips patates kızartması
[kuhzartmas**uh**]
(US) çips [cheeps]
chocolate çikolata [cheekolata]
milk chocolate sütlü çikolata
[sewt**lew**]
plain chocolate sade çikolata
[sa-d**eh**]
a hot chocolate kakao
choose seçmek [sechmek]
Christian Hıristiyan
[huhreestee-ya**n**]
Christian name ad

Christmas Noel
Christmas Eve Noel Gecesi
[gejes**ee**]
merry Christmas! İyi Noeller! [ee-y**ee**]
church kilise [keelees**eh**]
cider elma şırası [shuhras**uh**]
cigar puro
cigarette sigara

Turkish cigarettes can be rough, but if you're keen to try them, **İkibin** are the mildest followed by **Maltepe**. Better are the cigarettes made in Turkey under licence from foreign brands, notably Marlboro.

cigarette lighter çakmak
[chakmak]
cinema sinema

There are fewer than thirty cinemas remaining in all of Turkey, concentrated in İstanbul, Ankara and İzmir. Most foreign films are dubbed, but you may find a film in English in İstanbul, Ankara or İzmir. Examine the posters outside: **orijinal** means 'original voice' and **alt yazılı** means 'sub-titles'.

circle daire [da-eer**eh**]
(in theatre) balkon
citadel iç kale [eech kal**eh**]
city şehir [sheh-h**eer**]
city centre şehir merkezi
clean (adj) temiz

can you clean these for me?
lütfen bana bunları temizler
misiniz? [**lewt**fen – bunlar**uh**]
cleaning solution (for contact
lenses) temizleme sıvısı
[temeezleme**h** suhvuhs**uh**]
cleansing lotion temizleme
losyonu
clear duru
(obvious) açık [ach**uhk**]
clever akıllı [ak**uhll**uh]
cliff yar
climbing dağcılık [da-juhl**uhk**]
cling film jelatin [**J**elateen]
clinic klinik
cloakroom vestiyer
clock saat [sa-**at**]
close (verb) kapatmak

dialogue

what time do you close?
saat kaçta
kapatıyorsunuz? [sa-**at**
ka**cht**a kapatuh-yor–]
we close at 8 p.m. on
weekdays and 6 p.m. on
Saturdays hafta içinde
akşam sekizde,
cumartesileri akşam
altıda kapatıyoruz
[eecheend**eh** aksham seke**ez**deh
joomarteseeler**ee** – alt**uh**da
kapatuh-yor**ooz**]
do you close for lunch?
öğlenleri kapatıyor
musunuz? [ur-lenler**ee**
kapatuh-**yor**]
yes, between 1 and 3.30

p.m. evet, saat birle
üçbuçuk arasında [sa-**at**
beerl**eh** ewchboochook
aras**uh**nda]

closed kapalı [kapal**uh**]
cloth (fabric) kumaş [**koo**mash]
(for cleaning etc) bez
clothes giysiler [gee-is**ee**ler]
clothes line çamaşır ipi
[chamash**uhr**]
clothes peg çamaşır mandalı
[mandal**uh**]
cloud bulut
cloudy bulutlu
clutch (in car) debriyaj
[debree-ya**J**]
coach (bus) yolcu otobüsü
[yol**joo** otobews**ew**]
(on train) vagon
see bus
coach station otobüs garajı
[gara**J**uh]
coach terminal otogar
coach trip otobüsle gezi
[otob**ews**leh]
coast sahil [sa**н**eel]
on the coast sahilde
[saнeeld**eh**]
coat (long coat) palto
(jacket) ceket [**J**eket]
coathanger askı [ask**uh**]
cockroach hamam böceği
[burjeh-ee]
cocoa kakao
coconut hindistancevizi
–jeveez**ee**]
code (for phoning) kod
numarası [noomaras**uh**]

what's the (dialling) code for İzmir? İzmir'in kodu nedir?
coffee kahve [kaнveh]
two coffees, please iki kahve, lütfen [**lewt**fen]

Coffee is not as commonly drunk in Turkey as tea. Instant coffee (**nescafe** [neskaf**eh**]) is relatively costly but increasingly popular; much better is the traditional, fine-ground Turkish coffee, which is usually served with a glass of water – a little cold water added to the coffee will help the grounds settle. For an extended session of drinking either tea or coffee, you retire to a **çay bahçesi** (tea garden), which often will also serve ice cream and soft drinks. Useful terms are as follows:

Türk kahvesi [tewrk kaнv esee] Turkish coffee
sade [sa-deh] without sugar
orta şekerli [orta shekerlee] medium sweet
çok şekerli [chok] very sweet

coin madeni para
Coke® Koka Kola
cold soğuk [so-**ook**]
I'm cold üşüyorum [ewsh**ew**-yoroom]
I have a cold soğuk aldım [ald**uhm**]
collapse: he's collapsed yığılıverdi [yuh-uhl**uh**verdee]
collar yaka

collect toplamak, biriktirmek
I've come to collect ... ...-ı almaya geldim [-uh almī-**a**]
collect call ödemeli konuşma [urdemel**ee** konooshma]
college kolej [kole**J**]
colour renk
do you have this in other colours? bunun başka renkleri de bulunur mu sizde? [**bashka** – **deh** – seezd**eh**]
colour film renkli film
comb tarak
come (arrive) gelmek

dialogue

where do you come from? siz nerelisiniz?
I come from Edinburgh ben Edinburgluyum

come back dönmek [durnmek]
I'll come back tomorrow yarın tekrar gelirim
come in girmek
comfortable rahat
compact disc Compact Disc, CD [see dee]
company (business) şirket [sheerket]
compartment (on train) kompartıman [kompartuhman]
compass pusula
complain şikayet etmek [sheekī-et]
complaint şikayet

I have a complaint bir
şikayetim var
completely tamamen
computer bilgisayar
[beelgeesi-**ar**]
concert konser
concussion beyin sarsıntısı
[bay**ee**n sarsuhn-tuhs**uh**]
conditioner (for hair) saç kremi
[sa**ch**]
condom prezervatif
conference konferans
confirm doğrulamak
[doh-roolamak]
congratulations! tebrikler!
connecting flight aktarmalı
sefer [aktarmal**uh**]
connection bağlantı
[ba-lant**uh**]
conscious şuuru yerinde
[shoo-oor**oo** yereend**eh**]
constipation kabızlık
[kabuhzl**uh**k]
consulate konsolosluk
contact (verb) ilişki kurmak
[eeleeshk**ee**]
contact lenses kontak
lensleri
contraceptive prezervatif,
koruyucu [kor**oo**-yoo**joo**]
convenient uygun [**oo**-ig**oo**n]
that's not convenient o pek
uygun değil [deh-**eel**]
cook (verb) pişirmek
[peesheerm**ek**]
not cooked pişmemiş
[**pee**shmemeesh]
cooker ocak [**o**jak]
cookie bisküvi [beesk**ew**vee]

cooking utensils mutfak
aletleri
cool serin
copper bakır [bak**uhr**]
cork mantar
corkscrew tirbuşon
[teerboosh**on**]
corner: on the corner köşe
başında [kursh**eh** bash**uh**nda]
in the corner köşede
[kurshed**eh**]
cornflakes mısır gevreği
[muhs**uhr** gevreh-**ee**]
correct (right) doğru [doh-**roo**]
corridor koridor
cosmetics makyaj malzemesi
cost (verb) mal olmak
how much does it cost?
fiyatı nedir? [fee-yat**uh**]
cot çocuk yatağı [cho**jo**ok
yata-uh]
cotton pamuk
cotton wool hidrofil pamuk
couch (sofa) kanape [kanap**eh**]
couchette yatak, kuşet
cough (noun) öksürük
[**u**rksew-r**ewk**]
cough medicine öksürük
şurubu [shooroob**oo**]
could: could you
give ...? ... verebilir misiniz?
could I have ...? ... alabilir
miyim?
I couldn't ... ...–amadım
[-amaduhm]
country (nation) ülke [ewlk**eh**]
(countryside) kırsal alanlar
[kuhrsal]
countryside kırlar [kuhrlar],

şehir dışı [sheh-heer duhshuh]
couple (two people) çift [cheeft]
  a couple of ... (two) bir
  çift ...
  (a few) bir iki tane ... [taneh]
courgette kabak
courier kurye [koor-yeh]
course (main course etc) yemek
  çeşidi [chesheedee]
  of course elbette [elbetteh]
  of course not tabii değil
  [tabee-ee deh-eel]
courtyard avlu
cousin (male) kuzen
  (female) kuzin
cow inek
crab yengeç [yengech]
cracker (biscuit) kraker
craft shop el sanatları
  dükkanı [sanatlaruh
  dewk-kanuh]
crash (noun) çarpışma
  [charpuhshma]
  I've had a crash kaza yaptım
  [yaptuhm]
crazy deli
cream (in cake etc) krema
  (lotion) krem
  (colour) krem rengi
creche kreş [kresh]
credit card kredi kartı [kartuh]
  do you take credit cards?
  kredi kartı kabul ediyor
  musunuz?

A major credit card is
invaluable for domestic
ferry and plane tickets,
and also as a waiver for a huge cash

deposit when renting a car. You can
also normally get cash advances at
any bank displaying the appropriate
sign, either over the counter or from
the increasingly common ATMs. Visa
and Mastercard/Access are widely
accepted for fuel purchases in much
of Turkey.

dialogue

can I pay by credit card?
kredi kartıyla ödeyebilir
miyim? [kartuh-ila
urdayebeeleer]
which card do you want to
use? hangi kartla
ödemek istersiniz?
[urdemek]
Access/Visa
Access'le/Visa'yla
yes, sir peki efendim
what's the number?
numarası nedir?
[noomarasuh]
and the expiry date? ve ne
zamana kadar geçerli?
[veh neh – gecherlee]

Crete Girit [geereet]
crisps çips [cheeps]
crockery tabak takımları
  [takuhmlaruh]
crossing (by sea) geçiş
  [gecheesh]
crossroads kavşak [kavshak]
crowd kalabalık [kalabaluhk]
crowded kalabalık
crown (on tooth) kuron

cruise vapur gezisi
crutches koltuk değnekleri
[deh-nekleree]
cry (verb) ağlamak [a-lamak]
cucumber salatalık [salataluhk]
cup fincan [feenjan]
 a cup of ..., please lütfen bir
 fincan ... [lewtfen]
cupboard dolap
cure (verb) tedavi etmek
curly kıvırcık [kuhvuhrjuhk]
current (electrical) akım
 [akuhm]
 (in water) akıntı [akuhntuh]
curtains perdeler
cushion yastık [yastuhk]
custom gelenek
Customs Gümrük [gewmrewk]

Entering Turkey usually
entails a cursory Customs
inspection: a record of
laptop computers, video cameras
etc, may be made in your passport
to ensure that you take them out
with you when you leave. Checks on
the way out may be more thorough,
and you should arrive at the airport
or ferry dock in good time. Only an
idiot would try to take drugs through
Turkish Customs.

cut (noun) kesik
 (verb) kesmek
 I've cut my finger parmağımı
 kestim [parma-uhmuh]
cutlery çatal bıçak [chatal
 buhchak]
cycling bisiklete binmek

[beeseekleteh]
cyclist bisikletli
Cypriot (adj) Kıbrıs [kuhbruhs]
 (person) Kıbrıslı [kuhbruhsluh]
Cyprus Kıbrıs

D

dad baba
daily her gün [gewn]
 (adj) günlük [gewnlewk]
damage (verb) zarar vermek
damaged hasar görmüş
 [gurmewsh]
 I'm sorry, I've damaged this
 özür dilerim, bunu bozdum
 [urzewr]
damn! Allah kahretsin!
damp (adj) nemli
dance (noun) dans
 (verb) dans etmek
 would you like to dance?
 dans etmek ister misiniz?
dangerous tehlikeli
Danish (adj) Danimarka
 (language) Danimarkaca
 [–markaja]
Dardanelles Çanakkale
 Boğazı [chanakkaleh bo-azuh]
dark (adj: colour) koyu
 (skin, hair) esmer
 it's getting dark hava
 kararıyor [kararuh-yor]
date*: what's the date today?
 bugün ayın kaçı? [boogewn
 ī-uhn kachuh]
 let's make a date for next
 Monday gelecek pazartesi

için randevulaşalım [gelejek – eecheen randevoolashaluhm]

dates (fruit) hurma

daughter kız evlat [kuhz]

daughter-in-law gelin

dawn (noun) şafak [shafak]
 at dawn gün ağarırken [gewn a-aruhrken]

day gün [gewn]
 the day after ertesi gün
 the day after tomorrow öbür gün [urbewr]
 the day before bir gün önce [urnjeh]
 the day before yesterday evvelki gün
 every day her gün
 all day bütün gün [bewtewn]
 in two days' time iki gün içinde [gewn eecheendeh]
 have a nice day! iyi günler!

day trip günlük gezi gewnlewk

dead ölü [urlew]

deaf sağır [sa-uhr]

deal (business) iş [eesh]
 it's a deal anlaştık [anlashtuhk]

death ölüm [urlewm]

decaffeinated coffee kafeinsiz kahve [kafeh-eenseez kaнveh]

December aralık [araluhk]

decide karar vermek
 we haven't decided yet henüz karar vermedik [henewz]

decision karar

deck (on ship) güverte [gewverteh]

deckchair şezlong [shezlong]

deep derin

definitely kesinlikle [keseenleekleh]
 definitely not kesinlikle değil [deh-eel]

degree (qualification) diploma

delay (noun) gecikme [gejeekmeh]

deliberately kasten

delicatessen şarküteri [sharkewteree]

delicious nefis

deliver teslim etmek

delivery (of mail) dağıtım [da-uhtuhm]

Denmark Danimarka

dental floss diş ipi [deesh]

dentist dişçi [deesh-chee]

 Turkish dentists are called **diş doktoru, diş tabibi** or **hekimi** and are well qualified and experienced. Foreign visitors usually have to pay for medication and treatment by private dentists. However, the cost of treatment is low and can be claimed against insurance if receipts are obtained.

dialogue

it's this one here işte buradaki [eeshteh buradaki]
this one? bu mu?
no, that one hayır, şu [hï-**uhr** shoo]
here? buradaki mi?
yes evet

dentures takma diş [deesh]
deodorant deodoran
department bölüm [burlewm]
department store büyük mağaza [bew-yewk ma-aza]
departure kalkış [kalkuhsh]
departure lounge giden yolcular salonu
depend: it depends duruma göre [gur-reh]
it depends on ... ...-a bağlı [ba-luh]
deposit (noun) depozito
dervish derviş [derveesh]
description tanım [tanuhm]
dessert tatlı [tatluh]
destination gidilecek yer [geedeelejek]
develop (film) banyo etmek

dialogue

> **could you develop these films?** bu filmleri banyo edebilir misiniz?
> **yes, certainly** evet, tabi
> **when will they be ready?** ne zaman hazır olurlar? [neh – hazuhr]
> **tomorrow afternoon** yarın öğleden sonra
> **how much is the four-hour service?** dört saatlik servisin ücreti nedir? [durt sa-atleek – ewjretee]

diabetic (noun) şeker hastası [sheker hastasuh]
diabetic foods şeker hastaları

için diyet yemeği [–laruh eecheen – yemeh-ee]
dial (verb) çevirmek [cheveermek]
dialling code telefon kodu
dialling tone çevir sesi [cheveer]

 For direct international calls from Turkey, dial 00, then the country code (given below), the area code minus the first 0, and finally the subscriber number:

USA and Canada 1 Britain 44
Ireland 353 Australia 63
New Zealand 64

diamond elmas
diaper çocuk bezi [chojook]
diarrhoea ishal
do you have something for diarrhoea? sizde ishale karşı bir ilaç var mı? [seezdeh eeshaleh karshuh beer eelach var muh]
diary (business etc) ajanda [ajanda]
(for personal experiences) günce [gewnjeh]
dictionary sözlük [surzlewk]
didn't see **not**
Didyma Didim
die ölmek [urlmek]
diesel mazot
diet perhiz [perheez]
I'm on a diet perhiz yapıyorum [yapuh-yoroom]
I have to follow a special diet

özel bir rejim izlemem gerekiyor [urzel beer reJeem]

difference fark
what's the difference? ne fark var? [neh]

different başka [bashka]
this one is different bu farklı [farkluh]
a different table başka bir masa

difficult zor

difficulty zorluk

dinghy sandal

dining room yemek salonu

dinner (evening meal) akşam yemeği [aksham yemeh-ee] (midday meal) öğle yemeği [urleh]
to have dinner akşam yemeği yemek

direct (adj) direkt
is there a direct train? direkt giden bir tren var mı? [muh]

direction yön [yurn]
which direction is it? hangi yönde? [yurndeh]
is it in this direction? bu yönde mi?

directory enquiries bilinmeyen numaralar [beeleenmayen]

Directory assistance 118
Inter-city operator 131
International operator 115

dirt pislik, kir

dirty kirli

disabled özürlü [urzewrlew]

is there access for the disabled? özürlüler için giriş var mı? [urzewrlewler eecheen geereesh var muh]

disappear kaybolmak [kibolmak]
it's disappeared ortadan kayboldu [kiboldoo]

disappointed hayal kırıklığına uğramış [hī-al kuhruhkluh-uhna oo-ramuhsh]

disappointing düş kırıcı [dewsh kuhruhjuh]

disaster felaket

disco disko

discount indirim
is there a discount? indirim var mı? [muh]

disease hastalık [hastaluhk]

disgusting iğrenç [eerench]

dish (meal) yemek (bowl) tabak

dishcloth bulaşık bezi [boolashuhk]

disinfectant (noun) dezenfektan

disk (for computer) disket

disposable diapers/nappies kâğıt çocuk bezi [ka-uht chojook]

distance uzaklık [oozakluhk]
in the distance uzakta

distilled water arı su [aruh soo]

district semt

disturb rahatsız etmek [rahatsuhz]

diversion (detour) geçici güzergah [gecheejee gewzergaH]

diving board tramplen
divorced boşanmış
[boshanm**uhsh**]
dizzy: I feel dizzy başım
dönüyor [bash**uhm** durnew-y**or**]
do (verb) yapmak
  what shall we do? ne
  yapalım? [neh yapal**uhm**]
  how do you do it? onu nasıl
  yapıyorsunuz? [nas**uhl** yap**uh**–]
  will you do it for me? benim
  için bunu yapar mısınız?
  [eech**ee**n – muhsuhn**uh**]

I do, but she doesn't ben
isterim ama o istemiyor

doctor dok**t**or
  we need a doctor bize bir
  doktor lazım [beez**eh** –
  laz**uhm**]
  please call a doctor lütfen
  bir doktor çağırın [**lew**tfen –
  cha-uhr**uhn**]

You'll find well-trained doctors in larger towns and cities. Most of these are specialists, advertising themselves by means of signs outside their premises. Look for the words **dahiliye mütehassısı** or **iç hastalıkları mütehassısı**: both mean 'specialist in internal diseases' and are the nearest to a general doctor.

If you're not sure what's wrong with you, it's best to go instead to one of the free state clinics (who can give diagnoses and prescriptions) or a hospital. Hospitals are either public (**Devlet Hastanesi** or **SSK Hastanesi**) or private (**Özel Hastane**); the latter are vastly preferable in terms of cleanliness, shortness of queues and standard of care, and since all foreigners must pay for any attention anyway, you may as well get the best available. You should take out an insurance policy to cover against illness or injury before travelling to Turkey.

dialogue

  how do you do?
  nasılsınız? [nas**uhl**-suhnuhz]
  nice to meet you
  tanıştığımıza memnun
  oldum [tanuhshtuh-uhm**uh**za]
  what do you do? (work) ne
  iş yapıyorsunuz? [neh eesh]
  I'm a teacher, and you?
  öğretmenim, ya siz?
  [ur-retmen**ee**m]
  I'm a student öğrenciyim
  [**ur**-renj**ee**-veem]
  **what are you doing this
  evening?** bu akşam ne
  yapıyorsunuz?
  **we're going out for a drink,
  do you want to join us?** bir
  şey içmeye gidiyoruz,
  bize katılmak ister
  misiniz? [shay eechmay**eh** –
  beez**eh** katuhlmak]
  do you want cream?
  krema ister misiniz?

dialogue

where does it hurt? neresi
acıyor? [ajuh-**yor**]
right here tam burası
[booras**uh**]
does that hurt now? şimdi
acıyor mu? [sheemd**ee**]
yes evet
take this to the chemist
alın bunu, eczaneye
götürün [al**uh**n – ejzanay**eh**
gurtewr**ewn**]

document belge [belg**eh**]
dog köpek [kurp**ek**]
doll bebek
dome kubbe [koobb**eh**]
domestic flight iç hat seferi
[**eech**]
donkey eşek [**esh**ek]
don't!* yapma!
 don't do that! onu yapma!
 see **not**
door kapı [kap**uh**]
doorman kapıcı [kapuhj**uh**]
double çift [cheeft]
double bed iki kişilik yatak
 [keeshee**leek**]
double room iki kişilik oda
down (direction) aşağı [asha-**uh**]
 down here burda aşağıda
 put it down over there onu
 şuraya bırakın [shoorï-**a**
 buhrak**uh**n]
 it's down there on the right
 şurada, aşağıda sağda
 [shoora**da** – sa-**da**]
 it's further down the road

yolun daha aşağısında
[asha-uhsuhnd**a**]
downmarket (restaurant etc)
gösterişsiz [gurstereesh-s**eez**]
downstairs alt kat
dozen düzine [dewz**ee**neh]
 half a dozen yarım düzine
 [yar**uh**m]
drain (in sink) pis su borusu
 (in street) kanalizasyon
draught beer fıçı birası
 [fuhch**uh** beeras**uh**]
draughty: **it's draughty**
cereyan yapıyor [jeray**an**
yapuh-**yor**]
drawer çekmece [chekmej**eh**]
drawing çizim [cheez**eem**]
dreadful berbat
dream (noun) rüya [rew-**ya**]
dress (noun) elbise [elbis**eh**]
dressed: **to get dressed**
giyinmek
dressing (for cut) pansuman
 salad dressing sos
dressing gown (for women)
sabahlık [sabaH**luh**k]
 (for men) robdöşambr
 [robdursh**ambr**]
drink (alcoholic) içki [**eech**kee]
 (non-alcoholic) içecek
 [eechej**ek**], meşrubat
 [meshroob**at**]
 (verb) içmek [eech**mek**]
 a cold drink soğuk meşrubat
 [so-**ook**]
 can I get you a drink? içecek
 bir şey ister misiniz? [shay]
 **what would you like (to
 drink)?** ne içki alırsınız? [neh

eechk**ee** aluhrsuhn**uh**z]
no thanks, I don't drink hayır
teşekkür, ederim alkol
almıyorum [hī-**uh**r teshekk**ew**r
– **a**lmuh-yoroom]
I'll just have a drink of water
sadece bir**a**z su istiyorum
[sa-dej**eh**]
see **bar**
drinking water içme suyu
[eechm**eh**]
is this drinking water? bu
içme suyu mu?

 It's probably best to
avoid drinking tap
water, heavily chlorinated
though it is, and with bottled water
widely available you shouldn't
need to.

drive (verb) sürmek [sewrm**ek**]
we drove here buraya
arabayla geldik [b**oo**rī-a
arab**ī**la]
I'll drive you home ben sizi
arabayla evinize
götürürüm [cvconoozo**h**
yurtewr-ewr**aw**m]

You drive on the right, and
always yield to those
approaching from the
right. Speed limits are 50km/hr
within towns, 90km/hr on the open
road for saloon cars and 80km/hr for
lorries and vans. Major violations
such as jumping red lights, speeding
or drink driving carry very heavy on-

the-spot fines. Breathalyzers
(**üfleme cihazı**) are widely used by
the traffic police. The legal limit for
blood alcohol level when driving a
car is .05% but do not drink and
drive.

driver (of car) sürücü
[sewrewj**ew**]
(of bus) şoför [shof**u**r]
driving licence şoför ehliyeti
drop: just a drop, please (of
drink) yalnız bir damla,
lütfen [yaln**uh**z – l**ew**tfen]
drugs (narcotics) uyuşturucu
[oo-yooshtoorooj**oo**]
drunk (adj) sarhoş [sarh**osh**]
drunken driving içkili araba
kullanmak [eechkeel**ee**]
dry (adj) kuru
(wine) sek
dry-cleaner kuru temizleyici
[temeezl**ay**eejee]
duck ördek [**u**rdek]
**due: he/she was due to arrive
yesterday** dün gelmesi
gerekiyordu [d**ew**n]
when is the train due? tren
kaçta gelecek? [k**a**chta
gelej**ek**]
dull (pain) donuk
(weather) sıkıntılı
[suhkuhntuhl**uh**]
dummy (baby's) emzik
during sırasında [suhra-s**uh**nda]
dust toz
dustbin çöp tenekesi [churp]
dusty tozlu
Dutch (adj) Hollanda

(language) Hollandaca
[hollandaja]
duty-free (goods) gümrüksüz
eşya [gewmr**ew**ksewz esh-ya]
duty-free shop duty-free
duvet yorgan

E

each (every) her
  how much are they each?
  tanesi kaça? [kacha]
ear kulak
earache: I have earache
  kulağım ağrıyor [koola-**uh**m
  a-ruh-yor]
early erken
  early in the morning sabah
  erkenden [saba**H**]
  I called by earlier daha önce
  uğramıştım [**u**rnjeh
  oo-ramuhshtuhm]
earring(s) küpe [kewpeh]
east doğu [doh-**oo**]
  in the east doğuda
Easter Paskalya
easy kolay [ko-l**ī**]
eat yemek
  we've already eaten, thanks
  biz yedik, teşekkür ederiz
  [teshekk**ewr**]

eating habits
Breakfasts usually
consist of well-brewed
tea (without milk), bread or toast,
butter, jam or honey, olives and
sheep's cheese. Sometimes sliced
tomatoes, cucumber and boiled
eggs are also available, as is soup.
Tripe soup for early starters is also
appreciated by many after a late
night out.

Lunch (**öğle yemeği**) can be a
simple toasted sandwich or **börek**
(flaky, layered pastry containing
cheese, spinach or minced meat)
washed down with **ayran** (yoghurt
drink). Otherwise it is very similar to
dinner (**akşam yemeği**) which is
usually the main meal of the day.
They both start with soup followed
by a meat dish served with rice or
potatoes and a salad. Turkish
cuisine is rich in vegetable dishes –
some of which are cooked with
meat.

A vegetable dish follows the meat
dish. Some vegetable dishes are
cooked with olive oil (**zeytinyağlı**)
and are served cold. The meal ends
with dessert (**tatlı**) or fruit (**meyva**).
The most famous desserts are
baklava (layers of filo pastry filled
with pistachio nuts or walnuts and
soaked in syrup), **sütlaç** (rice
pudding) and **tavuk göğsü** (milk
pudding).

Most Turks, being Muslim, either do
not drink alcohol or drink very little.
Turkish men sometimes drink **rakı**
and water when out in restaurants
but in general and when at home
most people drink water with meals.
If Turks do drink in the evening, they
will usually accompany the alcohol
with **mezes** (hors d'œuvres). There

are lots of different mezes and a typical selection might include **sigara böreği** (cigarette-shaped filo pastry with cheese and parsley filling), **cacık** (yoghurt, cucumber and garlic dip), **patlıcan salatası** (aubergine purée salad), **zeytinyağlı dolma** (stuffed vine leaves or green peppers), **imam bayıldı** (an aubergine dish cooked with olive oil), sheep's cheese and olives. Sometimes mezes form a starter to a main meal.

eau de toilette kolonya
EC AT [a teh]
economy class ekonomi sınıfı [suhnuhf**uh**]
Edinburgh Edinburg
egg yumurta
eggplant patlıcan [patl**uh**jan]
either: either ... or ... ya ... ya ...
  either of them ikisinden biri
elastic (noun) lastik
elastic band lastik bant
elbow dirsek
electric elektrikli
electrical appliances elektrikli aletler
electric fire elektrik sobası [sobas**uh**]
electrician elektrikçi [elektreekch**ee**]
electricity elektrik
  see voltage
elevator asansör [asans**ur**]
else: something else başka bir şey [b**a**shka beer shay]

somewhere else başka bir yer

dialogue

> **would you like anything else?** başka bir şey ister misiniz?
> **no, nothing else, thanks** hayır, hepsi bu kadar, teşekkür ederim [hī-**uh**r – teshekk**ewr**]

e-mail email
embassy elçilik [elchee**leek**]
emergency acil durum [ajeel]
  this is an emergency! bu acildir! [ajeel**deer**]
emergency exit tehlike çıkışı [tehleek**eh** chukuhsh**uh**]
empty boş [bosh]
end (noun) son
  (verb) bitmek
  at the end of the ... (street etc) ...-un sonunda
  when does it end? ne zaman bitiyor?
engaged (toilet, telephone) meşgul [meshg**ool**]
  (to be married) nişanlı [neeshanl**uh**]
engine (car) motor
England İngiltere [eengeelt**ereh**]
English (adj) İngiliz [**ee**ngeeleez]
  (language) İngilizce [eengeel**ee**zjeh]
I'm English ben İngilizim

do you speak English?
İngilizce biliyor musunuz?
enjoy: to enjoy oneself
eğlenmek [eh-lenmek]

dialogue

how did you like the film?
filmi nasıl buldunuz?
[nasuhl]
I enjoyed it very much, did
you enjoy it? benim çok
hoşuma gitti, ya sizin?
[chok hoshooma]

enjoyable zevkli
enlargement (of photo)
büyültme [bew-yewltmeh]
enormous dev
enough yeter
there's not enough yetmez
it's not big enough yeterince
büyük değil [yetereenjeh bew-
yewk deh-eel]
that's enough bu kadar yeter
entrance giriş [geereesh]
envelope zarf
Ephesus Efes
epileptic (adj) saralı [saraluh]
equipment donatım
[donatuhm]
error hata
especially özellikle
[urzelleekleh]
essential şart [shart]
it is essential that ... ...-sı
şarttır [-shuh sharttuhr]
EU AB [a beh]
Eurocheque Eurocheque

Eurocheque card
Eurocheque kardı [karduh]
Europe Avrupa
European (adj) Avrupa
(person) Avrupalı [avroopaluh]
even ... ... bile [beeleh]
even if ... ...-se bile [-seh]
evening akşam [aksham]
this evening bu akşam
in the evening akşamleyin
[akshamlayeen]
evening meal akşam yemeği
[yemeh-ee]
eventually sonunda
ever hiç [heech]

dialogue

have you ever been to
Antalya? hiç Antalya'ya
gittiniz mi?
yes, I was there two years
ago evet, iki yıl önce
ordaydım [yuhl urnjeh
ordíduhm]

every her
every day her gün [gewn]
everyone herkes
everything her şey [shay]
everywhere her yer
exactly! çok doğru! [chok doh-
roo]
exam sınav [suhnav]
example örnek [urnek]
for example örneğin
[urneh-een]
excellent mükemmel
[mewkemmel]

(food) nefis
(hotel) çok güzel [chok gewzel]
excellent! mükemmel!
except ... ... hariç [hareech]
excess baggage fazla bagaj
[bagaJ]
exchange rate döviz kuru
[durveez]
exciting heyecan verici
[hayejan vereejee]
excuse me (to get past) pardon
(to get attention) affedersiniz
(to say sorry) özür dilerim
[urzewr]
exhaust (pipe) egzos borusu
exhausted (tired) bitkin
exhibition sergi
exit çıkış [chuhkuhsh]
  where's the nearest exit? en
  yakın çıkış nerede? [yakuhn –
  neredeh]
expect beklemek
expensive pahalı [paнaluh]
experienced tecrübeli
[tejrewbelee]
explain açıklamak
[achuhklamak]
  can you explain that? onu
  açıklar mısınız? [achuhklar
  muhsuhnuhz]
express (mail, train) ekspres
extension (telephone) dahili
numara [daнeelee]
  what is your extension?
  dahili numaranız nedir?
  [noomaranuhz]
  extension 221, please iki yüz
  yirmi bir numara, lütfen
  [yewz – lewtfen]

extension lead uzatma
kablosu
**extra: can we have an extra
one?** lütfen bir tane daha
[lewtfen – taneh]
  do you charge extra for that?
  bunun için ayrıca para
  alıyor musunuz? [eecheen
  īruhja para aluh-yor]
extraordinary çok garip [chok
gareep]
extremely son derece
[derejeh]
eye göz [gurz]
  **will you keep an eye on my
  suitcase for me?** benim için
  bavuluma göz kulak olur
  musunuz? [eecheen]
eyebrow pencil kaş kalemi
[kash]

eye contact
Local people often stare
blatantly at foreigners,
and such attention should not be
interpreted as rudeness. However,
staring back is likely to be
interpreted as hostility or – if you're
a woman – an invitation to further
interaction. Scrupulously avoiding
eye contact is one of the best
defences against sexual
harassment.

eye drops göz damlası [gurz
damlasuh]
eyeglasses (US) gözlük
[gurzlewk]
eyeliner eyeliner

eye make-up remover göz
makyajı çıkarıcısı [gurz
makyaJ**uh** chuhkaruh-juhs**uh**]
eye shadow far

F

face yüz [yewz]
factory fabrika
Fahrenheit* Fahrenhayt [–hīt]
faint (verb) bayılmak
  [bī-uhlmak]
  she's fainted bayıldı
  [bī-uhld**uh**]
  I feel faint kendimi çok
  halsiz hissediyorum [chok]
fair (funfair) panayır [panī-**uhr**]
  (trade) fuar [fwar]
  (adj: just) adil, haklı [hakl**uh**]
fairly oldukça [old**oo**kcha]
fake taklit
fall (verb) düşmek [dewshmek]
  she's had a fall düştü
  [dewshtew]
  (US: noun) sonbahar
  in the fall sonbaharda
false sahte [saHt**eh**]
Famagusta Magosa
family aile [a-**ee**leh]
famous ünlü [ewnl**ew**]
fan (electrical) vantilatör
  [vanteelat**ur**]
  (handheld) yelpaze [yelpaz**eh**]
  (sports) taraftar
  (of pop star etc) hayran [hīran]
fanbelt vantilatör kayışı
  [vanteelat**ur** kī-uhsh**uh**]
fantastic fantastik, hayali

far uzak

dialogue

is it far from here?
buradan uzak mı? [muh]
no, not very far hayır, pek
uzak değil [hī-**uhr** – deh-**eel**]
well, how far? peki ne
kadar uzak? [neh]
it's about 20 kilometres
yaklaşık yirmi kilometre
[yaklashu**h**k – keelometr**eh**]

fare yol parası [paras**uh**]
farm çiftlik [cheeftl**eek**]
fashionable moda
fast hızlı [huhzl**uh**]
fat (person) şişman [sheeshman]
  (on meat) yağ [ya]
father baba
father-in-law kayınpeder
  [kī-**uh**npeder]
faucet musluk
fault hata
  sorry, it was my fault özür
  dilerim, hata bendeydi
  [urz**ewr** – benda**ydee**]
  it's not my fault hata bende
  değil [bend**eh** deh-**eel**]
faulty arızalı [aruhzal**uh**]
favourite gözde [gurzd**eh**]
fax faks
fax (verb: person) –a faks
  çekmek [chekmek]
  (document) fakslamak
February şubat [shoobat]
feel hissetmek
  I feel hot sıcak bastı [suhjak

bast**uh**]
I feel unwell kendimi kötü
hissediy**o**rum [kurt**ew**]
I feel like going for a walk
canım yürüyüşe çıkmak
istiyor [jan**uh**m yewrew-yewsheh
ch**uh**kmak]
how are you feeling?
kendin**i**zi nasıl
hissediy**o**rsunuz? [nas**uhl**]
I'm feeling better kendimi
daha iyi hissediy**o**rum
felt-tip (pen) keçe uçlu kalem
[kech**eh** oochl**oo**]
fence parmaklık [parmakl**uhk**]
fender tampon
ferry feribot

City ferries, mainly
serving foot passengers
and connecting points
within places like İstanbul and İzmir,
are frequent, cheap and efficient,
running to very tight schedules. In
addition to these are short-hop
ferries, some of which serve foot
passengers only, while others have
provision for vehicles. Long-haul
domestic ferries are now restricted
to the coastal stretches where the
road network is substandard,
specifically between İstanbul and
Trabzon – with intermediate stops –
and direct from İstanbul to İzmir. All
long-haul services are very popular,
and reservations must be made well
in advance through one of the
authorized TML agencies in the
appropriate ports.

festival festival
fetch gidip getirmek
I'll fetch him/her gidip onu
çağırayım [cha-uhrı-**uhm**]
will you come and fetch me
later? sonra gelip beni alır
mısınız? [al**uhr** muhsuhn**uhz**]
feverish ateşli [ateshl**ee**]
few: a few birkaç [beerk**ach**]
a few days birkaç gün
[g**ewn**]
fiancé(e) nişanlı [neeshanl**uh**]
field tarla
fight (noun) kavga
figs incir [eenje**er**]
fill in doldurmak
do I have to fill this in?
bunu doldurmam gerekli
mi?
fill up doldurmak
fill it up, please lütfen
depoyu doldur**u**n [**lew**tfen
depo-y**oo**]
filling (in cake, sandwich) iç
[eech]
(in tooth) dolg**u**
film film

dialogue

do you have this kind of
film? sizde bu tip film var
mı? [seezd**eh** boo teep – m**uh**]
yes, how many exposures?
evet, kaç pozluk? [kach
pozl**ook**]
36 otuz altı

film processing film banyos**u**

filter coffee süzme kahve
[sewzmeh kahveh]
filter papers filtre kağıdı
[feeltreh ka-uhduh]
filthy pis [pees]
find (verb) bulmak
I can't find it bulamıyorum
[boolamuh-yoroom]
I've found it buldum
find out sorup öğrenmek
[ur-renmek]
could you find out for me?
benim için öğrenir misiniz?
[eecheen ur-reneer]
fine (weather) güzel [gewzel]
(punishment) ceza [jeza]

dialogues

how are you? nasılsınız?
[nasuhl-suhnuhz]
I'm fine, thanks iyiyim,
teşekkür ederim
[teshekkewr]

is that OK? nasıl, olur mu?
that's fine, thanks tamam,
teşekkür ederim

finger parmak
finish (verb) bitirmek
I haven't finished yet henüz
bitirmedim [henewz]
when does it finish? ne
zaman bitiyor? [neh]
fire (in hearth, campfire etc) ateş
[atesh]
(blaze) yangın [yanguhn]
fire! yangın var!

can we light a fire here?
burada ateş yakabilir miyiz?
it's on fire yanıyor [yanuh-yor]
fire alarm yangın alarmı
[yanguhn alarmuh]
fire brigade itfaiye [eetfa-ee-
yeh]

Dial 110 for the fire
brigade. This call costs
one small jeton, or one
phonecard unit.

fire escape yangın merdiveni
[yanguhn]
fire extinguisher yangın
söndürücü [surndewrew-jew]
first ilk, birinci [beereenjee]
I was first ilk bendim
at first ilk önce [urnjeh]
the first time ilk kez
first on the left soldan birinci
first aid ilk yardım [yarduhm]
first aid kit ilk yardım çantası
[chantasuh]
first class (travel etc) birinci
sınıf [beereenjee suhnuhf]
first floor birinci kat
(US) zemin kat
first name ad
fish (noun) balık [baluhk]
fish restaurant balık lokantası
[baluhk lokantasuh]
fishing village balıkçı köyü
[baluhkchuh kur-yew]
fishmonger's balıkçı
fit (attack) nöbet [nurbet]
fit: it doesn't fit me bana
uymuyor [oo-imoo-yor]

fitting room soyunma odası
[odas**uh**]
fix (arrange) halletmek
 can you fix this? (repair) bunu
 tamir edebilir misiniz?
fizzy gazlı [gazl**uh**]
flag bayrak [bīrak]
flannel el havlusu
flash (for camera) flaş [flash]
flat (noun: apartment) apartman
 dairesi [da-**ee**resee], daire
 [da-**ee**reh]
 (adj) düz [dewz]
 I've got a flat tyre lastiğim
 patladı [lastee-**ee**m patlad**uh**]
flavour tat
flea pire [peer**eh**]
flight uçak seferi [**oo**chak]
flight number sefer sayısı
 [si-uhs**uh**]
flippers paletler
flood sel
floor (of room) yer
 (storey) kat
 on the floor yerde [yerd**eh**]
florist çiçekçi [cheechekchee]
flour un
flower çiçek [cheechek]
flu grip [gr**oo**p]
fluent: he speaks fluent
 Turkish akıcı bir Türkçesi
 var [akuhj**uh** beer tewrkchesee]
fly (noun) sinek
 (verb) uçmak [**oo**chmak]
fly in inmek
fly out uçmak [**oo**chmak]
fog sis
foggy: it's foggy sisli
folk dancing halk oyunları

[oyunlar**uh**]
folk music halk müziği
 [mewz**ee**-ee]
follow takip etmek
 follow me beni takip edin
food yiyecek [yee-yejek]
food poisoning gıda
 zehirlenmesi [g**uh**da]
food shop/store bakkal
foot* (of person, measurement)
 ayak [ī-ak]
 on foot yayan [yī-an]
football (game) futbol
 (ball) top
football match futbol maçı
 [mach**uh**]
for için [eecheen]
 do you have something
 for ...? (headache/diarrhoea
 etc) ...için bir şeyiniz var
 mı? [shayeen**eez** var muh]

dialogues

who's the imam bayıldı
for? imam bayıldı kim
için? [bī-uhld**uh**]
that's for me o benim için
and this one? ya bu?
that's for her o, bayanın
 [bī-an**uh**n]

where do I get the bus for
İzmir? İzmir otobüsüne
nereden binebilirim?
[**ee**zmeer otob**ew**sewneh]
the bus for İzmir leaves
from İstiklal Caddesi İzmir
otobüsü İstiklal

Caddesi'nden kalkıyor
[kalk**uh**-yor]

how long have you been here for? ne zamandan beri buradasınız? [neh – boo**radasuhnuhz**]

I've been here for two days, how about you? ben iki gündür buradayım, ya siz? [gewnd**ewr boo**radī-uhm]

I've been here for a week bir haftadır buradayım [haftad**uhr boo**radī-uhm]

forehead alın [al**uhn**]
foreign yabancı [yabanj**uh**]
foreigner yabancı
forest orman
forget unutmak
  I forget, I've forgotten unuttum
fork çatal [**chatal**]
  (in road) iki yol ağzı [**a**-zuh]
form (document) form, formüler [**formewl**er]
formal (dress) resmi
fortnight on beş gün [besh gewn]
fortress kale [kal**eh**]
fortunately bereket versin
forward: could you forward my mail? mektuplarımı yeni adresime gönderir misiniz? [–lar**uhm**uh – **a**dreseemeh gurnder**eer**]
forwarding address gönderilecek adres [gurndereel**e**jek]

foundation cream fondöten [**fondurt**en]
fountain çeşme [cheshm**eh**]
foyer giriş holü [geer**ee**sh hol**ew**], fuaye [fwī-eh]
fracture (noun) kırık [k**uhruhk**]
France Fransa
free serbest
  (no charge) bedava
  is it free (of charge)? ücretsiz mi? [ewjrets**eez**]
freeway otoyol
  see **road**
freezer buzluk
French (adj) Fransız [frans**uhz**]
  (language) Fransızca [frans**uhz**ja]
French fries patates kızartması [kuhzartmas**uh**]
frequent sık [suhk]
  how frequent is the bus to Edirne? Edirne'ye kaç saatte bir otobüs var? [edeern**eh**-yeh kach sa-att**eh**]
fresh (breeze) serin
  (fruit etc) taze [taz**eh**]
fresh orange juice taze portakal suy**u**
Friday cuma [jooma]
fridge buzdolabı [**boo**zdolabuh]
fried kızarmış [kuhzarm**uhsh**]
fried egg yağda yumurta [ya-da]
friend arkadaş [**arkadash**]
friendly (person, animal) sokulgan
  (behaviour) dostça [**dost**cha]
from –den
  when does the next train

from Eskişehir arrive?
Eskişehir'den bir sonraki
tren ne zaman geliyor?
[eskiseheer-**den** – neh]
from Monday to Friday
Pazartesiden Cumaya
from next Thursday bir
dahaki Perşembeden
itibaren

dialogue

> **where are you from?**
> nerelisiniz?
> **I'm from Slough** ben
> Slough'lıyım [–luh-y**uhm**]

front ön [urn]
  in front önde [urn**deh**]
  in front of the hotel otelin
  önünde [urnewnd**eh**]
  at the front ön tarafta
frost don
frozen donmuş [don**moo**sh]
  frozen food dondurulmuş
  yiyecekler [dondoorool-m**oo**sh
  yee-yejekl**er**]
fruit meyva [**mayva**]
fruit juice meyva suyu
fry kızartmak [k**uh**zartmak]
frying pan tava
full dolu
  it's full of ... ... ile dolu
  [eel**eh**]
  I'm full doydum
full board tam pansiyon
fun: it was fun eğlendik
  [eh-lend**eek**]
funeral cenaze [jenaz**eh**]

funny (strange) garip
  (amusing) komik
furniture mobilya
further ileride [ilereed**eh**]
  it's further down the road
  yolun ilerisinde [eeleree-
  seend**eh**]

dialogue

> **how much further is it to**
> **Troy?** Truva'ya daha ne
> kadar var? [neh]
> **about 5 kilometres**
> yaklaşık beş kilometre
> [yaklash**uhk** – keelometr**eh**]

fuse sigorta
  the lights have fused sigorta
  attı [att**uh**]
fuse box sigorta kutusu
fuse wire sigorta teli
future gelecek [gelej**ek**]
  in future gelecekte
  [gelejekt**eh**]

G

Gallipoli Gelibolu
gallon* galon
game (cards etc) oyun
  (match) maç [mach]
  (meat) av eti
garage (for fuel) benzin
  istasyonu
  (for repairs) tamirhane
  [tameerhan**eh**]
  (for parking) garaj [gara**J**]

Filling stations are amazingly numerous throughout most of the country, and open long hours. On the main roads they are often advertised a few miles in advance and are open 24 hours. Some also have adjoining service facilities which are also open 24 hours. Self service is unusual and a tip is appreciated. Diesel is **mazot**, while petrol is **benzin**, available in **normal** (3-star/regular) or **süper** (4-star/premium) grades. **Kurşunsuz** (lead-free) is becoming increasingly common, but is still almost impossible to come by in the remote east.

Avoid **Petrol Ofisi** and its affiliate **Türkpetrol** in favour of private filling stations run by BP, Shell or Mobil.

garden bahçe [baʜch**eh**]
garlic sarmısak [sarmuʜs**ak**]
gas gaz
 (US: petrol) benzin
 see **garage**
gas cylinder (camping gas) gaz tüpü [tewp**ew**]
gasoline benzin
 see **garage**
gas permeable lenses gaz geçirgen lensler [gecheerg**en**]
gas station benzin istasyon**u**
gate kapı [kap**uh**]
 (at airport) çıkış kapısı [chuʜk**uh**sh kapuʜs**uh**]
gay homoseksüel [homoseksew**el**]

gay bar eşcinsellerin barı [eshjeensellere**en** bar**uh**]
gearbox vites kutusu
gear lever vites kol**u**
gears vitesl**er**
general (adj) genel
gents (toilet) erkekler (tuvaleti)
genuine (antique etc) gerçek [gerch**ek**]
Georgia Gürcistan [gewrjeestan]
Georgian (adj) Gürcü [gewrj**ew**]
German (adj) Alman (language) Almanca [alman**ja**]
German measles kızamıkçık [kuhzamuhk-ch**uhk**]
Germany Almanya
get (fetch) getirmek (obtain, buy) almak, bulmak **will you get me another one, please?** bana bir tane daha getirir misiniz, lütfen? [tan**eh** – l**ew**tfen]
how do I get to ...? ...'e nasıl gidebilirim? [-eh nas**uhl**]
do you know where I can get them? onlardan nerede bulabilirim acaba, biliyor musunuz? [n**e**redeh – aj**aba**]

dialogue

can I get you a drink? bir şey içmek ister misiniz? [shay eechm**ek**]
no, I'll get this one, what would you like? olmaz, bu

sefer ben alacağım, ne istersiniz? [alaja-**uhm** neh]
a glass of red wine bir bardak kırmızı şarap

get back (return) dönmek [durn**mek**]
get in (arrive) gelmek
get off inmek
  where do I get off? nerede inmem lazım? [**ne**redeh – la**zuhm**]
get on (to train etc) binmek
get out (of car etc) inmek
get up (in the morning) kalkmak
gift hediye [hedee-**yeh**]
gift shop hediyelik eşya dükkanı [esh-ya dewkkan**uh**]
gin cin [jeen]
  a gin and tonic, please bir cintonik, lütfen [**lew**tfen]
girl kız [kuhz]
girlfriend kız arkadaş [arka**dash**]
give vermek
  can you give me some bread/milk? bana biraz ekmek/süt verebilir misiniz?
  I gave it to him/her ona verdim
  will you give this to ...? bunu ...-e verir misiniz? [-**eh**]
give back iade etmek [ee-a**deh**]
glad memnun
glass (material) cam [jam]
  (tumbler) bardak

(wine glass) kadeh
a glass of wine bir kadeh şarap
a glass of tea bir bardak çay
glasses gözlük [gurzl**ewk**]
gloves eldiven
glue (noun) zamk
go gitmek
  we'd like to go to the Topkapı Palace Topkapı Sarayı'na gitmek istiyoruz [**to**pkapuh sarī-uh-**na**]
  where are you going? nereye gidiyorsunuz? [**ne**rayeh]
  where does this bus go? bu otobüs nereye gidiyor?
  let's go! haydi gidelim! [hīdee]
  he/she's gone (left) gitti
  where has he gone? nereye gitti?
  I went there last week oraya geçen hafta gittim [orī-a gechen]
  hamburger to go paket hamburger
go away çekilip gitmek [chekee**leep**]
  go away! çekil git! [chek**eel** geet]
go back (return) dönmek [durn**mek**]
go down (the stairs etc) inmek
go in girmek
go out çıkmak [chuhk**mak**]
  do you want to go out tonight? bu akşam çıkmak ister misiniz? [aksham chuhk**mak**]

go through geçmek [gechmek]
go up (the stairs etc) çıkmak
[chuhkmak]
goat keçi [kechee]
goat's cheese keçi peyniri
[payneeree]
God Allah
god tanrı [tanruh]
goddess tanrıça [tanruhcha]
goggles koruyucu gözlük
[koroo-yoojoo gurzlewk]
gold altın [altuhn]
golf golf
golf course golf sahası
[sahasuh]
good iyi
good! iyi!
it's no good boşuna, yararsız
[boshoona yararsuhz]
goodbye (general use) hoşça
kalın [hosh-cha kaluhn]
(said by person leaving)
Allahaısmarladık [alaha-
uhsmarladuhk]
(said to person leaving) güle güle
[gewleh]
good evening iyi akşamlar
[akshamlar]
good morning günaydın
[gewnīduhn]
good night iyi geceler [gejeler]
goose kaz
got: we've got to leave
gitmemiz gerek
have you got any ...?
hiç ...-nız var mı?
[heech ...-nuhz var muh]
government hükümet
[hewkewmet]

gradually giderek
grammar gramer
gram(me)* gram
granddaughter torun
grandfather büyükbaba
[bewyewk-baba]
grandmother büyükanne
[bewyewk-anneh]
grandson torun
grapefruit greyfrut [grayfroot]
grapefruit juice greyfrut suyu
grapes üzüm [ewzewm]
grass ot
grateful minnettar
gravy sos
great (excellent) fevkalade
[fevkaladeh]
that's great! mükemmel!
[mewkemmel]
a great success büyük bir
başarı [bewyewk beer basharuh]
Great Britain Büyük
Britanya
Greece Yunanistan
greedy açgözlü [achgurzlew]
Greek (adj) Yunan
(language) Rumca [roomja]
(person) Yunanlı [yoonanluh]
(adj, person: living in Turkey)
Rum [room]
Greek Cypriot (adj) Kıbrıs
Rum [kuhbruhs]
(person) Kıbrıslı Rum
[kuhbruhsluh]
Greek Orthodox Rum
Ortodoks
green yeşil [yesheel]
green card (car insurance) yeşil
kart

greengrocer's manav

greeting people
On meeting or leaving a person of the same gender, men and women kiss on the cheeks, at least once each side – but when greeting a person of the opposite sex you should just shake hands, unless you know them very well. You will please many old people if you kiss their hand when introduced. For this you do not really kiss but put the hand first towards your lips then to your forehead. If you are a woman, some older men may not give their hand at all.

grey gri [gree]
grill (noun) ızgara [uhzgara]
grilled ızgara [uhzgara]
grocer's bakkal
ground yer
 on the ground yerde [yerdeh]
ground floor zemin kat
group grup
guarantee (noun) garanti
 is it guaranteed? garantisi var mı? [muh]
guest misafir
guesthouse pansiyon

Often the most pleasant places to stay are **pansiyons**, small guesthouses which increasingly have en suite facilities. If there are vacancies in season, touts in the coastal resorts and other tourist targets descend on every incoming bus, **dolmuş** or boat; at other places or times, look for the sign **boş oda var** (literally: empty rooms free). The Turkish pansiyon breakfast is often served in the common gardens or terraces that are this kind of accommodation's strong point. Rooms tend to be sparse but clean. Laundry facilities – even if just a drying line and a plastic bucket – are almost always present. Hot showers are rarely charged for separately; if they are, count on an extra dollar a go, as in modest hotels.

guide (person, book) rehber [reHber]
guidebook rehber
guided tour rehberli tur
guitar gitar
gum (in mouth) dişeti [deeshetee]
gun (rifle) tüfek [tewfek]
 (pistol) tabanca [tabanja]
gym spor salonu
gypsy çingene [cheegeneh]

H

hair saç [sach]
hairbrush saç fırçası [fuhrchasuh]
haircut (man's) saç tıraşı [tuhrashuh]
 (woman's) saç kesme [kesmeh]

hairdresser's (men's) berber
(women's) kuaför [kwafur]

In Turkey most
hairdressers are open
long hours every day of
the week except Sundays. However,
some hairdressers and barbers at
resorts may open on Sundays if they
think they may get customers.

hairdryer saç kurutma
makinesi [sach]
hair gel jel [Jel]
hairgrips saç tokaları [sach
tokalaruh]
hair spray saç spreyi [sprayee]
half yarım [yaruhm]
half an hour yarım saat
[sa-at]
half a litre yarım litre [leetreh]
about half that onun yarısı
kadar [yaruhsuh]
half board yarım pansiyon
half-bottle yarım şişe
[sheesheh]
half fare yarım tarife [tareefeh]
half price yarı fiyat [yaruh]
ham jambon [Jambon]
hamburger hamburger
[hamboorger]
hammer (noun) çekiç
[chekeech]
hand el
handbag el çantası [chantasuh]
handbrake el freni
handkerchief mendil
handle (on door) kol
(on suitcase etc) sap

hand luggage el bagajı
[bagaJuh]
hang-gliding hang-gliding
hangover içkiden gelen baş
ağrısı [eechkeeden – bash
a-ruhsuh]
I've got a hangover çok
içtiğim için başım ağrıyor
[chok eechtee-eem eecheen
bashuhm]
happen olmak
what's happening? ne
oluyor? [neh]
what has happened? ne
oldu?
happy mutlu
I'm not happy about this bu
hiç hoşuma gitmiyor [heech
hoshooma]
harbour liman
hard sert
(difficult) zor
hard-boiled egg lop yumurta
hard lenses sert lensler
hardly ancak [anjak]
hardly ever hemen hemen
hiç [heech]
hardware shop nalbur
hat şapka [shapka]
hate (verb) nefret etmek
have* sahip olmak
can I have a ...? bir ... rica
edebilir miyim? [reeja]
can we have some ...?
biraz ... rica edebilir miyiz?
do you have ...? sizde ...
bulunur mu? [seezdeh – muh]
what'll you have? ne
alırsınız? [neh aluhrsuhnuhz]

I have to leave now şimdi
gitmek zorundayım
[sheemdee – zoroondī-**uhm**]
do I have to ...? ...-m lazım
mı? [laz**uh**m muh]
hayfever saman nezlesi
hazelnuts fındık [fuhnd**uhk**]
he* o
head baş [bash]
headache baş ağrısı [a-ruhs**uh**]
headlights farlar
headphones kulaklıklar
[koolakluhk**lar**]
healthy sağlıklı [sa-luhkl**uh**]
hear duymak [doo-imak]

dialogue

can you hear me? beni
duyabiliyor musunuz?
I can't hear you, could you
repeat that? sizi
duyamıyorum, tekrar
söyler misiniz? [doo-yamuh-
yoroom – **suh**-iler]

hearing aid işitme cihazı
[eesheetmeh jeehaz**uh**]
heart kalp
heart attack kalp krizi
heat sıcaklık [suhjakl**uh**k]
heater (in room) ısıtıcı
[uhsuhtuhj**uh**]
(in car) radyatör [radyat**ur**]
heating ısıtma [uhsuhtma]
heavy ağır [a-**uhr**]
heel (of foot, shoe) topuk
could you heel these?
bunların topuklarını yapar

mısınız? [boonlar**uhn**
top**oo**klaruhnuh – muhsuhn**uhz**]
heelbar kundura tamircisi
[tameerjees**ee**]
height (of person) boy
(of mountain) yükseklik
[yewksekl**eek**]
helicopter helikopter
hello merhaba
(answer on phone) alo
helmet (for motorcycle) kask
help (noun) yardım [yard**uhm**]
(verb) yardım etmek
help! imdat!
can you help me? bana
yardım edebilir misiniz?
thank you very much for your
help yardımınız için çok
teşekkür ederim
[yarduhmuhn**uh**z eech**een** chok
teshekk**ewr**]
helpful yardımcı [yarduhmj**uh**]
hepatitis hepatit
her*: her ... ...-i, ...-si
(emphatic) onun ...
it's her towel onun havlusu
I haven't seen her onu
görmedim [gurmedeem]
to her ona
with her onunla
for her onun için [eech**een**]
that's her işte o [eeshteh]
herbal tea bitkisel çay [chī]
herbs çeşni veren otlar
[cheshnee]
here burada
here is/are ... işte ... [eesht**eh**]
here you are (offering) buyrun
[boo-iroon]

hers* onunki
 that's hers şu onunki [shoo]
hey! hey!
hi! (hello) merhaba!
hide (verb) saklamak
high yüksek [yewksek]
highchair bebek iskemlesi
highway otoyol
 see road
hill tepe [tepeh]
him*: I haven't seen him onu
 görmedim [gurmedeem]
 to him ona
 with him onunla
 for him onun için [eecheen]
 that's him over there
 şuradaki o işte [shooradakee o
 eeshteh]
hip kalça [kalcha]
Hippodrome At Meydanı
 [maydanuh]
hire kiralamak
 for hire kiralık [keeraluhk]
 where can I hire a bike?
 nereden bir bisiklet
 kiralayabilirim? [keeralï-
 abeeleereem]
 see bargaining and rent
his*: his ... ...-i, ...-si
 (emphatic) onun ...
 it's his car onun otomobili
 that's his şu onunki [shoo]
hit (verb) vurmak
hitch-hike otostop yapmak
hobby merak
hold (verb) tutmak
hole delik
holiday tatil
 on holiday tatilde [tateeldeh]

Holland Hollanda
home ev
 at home (in my house etc) evde
 [evdeh]
 (in my country) bizde [beezdeh]
 we go home tomorrow yarın
 evimize gidiyoruz [yaruhn
 eveemeezeh]
honest dürüst [dewrewst]
honey bal
honeymoon balayı [balï-uh]
hood (US) motor kapağı
 [kapa-uh], kaput
hookah nargile [nargeeleh]
hope umut
 I hope so umarım öyledir
 [oomaruhm uh-iledeer]
 I hope not umarım öyle
 değildir [uh-ileh deh-eeldeer]
hopefully inşallah [eenshallah]
horn (of car) klakson, korna
horrible korkunç [korkoonch]
horse at
horse riding binicilik
 [beeneejeeleek]
hospital hastane [hastaneh]
hospitality konukseverlik
 thank you for your hospitality
 konukseverliğiniz için
 teşekkürler [konookseverlee-
 eeneez icheen teshekkewler]
hot sıcak [suhjak]
 (spicy) acı [ajuh]
 I'm hot sıcak bastı [bastuh]
 it's hot today bugün hava
 sıcak [boogewn – suhjak]
hotel otel

Turkish hotels are graded on a scale of one to five stars by the Ministry of Tourism; there is also a lower tier of unstarred establishments rated by municipalities. At the four- and five-star level you're talking Sheraton-type mod cons and prices. Two- or three-star outfits are less expensive and may have slightly more character; one-star establishments are basic but usually clean. Their exact price depends on the location and the presence or absence of a bath, and to some extent on the season; out of season you can often bargain prices down considerably in lower category hotels. Breakfast is often included in the rates, but it's almost invariably unexciting.

The unrated hotels licensed by municipalities can be virtually as good as the lower end of the one-star class. On average, though, expect spartan rooms with possibly a washbasin and certainly a shower (never a tub), with a squat toilet down the hall. Washbasins may not have plugs.

In remote areas, especially in the east, hoteliers may refuse to take unmarried couples. Wedding rings might convince some people, but documentary proof might be demanded. If the proprietor is adamant, there is nothing you can do except look for somewhere else.

hotel room otel odası [oda**suh**]

hour saat [sa-**at**]
house ev

 It is customary to remove your shoes when entering a house, even in households with a European lifestyle. Your host will usually offer you a pair of slippers; some hosts may tell you not to bother taking your shoes off but you should still remove them.

In rural areas single men should never enter a dwelling where only women and/or children are present, even if invited – you would be deemed to have violated the honour and good reputation of the family should the head of the household return, and you would be treated accordingly.

hovercraft hoverkraft
how nasıl [nas**uhl**]
 how many? kaç tane? [kach ta**neh**]
 how do you do? memnun oldum!

dialogues

 how are you? nasılsınız? [nas**uhl**-suhnuhz]
 fine, thanks, and you? iyiyim, teşekkür ederim, ya siz? [teshekk**ewr**]

 how much is it? kaça? [kach**a**]

1,5 milyon lira bir buçuk
milyon lira [boochook]
I'll take it alıyorum [aluh-
yoroom]

humid nemli
hungry: I'm hungry acıktım
[ajuhktuhm]
  are you hungry? acıktınız
  mı? [ajuhktuhnuhz muh]
hurry (verb) acele etmek
[ajeleh]
  I'm in a hurry acelem var
  [ajelem]
  there's no hurry aceleye
  gerek yok [ajelayeh]
  hurry up! çabuk ol! [chabook]
hurt (verb) incitmek
[eenjeetmek], acımak
[achuhmak]
  it really hurts gerçekten çok
  acıyor [gerchekten chok [ajuh-
  yor]
husband koca [koja]
hydrofoil kızaklı tekne
[kuhzakluh tekneh], hidrofoil
[heedrofoyl]

I

I ben
ice buz [booz]
  with ice buzlu
  no ice, thanks buz istemez,
  teşekkür ederim
  [teshekkewr]
ice cream dondurma
ice-cream cone dondurma

külahı [kewl-ahuh]
iced coffee buzlu kahve
[kaнveh]
ice lolly eskimo®
idea fikir
idiot aptal
if eğer [eh-er]
ignition kontak
ill hasta
  I feel ill kendimi hasta
  hissediyorum
illness hastalık [hastaluhk]
imitation (leather etc) taklit
immediately hemen
important önemli [urnemlee]
  it's very important çok
  önemlidir [chok]
  it's not important önemli
  değil [deh-eel]
impossible imkansız
[eemkansuhz]
impressive etkileyici [etkeelay-
eejee]
improve iyileştirmek
[eeyeelesh–], geliştirmek
[geleeshteermek]
  I want to improve my Turkish
  Türkçemi geliştirmek
  istiyorum [tewrkchemee
  geleeshteermek]
in: it's in the centre merkezde
[merkezdeh]
  in my car arabamda
  in İstanbul İstanbul'da
  in two days from now iki
  güne kadar [gewneh]
  in five minutes beş dakika
  içinde [eecheendeh]
  in May mayısta

in English İngilizce
[eengeeleezjeh]
in Turkish Türkçe [tewrkcheh]
is he in? orda mı? [muh]
inch* inç [eench]
include dahil etmek [daheel]
does that include meals?
buna yemekler dahil mi?
is that included? bu dahil
mi?
inconvenient elverişsiz
[elvereesh-seez]
incredible inanılmaz
[eenanuhlmaz]
Indian (adj) Hint
indicator sinyal
indigestion hazımsızlık
[hazuhm-suhzluhk]
indoor pool kapalı havuz
[kapaluh]
indoors içerde [eecherdeh]
inexpensive ucuz [oojooz]
infection enfeksiyon
infectious bulaşıcı
[boolashuhjuh]
inflammation iltihap
informal fazla resmı olmayan
[olmi-an]
information bilgi
do you have any information
about ...? sizde ... hakkında
bilgi var mı? [hakkuhnda – muh]
information desk danışma
masası [danuhshma masasuh]
injection enjeksiyon
enjeksee-yon]
injured yaralı [yaraluh]
she's been injured yaralandı
[yaralanduh]

inner tube (for tyre) iç lastik
[eech]
innocent masum
insect böcek [burjek]
insect bite böcek sokması
[sokmasuh]
do you have anything for
insect bites? sizde böcek
sokmasına karşı bir şey
bulunur mu? [seezdeh –
karshuh beer shay]
insect repellent böcek ilacı
[eelachuh]
inside: inside the hotel otelin
içinde [eecheendeh]
let's sit inside içerde
oturalım [eecherdeh
otooraluhm]
insist: I insist ısrar ediyorum
insomnia uykusuzluk
[oo-ikoosoozlook]
instant coffee neskafe
[neskafeh]
instead yerine [yereeneh]
give me that one instead
yerine şunu verin [shoonoo]
instead of ... ...-in yerine
insulin insülin [eensewleen]
insurance sigorta
intelligent zeki
interested: I'm interested in ...
...-e ilgi duyuyorum [-eh]
interesting ilginç [eelgeench]
that's very interesting çok
ilginç [chok]
international uluslararası
[oolooslararasuh]
Internet internet
interpret tercüme etmek

[terjewm**eh**]
interpreter tercüman
[terjewm**an**]
intersection kavşak [kavshak]
interval (at theatre) ara
into: into the ... ...-in içine
[eechee**neh**]
I'm not into ... ... ilgimi
çekmiyor [ch**ek**mee-yor]
introduce tanıştırmak
[tanuhshtuhr**mak**]
may I introduce ...? size ...-i
tanıştırabilir miyim?
[seez**eh** ...-ee
tanuhsh-tuhrabeel**eer**]
invitation davet
invite davet etmek
Iran İran [**ee**ran]
Iraq Irak [**uh**rak]
Ireland İrlanda [eer**landa**]
Irish İrlanda
I'm Irish İrlandalıyım
[eerlandal**uh**-yuhm]
iron (for ironing) ütü [**ew**tew]
can you iron these for me?
bunları benim için ütüler
misiniz? [boonlar**uh** – eech**een**
ewtewler]
is* -dir
Islam İslam [ees**lam**]
Islamic İslami
island ada
İstanbul İstanbul [eestan**bool**]
it o
it is ... o ...-dir
is it ...? ... mu?
where is it? nerede?
[**neredeh**]
it's him/her odur

it was ... ... idi
Italian (adj, person) İtalyan
[eetaly**an**]
(language) İtalyanca
[eetaly**anja**]
Italy İtalya
itch: it itches kaşınıyor
[kashuh**nuh**-yor]

J

jack (for car) kriko
jacket ceket [j**eket**]
jam reçel [r**echel**]
jammed: it's jammed takıldı
[takuhld**uh**]
January ocak [oj**ak**]
jar (noun) kavanoz
jaw çene [ch**eneh**]
jazz caz [jaz]
jealous kıskanç [kuhs**kanch**]
jeans blucin [bloojeen]
jellyfish denizanası [–s**uh**]
jersey kazak
jetty iskele [**ee**skeleh]
jeweller's kuyumcu [koo-
y**oom**joo]
jewellery mücevherat
[mew-jevher**at**]
Jewish Yahudi
job iş [eesh]
jogging koşu [kosh**oo**]
to go jogging koşu yapmak
joke şaka [sh**aka**]
journey yolculuk [yoljool**ook**]
have a good journey! iyi
yolculuklar!
jug sürahi [sewr**ahee**]

a jug of water bir sürahi su
juice: ... juice ... suyu
July temmuz
jump (verb) atlamak
jumper kazak
jump leads buji telleri
[booJee]
junction kavşak [kavshak]
June haziran
just (only) sadece [sa-dejeh]
just two sadece iki tane
[taneh]
just for me yalnız benim için
[yalnuhz – eecheen]
just here tam burada
not just now şimdi değil
[sheemdee deh-eel]
we've just arrived henüz
geldik [henewz]

K

kebab kebap
(mild) Bursa kebabı [kebabuh]
(very spicy) Urfa kebabı
keep tutmak
keep the change üstü kalsın
[ewstew kalsuhn]
can I keep it? bende kalabilir
mi? [bendeh]
please keep it sizde kalsın
[seezdeh]
ketchup keçap [kechap]
kettle çaydanlık [chidanluhk]
key anahtar [anaHtar]
the key for room 201, please
iki yüz bir numaralı odanın
anahtarı, lütfen [yewz beer
noomaraluh odanuhn anaHtaruh
lewtfen]
keyring anahtarlık
[anaHtarluhk]
kidneys (in body) böbrekler
[burbrekler]
(food) böbrek
kill (verb) öldürmek
[urldewrmek]
kilo* kilo
kilometre* kilometre
[keelometreh]
how many kilometres is it
to ...? ... buradan kaç
kilometre? [kach]
kind (generous) nazik, iyi
that's very kind çok
naziksiniz [chok]

dialogue

which kind do you want?
hangisinden istiyorsunuz?
I want this/that kind bu/şu
türden istiyorum [shoo
tewrden]

king kral
kiosk bufe [bewfeh]
kiss (noun) öpücük
[urpewjewk]
(verb) öpmek [urpmek]

kissing
Couples should not
indulge in visible displays
of affection beyond holding hands –
and in rural areas even that might
be thought improper. Kissing on a

park bench, for example, might get you pelted with a half-full soft-drink can, or worse.

kitchen mutfak
Kleenex® kâğıt mendil [ka-uht]
knee diz
knickers külot [kewlot]
knife bıçak [buhchak]
knitwear örgü [urgew]
knock (verb) vurmak
knock down çarpmak [charpmak]
he's been knocked down araba çarpmış [charpmuhsh]
knock over (object) devirmek (pedestrian) çarpmak [charpmak], çiğnemek [cheenemek]
know (somebody) tanımak [tanuhmak]
(something) bilmek
I don't know bilmiyorum
I didn't know that onu bilmiyordum
do you know where I can find ...? ...-i nerede bulabilirim, biliyor musunuz? [neredeh]

L

label etiket
ladies' (toilets) bayanlar [bī-anlar]
ladies' wear kadın giyim eşyası [kaduhn – esh-yasuh]

lady bayan [bī-an]
lager bira
see beer
lake göl [gurl]
lamb (meat) kuzu
lamp lamba
lane (motorway) şerit [shereet] (small road) dar yol
language dil
language course dil kursu
large büyük [bewyewk]
last (final) son
last week geçen hafta [gechen]
last Friday geçen Cuma
last night dün gece [dewn gejeh]
what time is the last train to Ankara? Ankara'ya son tren kaçta? [kachta]
late geç [gech]
sorry I'm late geciktiğim için özür dilerim [gejeektee-eem eecheen urzewr]
the train was late tren gecikti [gejeektee]
we must go – we'll be late gitmemiz gerek – geç kalacağız [kalaja-uhz]
it's getting late geç oluyor [gech]
later daha sonra
I'll come back later sonra tekrar gelirim
see you later görüşmek üzere [gurewshmek ewzereh]
later on daha sonra
latest en son
by Wednesday at the latest

en geç Çarşambaya kadar
[gech]
laugh (verb) gülmek
[gewlmek]
launderette, laundromat
otomatlı çamaşırhane
[otomatluh chamashuhr-haneh]
laundry (clothes) çamaşır
[chamashuhr]
(place) çamaşırhane
[chamashuhr-haneh]
lavatory tuvalet
law kanun
lawn çimen [cheemen]
lawyer avukat
laxative müshil [mews-heel],
laksatif
lazy tembel
lead (electrical) kablo
where does this lead to? bu
nereye çıkıyor? [nerayeh
chuhkuh-yor]
leaf yaprak
leaflet broşür [broshewr]
leak (noun) sızıntı [suhzuhntuh]
(verb) sızmak [suhzmak]
the roof leaks dam akıyor
[akuh-yor]
learn öğrenmek [ur renmek]
least: not in the least hiç de
değil [heech deh deh-eel]
at least en azından [en
azuhndan]
leather deri
leave (verb) bırakmak
[buhrakmak]
(go away) ayrılmak
[iruhlmak]
I am leaving tomorrow yarın

hareket ediyorum [yaruhn]
he left yesterday dün gitti
[dewn]
may I leave this here? bunu
burada bırakabilir miyim?
[buhraka-beeleer]
I left my coat in the bar
paltomu barda bıraktım
[buhraktuhm]
when does the bus for Bursa
leave? Bursa otobüsü ne
zaman kalkıyor? [neh –
kalkuh-yor]
Lebanon Lübnan [lewbnan]
leeks pırasa [puhrasa]
left sol
on the left solda
to the left sola
turn left sola dönün
[durnewn]
there's none left hiç kalmadı
[heech kalmaduh]
left-handed solak
left luggage (office) emanet
leg bacak [bajak]
lemon limon
lemonade limonata
lemon tea limonlu çay
[leemonloo chi]
lend ödünç vermek
· [urdewnch]
will you lend me your ... ?
...-inizi ödünç verir
misiniz? [urdewnch]
lens (of camera) objektif
[objekteef]
lesbian sevici [seveejee]
less daha az
less than ... ...-den daha az

less expensive daha az
pahalı
lesson ders
let (allow) -a izin vermek
  will you let me know? bana
  haber verir misiniz?
  I'll let you know ben size
  haber veririm [seezeh]
  let's go for something to eat
  hadi gidip bir şeyler yiyelim
  [shayler]
let off bırakmak [buhrakmak]
  will you let me off at ...?
  beni ...-da bırakır mısınız?
  [buhrakuhr muhsuhnuhz]
letter mektup
  **do you have any letters for
  me?** bana mektup var mı?
  [muh]
letterbox mektup kutusu

Letterboxes are yellow
and are clearly labelled
with categories of
destination: **yurtdışı** for overseas,
yurtiçi for inland, **şehiriçi** for local.
Street-corner letterboxes are rare so
you will need to go to a post office.

lettuce yeşil salata [yesheel]
lever (noun) manivela
library kütüphane
  [kewtewp-haneh]
licence izin belgesi
  (driving) ehliyet
lid kapak
lie (verb: tell untruth) yalan
  söylemek [suh-ilemek]
lie down uzanmak

life hayat [hī-at]
lifebelt can kemeri [jan]
lifeguard cankurtaran
  [jankoortaran]
life jacket can yeleği [jan
  yeleh-ee]
lift (in building) asansör
  [asansur]
  could you give me a lift? beni
  de arabanıza alır mısınız?
  [deh arabanuhza aluhr]
  would you like a lift? sizi de
  götürebilir miyim?
  [gurtewrebeeleer]
light (noun) ışık [uhshuhk]
  (not heavy) hafif
  do you have a light? (for
  cigarette) ateşiniz var mı?
  [atesheeneez var muh]
light green açık yeşil [achuhk
  yesheel]
light bulb ampul
  I need a new light bulb bana
  yeni bir ampul lazım
  [lazuhm]
lighter çakmak [chakmak]
lightning şimşek [sheemshek]
like (verb) hoşlanmak
  [hoshlanmak], sevmek
  I like it beğendim [beh-
  endeem]
  I like going for walks
  yürüyüşe çıkmayı severim
  [yewrew-yewsheh chuhkmī-uh]
  I like you sizden
  hoşlanıyorum
  [hoshlanuh-yoroom]
  I don't like it hoşuma
  gitmiyor [hoshooma]

do you like ...? ... sever
misiniz?
I'd like a beer bir bira
istiyorum
I'd like to go swimming
yüzmeye gitmek istiyorum
[yewzmay**eh**]
would you like a drink? bir
şey içmek ister misiniz?
[shay eechmek]
**would you like to go for a
walk?** yürüyüşe çıkmak
ister misiniz? [yewrew-yewsh**eh**
chuhmak]
what's it like? nasıl bir şey?
[nas**uhl**]
I want one like this bunun
gibi bir şey istiyorum
lime misket limonu
lime cordial konsantre limon
suyu [konsantr**eh**]
line (on paper) çizgi [cheezg**ee**]
(phone) hat
**could you give me an outside
line?** bana bir dış hat verir
misiniz? [d**uh**h]
lips dudaklar
lip salve dudak merhemi
lipstick ruj [rooj]
liqueur likör [leek**ur**]
listen dinlemek
listen! dinle! [deenl**eh**]
litre* litre [l**ee**treh]
a litre of white wine bir litre
beyaz şarap [bay**az** shar**ap**]
little küçük [kewch**ewk**]
just a little, thanks yalnız çok
az bir şey, teşekkür ederim
[**y**aln**uhz** chok – shay teshekk**ewr**]

a little milk biraz süt [sewt]
a little bit more biraz daha
live (verb) yaşamak [yashamak]
we live together birlikte
yaşıyoruz [beerleekt**eh** yashuh-
y**orooz**]

dialogue

where do you live? nerede
oturuyorsunuz? [neredeh]
I live in London Londra'da
oturuyorum

lively (person) canlı [janl**uh**]
(town) hareketli
liver (in body) karaciğer
[karajee-**er**]
(food) ciğer
loaf somun
lobby (in hotel) lobi
lobster istakoz
local yerel
**can you recommend a local
restaurant?** yörede bir
lokanta tavsiye edebilir
misiniz? [yured**eh** – tavsee-v**eh**]
lock (noun) kilit
(verb) kilitlemek
it's locked kilitli
lock in içeri kilitlemek
[eecher**ee**]
lock out dışarıda bırakmak
[duhsharuhda buhrakmak]
I've locked myself out
dışarıda kaldım [duhsharuhd**a**
kald**uhm**]
locker (for luggage etc) emanet
kasası [kasas**uh**]

lollipop lolipop

London Londra

long uzun

how long will it take to fix it?
tamir etmesi ne kadar
sürer? [neh – sewrer]

how long does it take? ne
kadar sürer?

a long time uzun süre
[sewreh]

one day/two days longer bir
gün/iki gün daha

long-distance call
şehirlerarası konuşma
[sheheerler-arasuh konooshma]

look: I'm just looking, thanks
şöyle bir bakıyorum,
teşekkür ederim [shuh-ileh
beer bakuh-yoroom teshekkewr]

you don't look well iyi
görünmüyorsunuz
[gurewnmew–]

look out! dikkat!

can I have a look? bir
bakabilir miyim?

look after –a bakmak

look at –a bakmak

look for aramak

I'm looking for ... ...-i
arıyorum [aruh-yoroom]

look forward to iple çekmek
[eepleh chekmek]

I'm looking forward to it onu
iple çekiyorum [eepleh
chekee-yoroom]

loose (handle etc) gevşek
[gevshek]

lorry kamyon

lose kaybetmek [kī-betmek]

I'm lost, I want to get to ...
yolumu kaybettim, ...-'e
gitmek istiyordum
[kibetteem ...-eh]

I've lost my bag çantamı
kaybettim [chantamuh]

lost property (office) kayıp
eşya [kī-uhp esh-ya]

lot: a lot, lots çok [chok]

not a lot çok değil [deh-eel]

a lot of people bir çok
insan

a lot bigger çok daha
büyük

I like it a lot çok beğendim
[beh-endeem]

lotion losyon

loud (noise) gürültülü
[gewrewl-tewlew]

(voice) yüksek sesle [yewksek
sesleh]

lounge (in house, hotel) salon
(airport) yolcu salonu [yoljoo]

love (noun) sevgi
(verb) sevmek

I love Turkey Türkiye'ye
aşığım [tewrkee-yeh-yeh ashuh-
uhm]

lovely çok güzel [chok gewzel]

low alçak [alchak]

luck şans [shans]

good luck! bol şanslar!

luggage bagaj [bagaJ]

luggage trolley eşya arabası
[esh-ya arabasuh]

lump (on body) yumru

lunch öğle yemeği [urleh
yemeh-ee]

lungs akciğerler [akjee-erler]

luxurious (hotel, furnishings) lüks
[lewks]
luxury lüks

M

macaroon acıbadem
kurabiyesi [ajuhbadem]
machine makina
mad (insane) deli
(angry) kızgın [kuhzguhn]
magazine dergi
maid (in hotel) oda hizmetçisi
[–cheesee]
maiden name kızlık adı
[kuhzluhk aduh]
mail (noun) posta
(verb) postalamak
is there any mail for me?
bana mektup var mı? [muh]
see post and post office
mailbox mektup kutusu
main esas
main course ana yemek
main post office merkez
postanesi
main road (in town) ana cadde
[jaddeh]
(in country) anayol
mains switch şalter [shalter]
make (brand name) marka
(verb) yapmak
I make it 5,000,000 lira benim
hesabıma göre beş milyon
lira ediyor [hesabuhma gureh]
what is it made of? neden
yapılmış? [yapuhlmuhsh]
make-up makyaj [makyaJ]

man adam
manager yönetici [yurneteejee]
can I see the manager?
yöneticiyi görebilir miyim?
[yurneteejee-yee gurebeeleer]
manageress yönetici bayan

manners
Invitations to drink tea are almost impossible to turn down without risking offence; offers of meals are rarer but can also create delicate situations. If the offer is perfunctory it will not be repeated after a polite refusal, but if it's repeated three times or more your benefactor is in earnest. Declining an invitation can be done with a polite excuse like '**hiç vaktim yok, kusura bakmayın**' [heech – bakmı-uhn] (I haven't got any time, please forgive me).

Other points to remember are: do not scrape your plates clean in a restaurant; it's considered polite to leave a small quantity of food. Do not smoke, chew gum or eat in public during Ramadan; foreigners are supposedly exempt from these restrictions, but there have been numerous attacks on unwitting offenders by fundamentalists.

manual düz [dewz]
(car) düz vitesli
many çok [chok]
not many az
map (city plan) şehir planı
[sheh-heer planuh]

(road map, geographical) harita

Stock up on touring maps before you leave, as Turkish ones are not very detailed or accurate. The tourist offices in İstanbul, Ankara, Antalya and İzmir stock reasonable city street plans.

March mart
margarine margarin
market pazar, çarşı [charshuh]
marmalade portakal reçeli [rehchelee]
married: I'm married evliyim
are you married? evli misiniz?
mascara rimel
match (football etc) maç [mach]
matches kibrit
material (fabric) kumaş [koomash]
matter: it doesn't matter önemli değil [urnemlee deh-eel]
what's the matter? ne oluyor? [neh]
mattress şilte [sheelteh]
May mayıs [mī-uhs]
may: may I have another one? bir tane daha alabilir miyim? [taneh]
may I come in? girebilir miyim?
may I see it? onu görebilir miyim? [gurebeeleer]
may I sit here? buraya oturabilir miyim? [boorī-a]

maybe belki
mayonnaise mayonez [mī-onez]
me* beni, bana
that's for me o benim için [eecheen]
send it to me onu bana gönderin
me too ben de [deh]
meal yemek

dialogue

did you enjoy your meal?
yemek hoşunuza gitti mi? [hoshoonooza]
it was excellent, thank you
mükemmeldi, teşekkür ederim [mewkemmeldee teshekkewr]

mean: what do you mean? ne demek istiyorsunuz? [neh]

dialogue

what does this word mean? bu kelimenin anlamı ne? [anlamuh neh]
it means ... in English
İngilizcede ... demektir [eengeeleezjedeh]

measles kızamık [kuhzamuhk]
meat et
meat restaurant kebapçı [kebapchuh]
mechanic tamirci [tameerjee]
medicine ilaç [eelach]

Ma

Mediterranean Akdeniz

medium (adj: size) orta

medium-dry dömi sek [dur**mee**]

medium-rare orta pişmiş [peesh**meesh**]

medium-sized orta büyüklükte [bewyew-klewk**teh**]

meet buluşmak [boo**loosh**mak]

(at airport) karşılamak [karshuhla**mak**]

nice to meet you memnun oldu**m**

where shall I meet you? nerede buluşalım? [**n**eredeh booloosha**luhm**]

meeting toplantı [toplant**uh**]

meeting place buluşma yeri [boo**loosh**ma]

melon kavun

men adamlar

mend onarmak

could you mend this for me? bunu benim için onarabilir misiniz? [ee**cheen**]

menswear erkek giyim eşyası [esh-**yasuh**]

mention (verb) bahsetmek [ba**H**setmek]

don't mention it bir şey değil [shay deh-**eel**]

menu yemek listesi

may I see the menu, please? yemek listesini görebilir miyim, lütfen? [gurebeel**eer** – **lewt**fen]

see **menu reader** page 240

message mesaj [mesa**J**]

are there any messages for me? bana mesaj var mı? [muh]

I want to leave a message for ... ... için bir mesaj bırakmak istiyorum [ee**cheen** – buh**rak**mak]

metal metal

metre* metre [**metreh**]

microwave (oven) mikro dalga

midday öğle üzeri [ur-**leh** ewzer**ee**]

at midday öğleyin [ur-lay**een**]

middle: in the middle ortada

in the middle of the night gece yarısı [gej**eh** yaruhs**uh**]

the middle one ortadaki

midnight gece yarısı

at midnight gece yarısı

might: I might come belki gelirim

I might not go gitmeyebilirim

I might want to stay another day bir gun daha kalmak isteyebilirim

migraine migren

mild (taste) hafif

(weather) ılıman [**uhl**uhman]

mile* mil

milk süt [sewt]

milkshake milkşeyk [meelksh**ayk**]

millimetre* milimetre [meeleem**etreh**]

minaret minare [meenar**eh**]

minced meat kıyma [kuh-**ima**]

mind: never mind zarar yok
I've changed my mind
fikrimi değiştirdim
[deh-eeshteerdeem]

dialogue

do you mind if I open the
window? pencereyi
açmamın bir mahzuru
var mı? [penjerayee
achmamuhn beer maHzorooo]
no, I don't mind hayır,
benim için farketmez
[hī-uhr eecheen]

mine*: it's mine o benim,
benimki
mineral water maden suyu
mints nane şekeri [naneh
shekeree]
minute dakika
in a minute birazdan
just a minute bir dakika
mirror ayna [īna]
Miss Bayan [bī-an]
miss: I missed the bus
otobüsü kaçırdım
[kachuhrduhm]
missing eksik [ekseek]
one of my ... is
missing ...lerimden biri
eksik
there's a suitcase missing bir
bavul eksik
mist sis
mistake (noun) hata
I think there's a mistake
sanırım bir yanlışlık var

[sanuhruhm – yanluhshluhk]
sorry, I've made a mistake
özür dilerim, hata yaptım
[urzewr – yaptuhm]
misunderstanding yanlış
anlama [–luhsh]
mix-up: sorry, there's been a
mix-up özür dilerim, bir
karışıklık olmuş [urzewr –
karuhshuhkluhk olmoosh]
mobile (phone) cep telefonu
[jep telefonoo]
modern modern [modairn]
modern art gallery çağdaş
sanat galerisi [cha-dash]
moisturizer nemlendirici
krem [–reejee]
moment: I'll be back in a
moment hemen geliyorum
monastery manastır
[manastuhr]
Monday pazartesi
money para
month ay [ī]
monument anıt [anuht]
moon ay [ī]
moped moped
more* daha
can I have some more water,
please? biraz daha su
alabilir miyim, lütfen?
[lewtfen]
more expensive/interesting
daha pahalı/ilginç
more than 50 elliden fazla
more than that ondan daha
fazla
a lot more çok daha fazla
[chok]

dialogue

would you like some more? biraz daha ister misiniz?
no, no more for me, thanks hayır, teşekkür ederim, bu kadar yeter bana [hī-**uh**r – teshekk**ew**r]
how about you? ya siz?
I don't want any more, thanks ben daha fazla istemiyorum, teşekkür ederim

morning sabah [saba**H**]
 this morning bu sabah [boo]
 in the morning sabahleyin [saba**H**layeen]
mosaic mozaik [moza-**eek**]
mosque cami [jam**ee**]

There's no admission fee for entry to mosques but you may be asked by the caretaker or imam to make a small donation. If 30, put it into the collection box rather than someone's hand. Larger mosques are frequented by tourists and are open all the time; others only for **namaz**, or Muslim prayer, five times a day. Whether or not you're required to, it's a courtesy for women to cover their heads before entering a mosque, and for both men and women to cover their legs (shorts are considered particularly offensive) and upper arms – in some

mosques pieces of material are distributed at the door. Shoes should always be removed.

mosquito sivrisinek
mosquito repellent sivrisinek ilacı [eelaj**uh**]
most: I like this one most of all en çok bundan hoşlanıyorum [chok – hoshlan**uh**-yoroom]
 most of the time çoğu zaman [choh-**oo**]
 most tourists çoğu turist
mostly çoğunlukla [choh-oonl**oo**kla]
mother anne [ann**eh**]
mother-in-law kayınvalide [kī-uhnvaleed**eh**]
motorbike motosiklet
motorboat deniz motoru
motorway otoyol
 see road
mountain dağ [da]
 in the mountains dağlarda [da-larda]
mountaineering dağcılık [da-juhl**uh**k]
mouse fare [**far**eh]
moustache bıyık [buhy**uh**k]
mouth ağız [a-**uh**z]
mouth ulcer aft, pamukçuk [pamookch**oo**k]
move (verb: oneself) hareket etmek
 (something) oynatmak
 (house) taşınmak [tash**uh**nmak]
 he's moved to another room başka bir odaya taşındı

[bashka beer odī-a tashuhnduh]
could you move your car?
arabanızı çeker misiniz?
[arabanuhzuh cheker]
could you move up a little?
biraz yukarı gider misiniz?
[yookaruh]
where has it moved to?
nereye taşındı? [nerayeh
tashuhnduh]
where has it been moved to?
(painting etc) nereye
kaldırıldı? [kalduhruhlduh]
movie film
movie theater sinema
see **cinema**
Mr Bay [bī]
Mrs Bayan [bī-an]
Ms Bayan
much çok [chok]
much better/worse çok daha
iyi/daha kötü
much hotter çok daha sıcak
not much pek değil
[deh-eel]
not very much çok fazla
değil
I don't want very much çok
fazla istemiyorum
mud çamur [chamoor]
mug (for drinking) kupa
I've been mugged saldırıya
uğradım [salduhruh-ya
oo-raduhm]
mum anne [anneh]
mumps kabakulak
museum müze [mewzeh]

Museums are generally
open from 8.30 or 9 a.m.
until 5 or 6 p.m., and
closed on Monday, though in the
case of some smaller museums you
may have to find the **bekçi**
(caretaker) yourself and ask him to
open up. All sites and museums are
closed on the mornings of public
holidays.
Major archeological sites have
variable opening hours, but are
generally open daily from just after
sunrise until just before sunset.
Some smaller archeological sites
are only guarded during the day, and
left unfenced, permitting a free
wander around in the evening.
Permission is required for
photographing and filming in
museums and ancient ruins and a
fee is charged in addition to the
entrance fee.

mushrooms mantar
music müzik [mewzeek]
musician müzisyen
Muslim (adj, person) Müslüman
[mewslewman]
mussels midye [meed-yeh]
must: I must ... ...-meliyim
I mustn't drink alcohol
alkol almamam lazım
[lazuhm]
mustard hardal
my* -im, -ım [-uhm], -um,
-üm [-ewm], -m
myself*: I'll do it myself
kendim yaparım [yaparuhm]

by myself yalnız başıma
[yaln**uh**z bash**uh**ma]

N

nail (finger) tırnak [tuhrnak]
  (metal) çivi [cheev**ee**]
nailbrush tırnak fırçası
  [tuhrnak fuhrchas**uh**]
nail varnish tırnak cilası
  [jeel**a**suh]
name ad
  my name's John adım John
  [ad**uh**m]
  what's your name? adınız
  nedir? [aduhn**uh**z]
  **what is the name of this
  street?** bu caddenin adı ne?
  [jadden**ee**n ad**uh** n**eh**]

In formal situations the
first name followed by
beyefendi equates to the
English Mr. The feminine version,
hanımefendi, is used in the same
way and equates to Mrs, Ms and
Miss. **Sayın** followed by the
surname is also used as a very
formal way of addressing a man or a
woman. Beyefendi and hanımefendi
are also used on their own when
inquiring very formally about absent
partners etc; for example,
'**hanımefendi nasıllar?**' is literally
'how is your (lady) wife?'
A less formal way of address is the
first name followed by **Bey** (Mr) or
Hanım (Mrs/Ms/Miss). First names

are only used between friends and
relatives. It is not usual to use first
names for much older people no
matter what the relationship is
unless you attach an **amca** (uncle),
teyze (aunty), **abla** (older sister) or
ağabey/abi (older brother) to the
first names, even if they are not
relatives.

napkin peçete [pecheteh]
nappy çocuk bezi [choj**oo**k]
narrow (street) dar
nasty (person, weather, taste)
  iğrenç [**ee**grench]
  (cut, accident) kötü [kurt**ew**]
national ulusal
nationality vatandaşlık
  [vatandashl**uh**k]
natural doğal [doh-**a**l]
nausea mide bulantısı
  [**mee**deh boolantuhs**uh**]
navy (blue) lacivert [lajeev**e**rt]
near: near the ... ...-in
  yakınında [yakuhn**uh**nda]
  is it near the city centre?
  şehir merkezine yakın mı?
  [m**uh**]
  do you go near Aya Sophia?
  Ayasofya'nın yakınından
  geçecek misiniz? [i-asofya-
  nuhn yakuhn**uh**ndan gechejek]
  where is the nearest ...? en
  yakın ... nerede? [n**e**redeh]
nearby yakında [yak**uh**nda]
nearly neredeyse [n**e**redayseh]
necessary gerekli
neck boy**u**n
necklace kolye [k**o**l-yeh]

necktie kravat
need: I need ... ...-e ihtiyacım
var [-eh eeнtee-yajuhm]
do I need to pay? para
ödemem gerekiyor mu?
[urdemem]
needle iğne [ee-neh]
negative (film) negatif
neither: neither (one) of them
hiç biri [heech]
neither ... nor ... ne ... ne ...
[neh]
nephew yeğen [yeh-en]
net (in sport) ağ [a]
Netherlands Hollanda
network map şebeke planı
[shebekeh planuh]
never hiçbir zaman
[heechbeer]

dialogue

have you ever been to
Bursa? Bursa'ya hiç
gittiniz mi?
no, never, I've never been
there hayır, oraya hiç
gitmedim [hī-**uhr** orī-a]

new yeni
news (radio, TV etc) haber
newsagent's gazete bayii
[gazeteh bī-ee-**ee**]
newspaper gazete
newspaper kiosk gazete satış
büfesi [satuhsh bewfesee]
New Year Yeni Yıl [yuhl]

New Year's Eve is widely
celebrated. This might be
at home with family and
friends perhaps with a special meal,
playing games, and watching special
programmes on the TV. Alternatively
Turks might go to a **gazino** (a
restaurant-cum-nightclub) or to a
dance. It is also quite common to
exchange presents on New Year's
Eve.

Happy New Year! Yeni
Yılınız Kutlu Olsun!
[yuhluhn**uhz**]
New Year's Eve Yılbaşı Gecesi
[yuhlbash**uh** gejes**ee**]
New Zealand Yeni Zelanda
New Zealander: I'm a New
Zealander Yeni
Zelandalıyım
[zelandal**uh**yuhm]
next bir sonraki
the next turning/street on the
left solda, bir sonraki
sapak/cadde
at the next stop bir sonraki
durakta
next week gelecek hafta
[gelejek]
next to ... ...-in bitişiğinde
[beeteeshee-eendeh]
nice (food, day) güzel [gewzel]
(person, looks, view) hoş [hosh]
Nicosia Lefkoşe [lefkosha]
niece yeğen [yeh-en]
night gece [gejeh]
at night geceleyin [gejelay-
een]

good night iyi geceler
[gejeler]

dialogue

do you have a single room
for one night? bir gece
için tek kişilik bir odanız
var mı? [gejeh eecheen tek
keesheeleek beer odanuhz var
muh]
yes, madam evet, efendim
how much is it per night?
gecesi ne kadar? [gejesee
neh]
it's 25,000,000 lira for one
night bir gece için yirmi
beş milyon lira
thank you, I'll take it
tutuyorum, teşekkür
ederim [teshekkewr]

nightclub gece kulübü
[koolewbew]
nightdress gecelik [gejeleek]
night porter gece bekcisi
[bekcheesee]
no hayır [hi-uhr]
I've no change hiç bozugum
yok [heech bozoo-oom]
there's no ... left
hiç ... kalmadı [kalmaduh]
no way! katiyen olmaz!
oh no! (upset) hay aksi! [hī]

The body language for
'no' is either raised
eyebrows, an abrupt
tilting back of the head, or a clicking

of the tongue against the teeth – or
sometimes all three at once.

nobody hiç kimse [heech
keemseh]
there's nobody there hiç
kimse yok orda
noise gürültü [gewrewltew]
noisy: it's too noisy fazla
gürültülü
non-alcoholic alkolsüz
[–sewz]
none hiç [heech]
nonsmoking compartment
sigara içmeyenlere mahsus
kompartıman
[eechmayenlereh maHsoos
kompartuhman]
noon öğle [ur-leh]
no-one hiç kimse [heech
keemseh]
nor: nor do I ne de ben [neh
deh]
normal normal [nor-mal]
north kuzey [koozay]
in the north kuzeyde
[koozaydeh]
to the north kuzeye
[koozayeh]
north of Ankara Ankara'nın
kuzeyi [ankara-nuhn]
northeast kuzeydoğu
[koozaydoh-oo]
northern kuzey
Northern Ireland Kuzey
İrlanda [eerlanda]
northwest kuzey batı [batuh]
Norway Norveç [norvech]
Norwegian (adj) Norveç

(language) Norveççe [norvech-**cheh**]

nose burun

nosebleed burun kanaması [kanamas**uh**]

not* değil [deh-**eel**]

no, I'm not hungry hayır, aç değilim [h**ī**-**uh**r ach deh-eel**eem**]

I don't want any, thank you hiç istemiyorum, teşekkür ederim [heech – teshekk**ewr**]

it's not necessary gerekli değil [deh-**eel**]

I didn't know that onu bilmiyordum

not that one – this one o değil – bu

note (banknote) kâğıt para [ka-**uh**t]

notebook not defteri

notepaper (for letters) mektup kağıdı [ka-uhd**uh**]

nothing hiç bir şey [heech beer shay]

nothing for me, thanks ben bir şey istemem, teşekkür ederim [teshekk**ewr**]

nothing else hepsi o kadar

novel roman

November kasım [kas**uh**m]

now şimdi [sheemdee]

number* (amount) sayı [s**ī**-**uh**]

(telephone) numara

I've got the wrong number yanlış numara [yanl**uh**sh]

what is your phone number? telefon numaranız nedir? [noomaran**uh**z]

number plate plaka

nurse hasta bakıcı [bakuhj**uh**]

nursery slope acemi pisti [ajem**ee**]

nut (for bolt) somun

nuts fıstık [fuhst**uh**k]

O

occupied (US) meşgul [meshg**ool**]

o'clock*: ... o'clock saat ... [sa-**at**]

October ekim

odd (strange) tuhaf

of* –in

off (lights) kapalı [kapal**uh**]

it's just off İstiklal Caddesi/Taksim Meydanı hemen daha İstiklal Caddesi'ne/Taksim Meydanı'na çıkmadan [eesteeklal jaddesee-**neh**/taks**eem** maydanuh-**na** chuhkmada**n**]

we're off tomorrow yarın ayrılıyoruz [yar**uh**n **ī**ruhl**uh**-yorooz]

offensive çirkin [cheerk**een**]

office büro [b**ew**ro]

officer (said to policeman) memur bey [bay]

often sık sık [s**uh**k]

not often ara sıra [s**uh**ra]

how often are the buses? otobüsler ne kadar sık? [neh]

oil (for car, for salad) yağ [ya]

ointment merhem

OK tamam

are you OK? iyi misin?
is that OK with you? siz ne
dersiniz? [neh]
is it OK to ...? ...-nin bir
mahzuru var mı? [muh]
that's OK, thanks tamam,
teşekkür ederim [teshekkewr]
I'm OK (nothing for me) ben
böyle iyiyim [buh-ileh]
(I feel OK) ben iyiyim
is this train OK for ...? ... için
bu tren doğru mu? [eecheen
– doh-roo]
I said I'm sorry, OK özür
diledim ya [urzewr]
old (person) yaşlı [yashluh]
(thing) eski

dialogue

how old are you? kaç
yaşındasınız? [kach
yashuhnda-suhnuhz]
I'm 25 yirmi beş
yaşındayım [yashuhndī-uhm]
and you? ya siz?

old-fashioned eski moda
old town (old part of town) eski
şehir [sheh-heer]
olive oil zeytinyağı
[zayteenya-uh]
olives zeytin
black/green olives siyah/
yeşil zeytin [yesheel]
omelette omlet
on*: on the ... ...-in üstünde
[ewstewndeh]
(light) açık [achuhk]

on the street/beach
caddede/plajda
[jaddedeh/plaJda]
is it on this road? bu yol
üzerinde mi? [ewzereendeh]
on the plane uçakta
[oochakta]
on Saturday Cumartesi
günü [gewnew]
on television televizyonda
I haven't got it on me
yanımda değil [yanuhmda
deh-eel]
this one's on me (drink) bu
benden
the light wasn't on ışık
yanmıyordu [uhshuhk yanmuh-
yordoo]
what's on tonight? bu akşam
ne var? [neh]
once (one time) bir kere [kereh]
at once (immediately) hemen
one* bir
the white one beyaz olan
one-way ticket gidiş bileti
[geedeesh]
onion soğan [soh-an]
only yalnız [yalnuhz]
only one yalnız bir tane
[taneh]
it's only 6 o'clock saat henüz
altı [sa-at henewz]
I've only just got here ancak
şimdi geldim [anjak sheemdee]
on/off switch açıp/kapama
düğmesi [achuhp – dew-mesee]
open (adj) açık [achuhk]
(verb) açmak [achmak]
when do you open? saat

kaçta açıyorsunuz? [sa-**at**
kachta achuh–]
I can't get it open
açamıyorum [acha**muh**–]
in the open air açık havada
opening times açılış ve
kapanış saatleri [a**ch**uh**luh**sh
veh kapan**uh**sh sa-**at**leree]
open ticket açık bilet [a**ch**u**hk**]
operation (medical) ameliyat
operator (telephone) santral
memur**u**
  see directory enquiries
opposite: the opposite
direction aksi yön [**yurn**]
  the bar opposite karşıdaki
  bar [karshuhda**kee**]
  opposite my hotel otelimin
  karşısında [karshuhs**uh**nda]
optician gözlükçü
[gurzlewk**chew**]
or veya [vay-**a**]
orange (fruit) portakal
  (colour) turuncu [tooroon**joo**]
orange juice portakal suy**u**
orchestra orkestra
order: can we order now? (in
restaurant) yemekleri şimdi
söyleyebilir miyiz? [sh**ee**mdee
suh-ilayebeel**eer**]
  I've already ordered, thanks
  ben ısmarladım, teşekkür
  ederim [uhsmarlad**uh**m
  teshekk**ewr**]
  I didn't order this ben bun**u**
  ısmarlamadım
  out of order bozuk
ordinary olağan [ola-**an**]
other diğer [dee-**er**]

  the other one öbürü
  [urbewr**ew**]
  the other day geçen gün
  [ge**ch**en ge**wn**]
  I'm waiting for the others
  diğerlerini bekliyorum
  do you have any others?
  başka var mı? [**bash**ka var muh]
  otherwise yoksa
our* –miz, –mız [-**muhz**],
  –muz, –müz [-**mewz**]
ours* bizimki
out: he's out yok, dışarda
  [duh**shar**da]
  three kilometres out of town
  şehrin üç kilometre dışında
  [sheh**reen** ewch keelometr**eh**
  duh**shuh**nda]
outdoors açık havada
a**ch**u**hk**]
outside: outside the ... ...–in
  dışında [duh**shuh**nda]
  can we sit outside? dışarda
  oturabilir miyiz? [duh**shar**da]
oven fırın [f**uh**ruhn]
over: over here burada
  over there orada
  over 500 beş yüzden fazla
  [**besh**]
  it's over bitti
overcharge: you've
  overcharged me benden
  fazla para aldınız [ald**uh**n**uhz**]
overcoat palto
overlooking: I'd like a room
  overlooking the courtyard
  avluya bakan bir oda
  istiyorum
overnight (travel) gece [ge**jeh**]

overtake geçmek [gechmek]
owe: how much do I owe you?
size borcum ne kadar?
[seezeh borjoom neh]
own: my own ... benim
kendi ...-m
are you on your own? tek
başına mısınız? [bashuhna
muhsuhnuhz]
I'm on my own tek
başımayım [bashuhmï-uhm]
owner sahibi

P

pack (verb) paketlemek
a pack of ... bir paket ...
package (parcel) paket, koli
package holiday paket tur
packed lunch piknik paketi
packet: a packet of cigarettes
bir paket sigara
padlock asma kilit
page (of book) sayfa [sïfa]
could you page Mr ...?
Sayın ...-i çağırtabilir
misiniz? [sï-uhn ...-ee cha-
uhrtabeeleer]
pain ağrı [a-ruh]
I have a pain here şuramda
bir ağrı var [shooramda beer
a-ruh var]
painful ızdıraplı [uhzduhrapluh]
painkillers ağrı kesiciler [a-ruh
keseejeeler]
paint (noun) boya
painting resim
pair: a pair of ... bir çift ...

[cheeft]
Pakistani (adj, person)
Pakistanlı [–luh]
palace saray [sarï]
pale solgun
pale blue uçuk mavi
[oochook]
pan tencere [tenjereh]
panties külot [kewlot]
pants (underwear: men's) don
(women's) külot [kewlot]
(US) pantolon
pantyhose külotlu çorap
[kewlotloo chorap]
paper kâğıt [ka-uht]
(newspaper) gazete [gazeteh]
a piece of paper bir parça
kağıt [parcha]
paper handkerchiefs kağıt
mendil
parcel koli
pardon (me)? (didn't
understand/hear) efendim?
parents anne baba [anneh]
park (noun) park
(verb) park etmek
can I park here? buraya park
edebilir miyim? [boorï-a]
parking lot otopark
part (noun) parça [parcha]
partner (boyfriend, girlfriend etc)
arkadaş [arkadash]
party (group) grup
(celebration) parti
pass (in mountains) geçit
[gecheet]
passenger yolcu [yoljoo]
passport pasaport

It is advisable to carry your passport with you at all times. Hotels ask for it when checking in. You probably won't need to produce it whilst on the beach at major resorts, but the police and military sometimes have road checks, where both Turks and foreigners are obliged to produce their ID cards or passports.

past: in the past geçmişte [gechmeeshteh]
just past the information office danışma bürosunu geçer geçmez [danuhshma bewrosoonoo gecher gechmez]
path patika, yol
pattern desen
pavement kaldırım [kalduhruhm]
on the pavement kaldırımda
pay (verb) ödemek [urdemek]
can I pay, please? ödeyebilir miyim, lütfen? [urdayebeeleer]
it's already paid for ödendi bile [urdendee beeleh]

dialogue

> who's paying? kim ödüyor? [urdew-yor]
> I'll pay ben ödeyeceğim [urdayejeh-eem]
> no, you paid last time, I'll pay olmaz, siz geçen sefer ödediniz, ben ödeyeceğim [gechen –

urdedeeneez ben urdayejeh-eem]

pay phone umumi telefon
peaceful sakin
peach şeftali [sheftalee]
peanuts yerfıstığı [yerfuhstuh-**uh**]
pear armut
peas bezelye [bezelyeh]
peculiar (strange) tuhaf
pedestrian crossing yaya geçidi [yī-a gecheedee]

 Be careful when crossing city roads: drivers, if they can get away with it, prefer not to stop at pedestrian crossings.

pedestrian precinct yayalara mahsus bölge [maHsoos burlgeh]
peg (for washing) mandal (for tent) kazık [kazuhk]
pen mürekkepli kalem [mewrek-keplee]
pencil kurşun kalem [koorshoon]
penfriend mektup arkadaşı [arkadashuh]
penicillin penisilin
penknife çakı [chakuh]
pensioner emekli
people insanlar
the other people in the hotel oteldeki diğer kişiler [dee-er keesheeler]
too many people fazla sayıda

insan [sī-**uh**da]
pepper biber
green pepper yeşil biber
[yesh**eel**]
red pepper kırmızı biber
[kuhrmuhrz**uh**]
peppermint (sweet) nane
şekeri [nan**eh** sheker**ee**]
per: per night bir gecesi
[geje**see**]
how much per day?
gündeliği kaça? [gewndelee-**ee**
ka**cha**]
per cent yüzde [yewzd**eh**]
perfect mükemmel
[mewkemm**el**]
perfume parfüm [parf**ew**m]
perhaps belki
perhaps not belki de değil
[deh deh-**eel**]
period (of time) süre [sewr**eh**]
(menstruation) adet dönemi
perm perma
permit (noun) izin
person kişi [keesh**ee**]
personal stereo walkman®
petrol benzin
see garage
petrol can benzin bidonu
petrol station
benzin istasyonu
pharmacy eczane [ejz**a**neh]

For minor complaints
head for the nearest
eczane (pharmacy) –
even the smallest town will have at
least one. Pharmacists in Turkey are
able to dispense medicines that
would ordinarily require a
prescription abroad. In larger towns,
eczane staff may know some
English or German. Foreign visitors
have to pay for prescriptions.
Medication prices are low, but you
may find it difficult to find exact
equivalents to your home
prescription, so take anything you
need with you. Night-duty
pharmacies are known as **nöbetçi**;
a list of the current rota is posted in
every pharmacist's front window.

phone (noun) telefon
(verb) telefon etmek

The best place to make
phone calls is the **PTT**
(post and telephone
office) or mobile PTT services in
holiday resorts. Inside or just
adjacent there is usually a range of
alternatives: a **jeton** (token) phone, a
cardphone and/or a **konturlu**
(metered, clerk-attended) phone,
sometimes in a closed booth.
Phones elsewhere are relatively
rare, though you will find them in
public parks and at filling stations.
Jetons theoretically come in small
(**küçük**), medium (**orta**) and large
(**büyük**) sizes, for local, trunk and
international use respectively,
though the medium-sized ones are
often in short supply. Partly used
tokens are not returned, so don't use
bigger sizes for local calls. While
you're in Turkey it's a good idea to

carry a few on you – they're not always on sale when you need them. Drop at least one token in the slot before dialling; when the red light comes on and a warning tone sounds, you have about ten seconds to feed in more. Never attempt to call from a jeton-operated phone box where the square, red 'out of service' light is illuminated. For trunk or overseas calls, phonecards (available in 30, 60 and 100 units) or metered booths inside PTTs are better value. Overseas rates are not cheap, but there is a 25 per cent discount on normal rates after 10 p.m. and on Sunday. Try not to make anything other than local calls from a hotel room – there is usually a one-hundred per cent surcharge on the already hefty rates.

phone book telefon rehberi [reHber**ee**]
phone box telefon kulübesi [koolewbes**ee**]
phonecard telefon kartı [kart**uh**]
phone number telefon numarası [noomaras**uh**]
photo fotoğraf [foto-r**af**]
  excuse me, could you take a photo of us? affedersiniz, bir fotoğrafımızı çekebilir misiniz? [foto-rafuhmuhz**uh** chekebeel**eer**]
phrasebook konuşma kılavuzu [konooshm**a** kuhlavooz**oo**]

piano piyano
pickpocket yankesici [yankeseej**ee**]
pick up: will you be there to pick me up? beni almaya gelecek misiniz? [almı-**a** gelej**ek**]
picnic piknik
picture resim
pie (meat) etli börek [bur-r**ek**] (fruit) turta
piece parça [parch**a**]
  a piece of ... bir parça ...
pill doğum kontrol hapı [doh-**oom** – hahp**uh**]
  I'm on the pill doğum kontrol hapı alıyorum [hap**uh** aluh-y**o**room]
pillow yastık [yast**uh**k]
pillow case yastık kılıfı [kuhluhf**uh**]
pin (noun) toplu iğne [ee-n**eh**]
pineapple ananas
pineapple juice ananas suyu
pink pembe [pemb**eh**]
pipe (for smoking) pipo (for water) boru
pistachio antep fıstığı [fuhst**uh**-uh]
pity: it's a pity yazık [yaz**uh**k]
pizza pizza
place (noun) yer
  is this place taken? bu yerin sahibi var mı? [m**uh**]
  at your place sende [send**eh**], sizin evde [evd**eh**]
  at his place onda, onun evinde [eveend**eh**]
plain (not patterned) düz [dewz]

plane uçak [oochak]
 by plane uçakla
plant bitki
plaster cast alçı [alchuh]
plasters flaster, yara bandı
 [banduh]
plastic plastik
 (credit cards) kredi kartları
 [kartlaruh]
plastic bag naylon torba
 [nilon]
plate tabak
platform peron
 which platform is it for
 Bursa? Bursa treni hangi
 perondan kalkıyor? [kalkuh-
 yor]
play (verb) oynamak
 (noun: in theatre) oyun
playground çocuk bahçesi
 [chojook baнchesee]
pleasant hoş [hosh]
please lütfen [lewtfen]
 yes please lütfen
 could you please ...?
 lütfen ,,,-ebilir miydiniz?
 [mee-ideeneez]
 please don't do that lütfen
 yapmayın
 pleased to meet you!
 tanıştığımıza memnun
 oldum! [tanuhshtuh-uhmunza]
pleasure: my pleasure rica
 ederim [reeja]
plenty: plenty of ... bol bol ...
 there's plenty of time bol bol
 vakit var
 that's plenty, thanks teşekkür
 ederim, yeter [teshekkewr]

pliers kerpeten
plug (electrical) fiş [feesh]
 (in sink) tıkaç [tuhkach]
 (for car) buji [booJee]
plumber tesisatçı [teseesatchuh]
p.m.*: ... p.m. (afternoon)
 öğleden sonra ... [ur-leden]
 (evening) akşam ... [aksham]
poached egg kaynar suya
 kırılmış yumurta [kinar –
 kuhruhlmuhsh]
pocket cep [jep]
point: two point five iki nokta
 beş
 there's no point anlamı yok
 [anlamuh]
points (in car) kesici platinler
 [keseejee]
poisonous zehirli
police polis
 call the police! polis çağırın!
 [cha-uhruhn]

Civilian police come in a
variety of subdivisions.
The green-uniformed
Polis are the everyday security force
in the towns and cities. The **Trafik
Polisi**, recognized by their white
caps, are a branch of this service.
The **Turizm Polisi** patrol tourist
areas dressed in beige uniforms and
maroon berets, and should have
some knowledge of English, German
or Arabic. In the towns you're also
likely to see the **Belediye Zabıtası**
or navy-clad market police, who
patrol the markets and bazaars to
ensure that tradesmen aren't ripping

off customers.

In most rural areas, particularly as you move further east, law enforcement is in the hands of the **Jandarma**, a division of the regular army charged with law enforcement duties. Dial 155 for the police, 156 for the Jandarma and 154 for the traffic police. The call costs one small jeton, or one phonecard unit.

policeman polis
police station polis karakolu
policewoman kadın polis [kad**uhn**]
polish (noun) cila [jeel**a**]
polite nazik
polluted kirli
pony midilli
pool (for swimming) havuz
poor (not rich) fakir
(quality) kalitesiz
pop music pop müzik [mewz**eek**]
pop singer pop şarkıcısı [sharkuhjuhs**uh**]
popular sevilen
population nüfus [newf**oos**]
pork domuz eti
port (for boats) liman
(drink) porto şarabı [sharab**uh**]
porter (in hotel) kapıcı [kapuhj**uh**]
portrait portre [**po**rtreh]
posh kibar
possible mümkün [mewmk**ewn**]
is it possible to ...? ...-mak

mümkün mü? [mew]
as ... as possible olduğunca ... [oldoo-oonj**a**]
post (noun: mail) posta
(verb) postalamak
could you post this for me? bunları benim postalayabilir miydiniz? [boonlar**uh** – eecheen postalí-abeel**eer** mee-ideen**eez**]
postbox posta kutusu
postcard kartpostal
postcode posta kodu
poster (for room) poster
(in street) afiş [af**eesh**]
poste restante postrestant
post office postane [post**a**neh]

 The Turkish postal and telephone service is run by the PTT (**Posta, Telgraf, Telefon**), easily identified by a black-on-yellow logo. In larger towns and tourist resorts, the phone division of the main PTT building is open 24 hours, with mail accepted from 8 a.m. until 7 p.m. Elsewhere expect both facilities to be available from 8 a.m. to 10 p.m. Monday to Saturday, and from 9 a.m. to 7 p.m. on Sunday.

The outgoing service is efficient, but make sure that the clerk has charged you for airmail (**uçakla** [ooch**akla**]) and not the cheaper and slower surface rate. The best advice on sending packages is not to send anything over two or three kilos. Boxes must be left open for inspection, though at main branches folded packing kits are sold.

potato patates
pots and pans mutfak eşyası [esh-yasuh]
pottery (objects) seramik, toprak eşya [esh-ya]
pound* (money) sterlin (weight) libre [leebreh]
power cut elektrik kesilmesi
power point priz
practise: I want to practise my Turkish Türkçe pratik yapmak istiyorum [tewrkcheh]
prawns karides
prayer dua
prayer mat seccade [sejjadeh]
prefer: I prefer ... ... tercih ederim [terjeeH]
pregnant gebe [gebeh]
premium süper [sewper]
prescription (for medicine) reçete [recheteh]
see pharmacy
present (gift) hediye [hedee-yeh]
president (of country) cumhurbaşkanı [joomHoor-bashkanuh]
pretty güzel [gewzel]
it's pretty expensive oldukça pahalı [oldookcha]
price fiyat
priest rahip
prime minister başbakan [bashbakan]
printed matter matbua

priority (in driving) öncelik [urnjeleek]
prison hapishane hapeeshaneh]
private özel [urzel]
private bathroom özel banyo
probably belki
problem problem
no problem! hiç sorun değil! [heech – deh-eel]
program(me) (noun) program
promise: I promise söz veriyorum [surz]
pronounce: how is this pronounced? bu nasıl telaffuz edilir? [nasuhl]
properly (repaired, locked etc) hakkıyla [hakkuh-yuhla], iyice [ee-yeejeh]
protection factor koruma faktörü [fakturew]
Protestant Protestan
public convenience umumi hela
public holiday resmi tatil
pudding (dessert) sütlü tatlı [sewtlew tatluh], puding
pull çekmek [chekmek]
pullover kazak
puncture (noun) lastik patlaması [patlamasuh]
purple eflatun
purse (for money) para çantası [chantasuh]
(US) el çantası [chantasuh]
push itmek
pushchair puset
put koymak
where can I put ...? ...-i

nereye koyabilirim? [nerayeh]
**could you put us up for the
night?** bu gece bizi konuk
edebilir misiniz? [gejeh]
pyjamas pijama [peeJama]

Q

quality kalite [kaleeteh]
quarantine karantina
quarter çeyrek [chayrek]
quayside: on the quayside
rıhtımda [ruHtuhmda]
question soru
queue (noun) kuyruk [koo-
irook]
quick çabuk [chabook]
that was quick ne kadar
çabuk oldu [neh]
what's the quickest way
there? oraya en çabuk nasıl
gidilir? [nasuhl]
fancy a quick drink? çabucak
bir şey içelim ister misin?
[chaboojak beer shay eecheleem]
quickly hızla [huhzla]
quiet (place, hotel) sakin
[sakeen]
quiet! gürültü yapmayın!
[gewrewltew yapmï-uhn]
quite (fairly) oldukça
[oldookcha]
(very) tamamen, pek, çok
[chok]
that's quite right çok doğru
[chok doh-roo]
quite a lot oldukça çok
[oldookcha]

R

rabbit tavşan [tavshan]
race (for runners, cars) yarış
[yaruhsh]
racket (tennis, squash) raket
radiator radyatör [rad-yatur]
radio radyo
on the radio radyoda
rail: by rail trenle [trenleh]
railway demiryolu
rain (noun) yağmur [ya-moor]
in the rain yağmurda
it's raining yağmur yağıyor
[ya-uh-yor]
raincoat yağmurluk
Ramadan Ramazan
rape (noun) ırza geçme [uhrza
gechmeh]
rare (uncommon) nadide
[nadeedeh]
(steak) az pişmiş [peeshmeesh]
rash (on skin) isilik
raspberry ahududu
[aHoodoodoo]
rat sıçan [suhchan]
rate (for changing money) kur
rather: it's rather good
oldukça iyi [oldookcha]
I'd rather ... ...-yi tercih
ederim [terjeeH]
razor ustura
(electric) elektrikli tıraş
makinesi [tuhrash]
razor blades jilet [Jeelet]
read okumak
ready hazır [hazuhr]
are you ready? hazır

mısınız? [muhsuhn**uh**z]
I'm not ready yet henüz
hazır değilim [hen**ew**z –
deh-**ee**leem]

dialogue

> when will it be ready? ne
> zaman hazır olur? [neh]
> it should be ready in a
> couple of days bir kaç
> güne kadar hazır olur
> [kach gewn**eh**]

real gerçek [ger**chek**]
really gerçekten [**ge**rchekten]
I'm really sorry gerçekten
üzgünüm [ewzgewn**ewm**]
that's really great gerçekten
çok iyi [chok]
really? (doubt) yok canım?
[jan**uhm**]
(polite interest) sahi mi?
rear lights arka lambalar
rearview mirror dikiz aynası
[inas**uh**]
reasonable (prices etc) akla
yakın [yak**uhn**]
receipt makbuz
recently geçenlerde
[gechenlerd**eh**]
reception (in hotel) resepsiyon
(for guests) davet
at reception resepsiyonda
reception desk resepsiyon
masası [masas**uh**]
receptionist resepsiyon
memur**u**
recognize tanımak [tan**uhmak**]

recommend: could you
recommend ...? ... tavsiye
edebilir misiniz? [tavsee-y**eh**]
record (noun: music) plak
red kırmızı [kuhrmuhz**uh**]
red wine kırmızı şarap
[shar**ap**]
refund (noun) iade [ee-ad**eh**]
can I have a refund? paramı
geri alabilir miyim?
[param**uh**]
region bölge [burlg**eh**]
registered: by registered mail
taahhütlü [ta-a-hewtl**ew**]
registration number kayıt
numarası [kī-**uht** noomaras**uh**]
regular gas normal [nor-mal]
relative (noun) akraba
religion din [deen]
remember: I don't remember
hatırlamıyorum [hatuhrlamuh-
yoroom]
I remember hatırlıyorum
[hatuhrluh-**yo**room]
do you remember? hatırlıyor
musunuz?
rent (noun: for apartment etc) kira
(verb: car etc) kiralamak
for rent kiralık [keeral**uhk**]

dialogue

> I'd like to rent a car bir
> otomobil kiralamak
> istiyorum
> for how long? ne kadar
> süre için? [neh – sewr**eh**
> eech**een**]
> two days iki gün [gewn]

this is our range
elimizdekiler bunlar
I'll take the ... ...-yi alayım
[alî-**uhm**]
is that with unlimited
mileage? kilometre sınırı
yok değil mi? [keelomet**reh**
suhnuh-ruh y**o**k deh-**eel**]
it is evet
can I see your licence
please? ehliyetinizi
görebilir miyim lütfen?
[eHlee-yeteeneez**ee** gurebeel**eer**
– le**w**tfen]
and your passport ve
pasaportunuzu [veh]
is insurance included?
sigorta içinde mi?
[eecheend**eh**]
yes, but you pay the first
50,000,000 lira evet, fakat
ilk elli milyon lirayı siz
ödeyeceksiniz [leerî-uh s**eez**
urdayejekse**eneez**]
can you leave a deposit of
20,000,000 lira? yirmi
milyon lira depozito
bırakabilir misiniz?
[buhrakabeel**eer**]

rented car kiralık otomobil
[keeral**uhk**]
repair (verb) onarmak
  can you repair it? onu
  onarabilir misiniz?
repeat tekrarlamak
  could you repeat that? onu
  tekrarlar mısınız?
  [muhsuhn**uhz**]

reservation rezervasyon
I'd like to make a reservation
bir rezervasyon yapmak
istiyorum

dialogue

I have a reservation
rezervasyonum var
yes sir, what name please?
evet efendim, isim neydi
lütfen? [nay**dee**]

reserve (verb) ayırtmak
[î-uhrtmak]

dialogue

can I reserve a table for
tonight? bu akşam için
bir masa ayırtabilir
miyim? [aksham eech**een** –
î-uhrtabeel**eer**]
yes madam, for how many
people? evet efendim,
kaç kişi için? [kach
kee**shee**]
for two iki kişi için
and for what time? ve saat
kaç için? [veh sa-**at**]
for eight o'clock sekiz için
and could I have your
name, please? adınızı
alabilir miyim, lütfen?
[aduhnuhzuh-abeel**eer** –
le**w**tfen]
see alphabet for spelling

rest: I need a rest dinlenmeye

ihtiyacım var [–may**eh** ee**H**tee-yaj**uh**m]
the rest of the group grubun geri kalan kısmı [kuhsm**uh**]
restaurant lokanta, restoran

A **lokanta** is a restaurant, as is a **restoran**. A **kebapçı** or **köfteci** specializes in the preparation of **kebabs** and **köfte** respectively, with a limited number of side dishes. Most budget-priced restaurants are **içkisiz** or alcohol-free; any place marked **içkili** (licensed) is likely to be more expensive. Many places don't have menus: you'll need to ascertain the prices of the main courses beforehand, and review bills carefully when finished.
In many restaurants lone women will be ushered into the family parlour, which is often upstairs or behind a curtain.

restaurant car yemekli vagon
restroom tuvalet [toovalet]
see **toilet**
retired: I'm retired emekliyim
return: a return to ... ...'e bir gidiş dönüş bilet [-eh beer geedeesh durnewsh]
return ticket gidiş dönüş bileti
see **ticket**
reverse charge call ödemeli konuşma [urdemelee konooshma]
reverse gear geri vites

revolting iğrenç [ee-rench]
Rhodes Rodos
rib kaburga
rice (uncooked) pirinç [peer**ee**nch]
(cooked) pilav
rich (person) zengin
(food) ağır [a-**uhr**]
ridiculous gülünç [gewlewnch]
right (correct) doğru [doh-r**oo**]
(not left) sağ [sa]
you were right haklıymışsınız [hakluh-imuhsh-suhn**uhz**]
that's right doğru
this can't be right bu doğru olamaz
right! tamam!
is this the right road for ...? bu yol ...-e gider mi? [-eh]
on the right sağda [sa-d**a**]
turn right sağa dönün [durn**ewn**]
right-hand drive sağdan direksiyonlu [sa-d**an**]
ring (on finger) yüzük [yewz**ewk**]
I'll ring you sizi telefonla ararım [ar**uh**m]
ring back geri aramak (telefonla)
ripe (fruit) olgun
rip-off: it's a rip-off tam bir kazık [kaz**uhk**]
rip-off prices kazık fiyatlar
risky rizikolu
river nehir [neh-**H**eer]
road yol

is this the road for ...?
bu ... yolu mudur?
down the road yolun
ilerisinde [eelereeseendeh]

 Ordinary main roads are usually adequately paved, but often dangerously narrow. Toll highways are springing up, and are well worth the modest tolls. International roads have 'E' before a number (meaning Europe) and state roads have 'D' (meaning 'devlet' state). The main motorway (otoyol) connecting İstanbul to Ankara is called the TEM (Trans European Motorway); a toll is charged depending on the distance travelled.

road accident trafik kazası
[kazasuh]
road map karayolu haritası
[hareetasuh]
roadsign trafik işareti
[eesharetee]
rob: I've been robbed
soyuldum
rock kaya [kī-a]
(music) rock müziği
[mewzee-ee]
on the rocks (with ice) buzlu
roll (bread) sandviç ekmeği
[sandveech ekmeh-ee]
roof dam
roof rack üst bagaj yeri [ewst bagaJ]
room oda
in my room odamda

dialogue

do you have any rooms?
boş odanız var mı? [bosh
odanuhz var muh]
for how many people? kaç
kişi için? [kach keeshee
eecheen]
for one/for two bir/iki kişi
için
yes, we have rooms free
evet, boş odamız var
[odamuhz]
for how many nights will it
be? kaç gece için olacak?
[gejeh – olajak]
just for one night sadece
bir gece için [sa-dejeh]
how much is it? ne kadar?
[neh]
... with bathroom
and ... without bathroom
banyolu ... ve banyosuz ...
[veh]
can I see a room with
bathroom? banyolu odayı
görebilir miyim? [odī-uh
gurebeeleer]
OK, I'll take it tamam,
tutuyorum

room service oda servisi
rope halat
rosé (wine) pembe şarap
[pembeh sharap]
roughly (approximately) kabaca
[kabaja]
round: it's my round bu sefer
sıra bende [suhra bendeh]

roundabout (for traffic) göbek
[gu**rbek**]

round trip ticket gidiş dönüş
bileti

route yol
what's the best route? en iyi
hangi yoldan gidilir?

rubber (material) lastik
(eraser) silgi

rubber band lastik bant

rubbish (waste) çöp [churp]
(poor quality goods) uyduruk
şeyler [oo-idoor**uh**k shayler]
rubbish! (nonsense) saçma!
[sach**ma**]

rucksack sırt çantası [suhrt
chantas**uh**]

rude kaba

rug (for floor) kilim
(blanket) battaniye [battanee-
yeh]

ruins harabeler

rum rom
rum and coke rom ve koka
kola [vch]

run (verb: person) koşmak
[kosh**mak**]
how often do the buses run?
otobüslerin arası ne kadar?
[arrasuh ne.h]
I've run out of money param
bitti

rush hour kalabalık saatler
[kalabal**uh**k sa-atler]

S

sad üzgün [ewzg**ewn**]

saddle (for horse) eyer [ay-er]
(for bike) sele [sel**eh**]

safe (not in danger) güvenli
[gewvenl**ee**]
(not dangerous) güvenilir

safety pin çengelli iğne
[chengell**ee** ee-neh]

sail (noun) yelken

sailboard (noun) yelkenli sörf
[surf]

sailboarding sörf yapmak

salad salata

salad dressing salata sosu

sale: for sale satılık [satuhl**uh**k]

salmon som balığı [baluh-**uh**]

salt tuz

same: the same aynı [**in**uh]
the same as this bunun
aynısı [**in**uhs**uh**]
the same again, please
aynısından bir tane daha,
lütfen [**in**uhsuhndan beer taneh –
l**ewt**fen]
it's all the same to me benim
için hepsi bir [eech**een**]

sand kum [koom]

sandals sandal

sandwich sandviç [sandv**eech**]

sanitary napkin kadın bağı
[kad**uh**n ba-**uh**]

sanitary towel kadın bağı

sardines sardalya

Saturday cumartesi
[joom**a**rtesee]

sauce sos

saucepan tencere [**ten**jereh]

saucer fincan tabağı [**feen**jan taba-**uh**]

sauna sauna [sa-**oo**na]

sausage sosis

say (verb) demek, söylemek [suh-ile**mek**]

how do you say ... in Turkish? Türkçe ... nasıl denir? [**tew**rkcheh ... **na**suhl]

what did he/she say? ne dedi? [neh]

he/she said ... ... dedi

could you say that again? tekrarlar mısınız? [muhsuhn**uh**z]

scarf (for neck) atkı [atk**uh**] (for head) eşarp [e**sharp**]

scenery manzara

schedule (US) tarife [taree**feh**]

scheduled flight tarifeli sefer

school okul

scissors: a pair of scissors makas

scooter küçük motosiklet [kewche**wk**]

scotch viski

Scotch tape® seloteyp [**selo**tayp]

Scotland İskoçya [eesko**ch**-ya]

Scottish İskoç

I'm Scottish İskoçyalıyım [eesko**ch**-yaluh-y**uh**m]

scrambled eggs karılmış sahanda yumurta [karuhl**muh**sh]

scratch (noun) çizik [chee**zeek**]

screw (noun) vida

screwdriver tornavida

sea deniz

by the sea deniz kıyısında [kuh-yuhsuhn**da**]

seafood deniz ürünleri [ewrewnler**ee**]

seafood restaurant balık lokantası [bal**uh**k lokantas**uh**]

seafront sahil [sa**Heel**]

on the seafront sahilde [saHeeld**eh**]

seagull martı [mart**uh**]

Sea of Marmara Marmara Denizi

search (verb) aramak

seashell deniz kabuğu [den**eez** kab**oo**-oo]

seasick: I feel seasick beni deniz tuttu

I get seasick beni deniz tutar

seaside: by the seaside deniz kenarında [kenaruhn**da**]

seat oturacak yer [otoora**jak**]

is this anyone's seat? bu yerin sahibi var mı? [muh]

seat belt emniyet kemeri

sea urchin deniz kestanesi

seaweed yosun

secluded kuytu [koo-it**oo**]

second (adj) ikinci [eek**een**jee] (of time) saniye [sanee-**yeh**]

just a second! bir saniye! [beer]

second class (travel) ikinci sınıf [eek**een**jee suhn**uh**f]

second floor ikinci kat [eek**een**jee] (US) birinci kat [beer**een**jee]

second-hand elden düşme
[dewshmeh]
see görmek [gurmek]
  can I see? görebilir miyim?
  [gurebeeleer]
  have you seen ...? ...-i
  gördünüz mü? [-ee
  gurdewnewz mew]
  I saw him/her this morning
  onu bu sabah gördüm
  [gurdewm]
  see you! görüşürüz!
  [gurewshewrewz]
  I see (I understand) anlıyorum
  [anluh-yoroom]
self-catering apartment
  pansiyon (yemek pişirme
  olanaklı) [peesheermeh
  olanakluh]
self-service self servis
sell satmak
  do you sell ...? ... satıyor
  musunuz? [satuh-yor]
Sellotape® seloteyp [selotayp]
send göndermek [gurndermek]
  I want to send this to England
  bunu İngiltere'ye
  göndermek istiyorum
  [gurndehrreh-yeh]
  senior citizen yaşlı vatandaş
  [yashluh vatandash]
separate ayrı [iruh]
separated: I'm separated
  eşimden ayrı yaşıyorum
  [esheemden – yashuh-yoroom]
separately (pay, travel) ayrı ayrı
  [iruh]
September eylül [aylewl]
septic mikroplu

serious ciddi [jeeddee]
service charge (in restaurant)
  servis ücreti [ewjretee]
service station servis
  istasyonu
serviette peçete [pecheteh]
set menu tabldot [tabldot]
several birkaç [beerkach]
sew dikmek
  could you sew this back on?
  bunu yerine dikebilir
  misiniz? [yereeneh]
sex seks
  (gender) cinsiyet [jeensee-yet]
sexy cazibeli [jazeebelee]
shade: in the shade gölgede
  [gurlgedeh]
shake: let's shake hands
  tokalaşalım [tokalashaluhm]
shallow (water) sığ [suh]
shame: what a shame! ne
  yazık! [neh yazuhk]
shampoo (noun) şampuan
  [shampoo-an]
shampoo and set yıkama ve
  mizanpli [yuhkama veh]
share (verb: room, table etc)
  paylaşmak [pilashmak]
sharp (taste, knife) keskin
  (pain) şiddetli [shuhddetlee]
shattered (very tired)
  yorgunluktan bitmiş
  [beetmeesh]
shaver tıraş makinesi [tuhrash]
shaving foam tıraş köpüğü
  [kurpew-ew]
shaving point tıraş makinesi
  prizi
she* o

131

is she here? o burada mı?
[muh]

sheep's cheese beyaz peynir
[bay**az** payn**eer**]

sheet (for bed) çarşaf [charsh**af**]

shelf raf

shellfish kabuklu deniz
ürünleri [ewrewnler**ee**]

sherry şeri [sh**eree**]

ship gemi

by ship gemiyle [gemee-il**eh**]

shirt gömlek [g**u**rmlek]

shit! şimdi hapı yuttuk!
[sheemdee hap**uh**]

shock (noun) şok [shok]

I got an electric shock from
the ... ...-den elektrik çarptı
[charpt**uh**]

shock-absorber amortisör
[amort**ee**s**ur**]

shocking korkunç [kork**oo**nch]

shoe ayakkabı [**i**-akkab**uh**]

a pair of shoes bir çift
ayakkabı [ch**ee**ft]

shoelaces ayakkabı bağı
[ba-**uh**]

shoe polish ayakkabı cilası
[jeelas**uh**]

shoe repairer kundura
tamircisi [–jees**ee**]

shop dükkân [dewkk**an**]

Ordinary shops are open
continuously from 8.30 or
9 a.m. until 7 or 8 p.m.,
depending on the owner. Craftsmen
and bazaar stallholders keep long
hours, often working from 9 a.m. to
8 or 9 p.m., Monday to Saturday,
with only the hastiest of breaks for
meals, tea or prayers. Even on
Sunday the tradesmen's area may
not be completely shut down –
though don't count on this.

shopping: I'm going shopping
ben alış-verişe çıkıyorum
[al**uh**sh-ver**ee**sheh chuhkuh-
y**o**room]

shopping centre alış-veriş
merkezi

shop window vitrin

shore sahil [sa**heel**]

short kısa [k**uh**sa]

shortcut kestirme [kesteerm**eh**]

shorts şort [short]

should: what should I do? ne
yapmam lazım? [neh –
laz**uh**m]

you should ... ...-malıydınız
[-mal**uh**-iduhn**uh**z]

you shouldn't ...
...-mamalıydınız

he should be back soon
birazdan gelmesi lazım

shoulder omuz [om**ooz**]

shout (verb) bağırmak
[ba-uhrm**ak**]

show (in theatre) gösteri
[gurster**ee**]

could you show me? bana
gösterebilir misiniz?
[gursterebeel**eer**]

shower (in bathroom) duş
[doosh]

(rain) sağanak [sa-an**ak**]

with shower duşlu [doosh**loo**]

shower gel duş jeli [doosh]

shut (verb) kapatmak
 when do you shut? saat kaçta
 kapatıyorsunuz? [sa-at kachta
 kapatuh-yorsoonooz]
 when does it shut? ne
 zaman kapanıyor? [neh
 kapanuh-yor]
 they're shut kapalılar
 [kapaluh-lar]
 I've shut myself out anahtarı
 içerde unuttum [anaHtaruh
 eecherdeh]
 shut up! kapa çeneni!
 [chenenee]
shutter (on camera) örtücü
 [urtewjew], obtüratör
 [obdewratur]
 (on window) kepenk
shy çekingen [chekeengen]
sick (ill) hasta
 I'm going to be sick (vomit)
 kusacağım galiba [koosaja-
 uhm]
side yan
 the other side of the street
 caddenin öbür tarafı [urbewr
 tarafuh]
 side lights park lambaları
 [lambalaruh]
 side salad garnitür salata
 [garneetewr]
 side street yan sokak
sidewalk kaldırım
 [kalduhruhm]
 on the sidewalk kaldırımda
sight: the sights of ... ...-nin
 görmeye değer yerleri
 [gurmayeh deh-er]
sightseeing: we're going

sightseeing geziye çıkıyoruz
 [gezee-yeh chuhkuh-yorooz]
sightseeing tour gezi, tur
sign (roadsign etc) işaret
 [eesharet]
signal: he/she didn't give a
 signal (driver, cyclist) işaret
 vermedi
signature imza
signpost işaret levhası [isharet
 levhasuh]
silence sessizlik
silk ipek
silly (person) sersem
 (thing to do) saçma [sachma]
silver (noun) gümüş
 [gewmewsh]
silver foil aluminyum folyo
similar benzer
simple (easy) kolay [kolī]
since: since last week geçen
 haftadan beri [gechen]
 since I got here buraya
 geldiğimden beri [boorī-a
 geldee-eemden]
sing şarkı söylemek [sharkuh
 suh-ilemek]
singer şarkıcı [sharkuhjuh]
single: a single to ... ... e bir
 gidiş bileti [... eh boor goodeesh]
 I'm single bekârım
 [bekaruhm]
 see ticket
single bed tek kişilik yatak
 [keesheeleek]
single room tek kişilik bir
 oda
sink (in kitchen) evye [ev-yeh],
 bulaşık lavabosu [boolashuhk]

sister kız kardeş [kuhz kardesh]
sister-in-law (wife's sister)
baldız [balduhz]
(husband's sister) görümce
[gurrewmjeh]
(brother's wife) yenge [yengeh]
sit: can I sit here? buraya
oturabilir miyim? [boorī-a]
is anyone sitting here?
burada oturan var mı? [muh]
sit down oturmak
sit down oturun
size boy
ski (noun) kayak [kī-ak]
(verb) kayak yapmak
a pair of skis bir çift kayak
[cheeft]
skiing kayakçılık [kī-ak-
chuhluhk]
ski-lift telesiyej [telesee-yeɹ]
skin cilt [jeelt]
skin-diving balık adamlık
[baluhk adamluhk]
skinny sıska [suhska]
skirt etek
sky gök [gurk]
sleep (verb) uyumak
[oo-yoomak]
did you sleep well? iyi
uyudunuz mu?
[oo-yoodoonooz]
sleeper (on train) yataklı vagon
[yatakluh]
sleeping bag uyku tulumu
[oo-ikoo]
sleeping car yataklı vagon
[yatakluh]
sleeping pill uyku hapı
[oo-ikoo hapuh]

sleepy: I'm feeling sleepy
uykum geldi
sleeve kol
slide (photographic) diya
slip (garment) kombinezon
slippers terlik
slippery kaygan [kīgan]
slow yavaş [yavash]
slow down! (driving, speaking)
yavaşla!
slowly yavaşça [yavash-cha]
very slowly çok yavaş [chok]
small küçük [kewchewk]
smell: it smells (smells bad)
kötü kokuyor [kurtew]
smile (verb) gülümsemek
[gewlewm-semek]
smoke (noun) duman
do you mind if I smoke?
izninizle sigara içebilir
miyim? [–leh – eechebeeleer]
I don't smoke ben sigara
kullanmıyorum
koollanmuh–]
do you smoke? sigara içiyor
musunuz? [eechee-yor]
snack hafif yemek, meze
[mezeh]
just a snack yalnız hafif bir
şeyler [yalnuhz – shayler]

Many workers start the
morning with a **börek**, a
rich, flaky, layered pastry
containing bits of mince or cheese;
these are sold either at a tiny **büfe**
(stall-café) or from street carts.
Others content themselves with a
simple **simit** (bread rings speckled

with sesame seeds) or a bowl of
çorba (soup) with lemon.
Later in the day, vendors hawk
lahmacun, small, round Arab-style
pizzas with a thin meat-based
topping. Also available are
sandwiches (**sandviç**) with various
fillings (spicy sausage, cheese,
kokoreç offal, or fish). In coastal
cities **midye tava** (deep-fried
mussels) are often available, as are
midye dolması (mussels stuffed
with rice, pine nuts and allspice).
At lunchtime you can buy **pide**,
Turkish pizza – flat bread with
various toppings, served in a **pideci**
or **pide salonu**.

sneeze (noun) hapşırık
  [hapshuhr**uh**k]
snorkel şnorkel [shn**o**rkel]
snow (noun) kar
  it's snowing kar yağıyor
  [ya-uh-y**o**r]
so: it's so good! oyle iyi ki!
  [uh il**eh**]
  it's so expensive! öyle pahalı
  ki!
  not so much o kadar çok
  değil [chok deh-**eel**]
  not so bad pek kötü değil
  [kurt**ew**]
  so am I ben de öyle [d**eh**]
  so do I ben de
so-so şöyle böyle [sh**uh**-ileh
  b**uh**-ileh]
soaking solution (for contact
  lenses) koruyucu sıvı [koroo-
  yoo**joo** suhv**uh**]

soap sabun
soap powder sabun tozu
sober ayık [**ī**-uh**k**]
sock çorap [ch**o**rap]
socket (electrical) priz
soda (water) maden sodası
  [sodas**uh**]
sofa divan
soft (material etc) yumuşak
  [yoomoosh**ak**]
soft-boiled egg rafadan
  yumurta
soft drink alkolsüz içecek
  [alkols**ewz** eechej**ek**], meşrubat
  [meshroob**at**]
soft lenses yumuşak kontak
  lensleri [yoomoosh**ak**]
sole (of shoe, of foot) taban
  **could you put new soles on
  these?** bunlara pençe yapar
  mısınız? [pench**eh** –
  muhsuhn**uhz**]
some: can I have some water?
  biraz su alabilir miyim?
  can I have some biscuits?
  birkaç bisküvi alabilir
  miyim? [beerkach**uh**]
  can I have some? biraz
  alabilir mıyım?
somebody, someone birisi
something bir şey [sh**ay**]
something to eat yiyecek bir
  şey [yee-yej**ek**]
sometimes bazen
somewhere bir yerde [beer
  yerd**eh**]
son oğul [o-**ool**]
song şarkı [sh**a**rk**uh**]
son-in-law damat

soon yakında [yakuhnda]
 I'll be back soon birazdan
 dönerim
 as soon as possible en kısa
 zamanda [kuhsa]
sore: it's sore acıyor [ajuh-yor]
sore throat boğaz ağrısı [bo-az
 a-ruhsuh]
sorry: (I'm) sorry özür dilerim
 [urzewr]
 sorry? (didn't hear etc)
 efendim?
sort: what sort of ...? ne
 tür ...? [neh tewr]
soup çorba [chorba]
sour (taste) ekşi [ekshee]
south güney [gewnay]
 in the south güneyde
 [gewnaydeh]
South Africa Güney Afrika
South African (adj) Güney
 Afrika
 I'm South African Güney
 Afrikalıyım [–luh-yuhm]
southeast güney doğu
 [doh-oo]
southwest güney batı [batuh]
souvenir hatıra [hahtuhra]
Spain İspanya [eespanya]
Spanish (adj, person) İspanyol
 (language) İspanyolca
 [eespanyolja]
spanner somun anahtarı
 [anaHtaruh]
spare part yedek parça
 [parcha]
spare tyre yedek lastik
spark plug buji [boojee]
speak: do you speak English?

İngilizce biliyor musunuz?
 [eengeeleezjeh]
I don't speak ...
 ... bilmiyorum
can I speak to ...? ... ile
 görüşebilir miyim? [eeleh
 gurew-shebeeleer]

dialogue

can I speak to Sinan?
 Sinan'la görüşebilir
 miyim? [gurewshebeeleer]
who's calling? kim arıyor?
 [aruh-yor]
it's Patricia Patricia
I'm sorry, he's not in, can I
 take a message?
 üzgünüm evde değil,
 mesaj alabilir miyim?
 [ewzgewnewm evdeh deh-eel
 mesaJ]
no thanks, I'll call back
 later hayır teşekkür
 ederim, ben sonra tekrar
 ararım [hī-uhr teshekkewr –
 araruhm]
please tell him I called
 lütfen aradığımı söyleyin
 [lewtfen araduh-uhmuh
 suh-ilayeen]

spectacles gözlük [gurzlewk]
speed (noun) hız [huhz]
speed limit azami hız
speedometer hızölçer
 [huhzurlcher]
spell: how do you spell it?
 nasıl yazılıyor? [nasuhl

136

yazuhluh-**yor**]
see **alphabet**
spend harcamak [harjamak]
spider örümcek [urewmjek]
spin-dryer santrifüjlü
kurutma makinesi
[santreefewJ**lew**]
splinter kıymık [kuh-im**uhk**]
spoke (in wheel) jant [Jant]
spoon kaşık [kash**uhk**]
sport spor
sprain: I've sprained my ...
...-m burkuld**u**
spring (season) ilkbahar
(of car, seat) yay [yī]
square (in town) meydan
[may**dan**]
stairs merdiven
stale bayat [bī-**at**]
stall: the engine keeps stalling
motor sık sık duru**yor** [**suhk**]
stamp (noun) pul

dialogue

a stamp for England,
please İngiltere'ye bir
pul, lütfen [eengeelterch-**yeh**
– l**ewtfen**]
what are you sending? ne
gönderiyorsunuz?
[gurnderee-yorsoon**ooz**]
this postcard bu
kartpostalı
–postal**uh**]

Stamps are only available
from the **PTT** (post and
telephone office).

standby yedek, standby
star yıldız [yuhld**uhz**]
(in film) film yıldızı
start (noun) başlangıç
[bashlang**uhch**]
(verb) başlamak [bashlam**ak**]
when does it start? ne
zaman başlayacak? [neh –
bashlī-aj**ak**]
the car won't start araba
çalışmıyor [chal**uh**shmuh-yor]
starter (of car) marş [marsh]
(food) ordövr [ord**urvr**], meze
[mez**eh**]
starving: I'm starving çok
acıktım [chok ajuhkt**uhm**]
state (country) devlet
the States (USA) Birleşik
Amerika [beerlesh**eek**]
station istasyon
statue heykel [**haykel**]
stay: where are you staying?
nerede kalıyorsunuz?
[neredeh kal**uh**-yorsoonooz]
I'm staying at ... ...-de
kalıyorum [doh kal**uh**-yoroom]
I'd like to stay another two
nights iki gece daha kalmak
istiyorum [g**ejeh**]
steak biftek
steal çalmak [chalmak]
my bag has been stolen
çantam çalındı [chantam
chal**uh**nd**uh**]
steep (hill) dik
steering direksiyon sistemi
step: on the steps
merdivende [merdeevend**eh**]
stereo stereo

sterling sterlin
steward (on plane) kabin
memuru
stewardess hostes
sticky tape seloteyp [selotayp]
sticking plaster flaster, yara
bandı [band**uh**]
still: I'm still here hâlâ
buradayım [hala booradī-**uhm**]
is he/she still there? hâlâ
orada mı? [muh]
keep still! kımıldamayın!
[kuhmuhl-damī-uhn]
sting: I've been stung beni
böcek soktu [burjek]
stockings çoraplar [choraplar]
stomach mide [meed**eh**]
stomach ache mide ağrısı
[a-ruhs**uh**]
stone (rock) taş [tash]
stop (verb) durmak
please, stop here (to taxi driver
etc) lütfen, burada durun
[**lew**tfen]
do you stop near ...?
... yakınında duruyor
musunuz? [yakuhnuhnda]
stop it! kes (artık)! [art**uhk**]
stopover ara durak
storm fırtına [fuhrtuhna]
straight (whisky etc) sek
it's straight ahead dümdüz
ilerde [dewmd**ewz** eelerd**eh**]
straightaway hemen şimdi
[sheemdee]
strange (odd) acayip [ajī-**eep**]
stranger yabancı [yabanj**uh**]
I'm a stranger here buranın
yabancısıyım [**boo**ranuhn
–s**uh**-yuhm]
strap (on watch, suitcase) kayış
[kī-**uh**sh]
(on dress) askı [ask**uh**]
strawberry çilek [cheelek]
stream dere [der**eh**]
street sokak
on the street sokakta
streetmap şehir planı [sheheer
plan**uh**]
string ip
strong (person) güçlü
[gewchl**ew**]
(drink) sert
stuck: it's stuck sıkıştı
[suhkuhsht**uh**]
student öğrenci [ur-renj**ee**]
stupid aptal
subway (US) metro
suburb banliyö [banlee-**yur**]
suddenly aniden
suede süet [sewet]
sugar şeker [sheker]
sugared almonds badem
şekeri
suit (man's) takım elbise
[tak**uhm** elbees**eh**]
(woman's) tayyör [tī-**ur**]
it doesn't suit me (jacket etc)
bana yakışmıyor
[yak**uh**shmuh-yor]
it suits you size yakışıyor
[seez**eh** yakuhshuh-yor]
suitcase bavul
summer yaz
in the summer yazın
[yaz**uhn**]
sun güneş [gewnesh]
in the sun güneşte

[gewnesht**eh**]
out of the sun gölgede
[gurlged**eh**]
sunbathe güneş banyosu
yapmak
sunblock (cream) güneş
merhemi [gewn**esh**]
sunburn güneş yanığı
[yanuh-**uh**]
sunburnt güneşte yanmış
[gewnesht**eh** yanm**uh**sh]
Sunday pazar
sunglasses güneş gözlüğü
[gewnesh gurzlew-**ew**]
sun lounger şezlong [shezl**o**ng]
sunny: it's sunny hava güneşli
[gewnesh**lee**]
sunroof (in car) güneşlik
[gewnesh**leek**], sunroof
sunset günbatımı [gewn-
batuhm**uh**]
sunshade gölgelik
[gurlgel**eek**], güneş şemsiyesi
[gewnesh shemsee-yes**ee**]
sunshine güneş ışığı
[**uh**sh**uh**-uh]
sunstroke guneş çarpması
[charpmas**uh**]
suntan bronz ten
suntan lotion güneş losyonu
[gewnesh los-yon**oo**]
suntanned bronzlaşmış
[bronzlashm**uh**sh]
suntan oil güneş yağı [gewnesh
ya-**uh**]
super fevkalade [**fev**kaladeh]
supermarket süpermarket
[sewpermark**et**]
supper akşam yemeği

[aksham yemeh-**ee**]
supplement (extra charge) ek
ücret [ewjr**et**]
sure: are you sure? emin
misiniz?
sure! tabii! [**tab**ee-ee]
surfboard sörf tahtası [surf
tahtas**uh**]
surname soyadı
swearword küfür [kewf**ewr**]
sweater kazak
sweatshirt svetşört [svetsh**u**rt]
Sweden İsveç [eesv**ech**]
Swedish (adj) İsveç
(language) İsveçce [eesvech-
cheh]
sweet (dessert) tatlı [tatl**uh**]
it's too sweet fazla tatlı
sweets şeker [shek**er**]
swelling şişlik [sheeshl**eek**]
swim (verb) yüzmek [yewzm**ek**]
I'm going for a swim
yüzmeye gidiyorum
[yewzmay**eh**]
let's go for a swim hadi
yüzmeye gidelim
swimming costume mayo
[m**ī**-o]
swimming pool yüzme
havuzu [yewzm**uh**]
swimming trunks mayo [mi-**o**]
switch (noun) elektrik
düğmesi [dewmes**ee**]
switch off kapamak
switch on açmak [achm**ak**]
swollen şişmiş [sheeshm**ee**sh]
Syria Suriye [**soo**ree-yeh]

T

table masa
a table for two iki kişilik bir
masa [keesheeleek]
tablecloth masa örtüsü
[urtewsew]
table tennis masatopu
table wine sofra şarabı
[sharabuh]
tailback (of traffic) taşıt
kuyruğu [tashuht koo-iroo-oo]
tailor terzi
take (verb: lead) götürmek
[gurtewmek]
(accept) almak
(room etc) tutmak
can you take me to the ...?
beni ...-'e götürür
müsünüz? [-eh gurtew-rewr
mewsewnewz]
do you take credit cards?
kredi kartı kabul ediyor
musunuz? [kartuh]
fine, I'll take it tamam,
alıyorum [aluh-yoroom]
(room) tamam, tutuyorum
can I take this? (leaflet etc)
bunu alabilir miyim?
how long does it take? ne
kadar sürer? [neh – sewrer]
it takes three hours üç saat
sürer [ewch sa-at]
is this seat taken? bu yerin
sahibi var mı? [muh]
hamburger to take away
paket hamburger
can you take a little off here?

(to hairdresser) buradan biraz
alır mısınız? [aluhr
muhsuhnuhz]
talcum powder talk pudrası
[tahlk poodrasuh]
talk (verb) konuşmak
[konooshmak]
tall (person) uzun boylu
(building) yüksek [yewksek]
tampons tampon
tan (noun) bronz ten
to get a tan güneşte yanmak
[gewneshteh], bronzlaşmak
[bronzlashmak]
tank (of car) depo
tap musluk
tape (for cassette) teyp [tayp]
tape measure şerit metre
[sheret metreh], mezür
[mezewr]
tape recorder teyp [tayp]
taste (noun) tat
can I taste it? tadına
bakabilir miyim? [taduhna]
taxi taksi
will you get me a taxi?
bana bir taksi bulur
musunuz?
where can I find a taxi?
nerede bir taksi bulabilirim?
[neredeh]

dialogue

to the airport/to
the ... Hotel, please
havaalanına/Hotel ...-'e,
lütfen [hava-alanuhna – ...-eh
lewtfen]

how much will it be? ne kadar tutar? [neh] **15,000,000 lira** on beş milyon lira **that's fine right here, thanks** tamam burası iyi, teşekkürler [boorasuh – teshekkewrler]

Yellow city taxis are everywhere, and ranks crop up at appropriate places, though in rush hour finding a free cab can be difficult. Hailing one in the street is the best way to find a cab, but in suburban areas there are useful street corner telephones from which you can call cabs if you can make yourself understood. Urban vehicles all have working, digital-display meters, and fares are among the lowest in the Mediterranean. Out in the country, you'll have to bargain.

A Turkish institution is the **dolmuş** or shared transport. This is a car or minibus which runs along set routes, picking passengers up and dropping them off along the way. To stop a dolmuş, give a hand signal as for a normal taxi, and if there's any room at all, they'll stop and let you on. Generally dolmuşes run between 7 or 8 a.m. and 7 p.m. in summer, stopping earlier to match the hour of sunset in winter or extending until 10 or 11 p.m. near popular resorts. Dolmuşes do not operate to a timetable but leave when they are full or when there is hope of picking up passengers en-route.

taxi-driver taksi şoförü [shofurew] **taxi rank** taksi durağı [doora-uh] **tea** (drink) çay [chï] **tea for one/two, please** bir/iki çay, lütfen [lewtfen]

Tea is the national drink and is properly prepared in a double-boiler apparatus, with a larger water chamber underneath the smaller receptacle (**demlik**) containing dry leaves, to which a small quantity of hot water is added. After a suitable wait the tea is decanted into tiny tulip-shaped glasses, then diluted with more water to taste: **açık** [achuhk] is weak, **demli** or **koyu** strong. Sugar comes as cubes on the side; milk is never added. If you're frustrated by the usual tiny glass at breakfast, ask for a **dublo çay** [doobleh] (a 'double', served in a juice glass).

Herbal teas are also popular in Turkey, particularly **ıhlamur** [uhHlamoor] (linden flower) and **ada çayı** [chï-uh] ('island' tea), an infusion of a type of sage. The much-touted **elma çayı** (apple tea) in fact contains only chemicals and not a trace of apple essence.

teabags torba çay

teach: could you teach me?
bana öğretir misiniz?
[ur-reteer]

teacher öğretmen [ur-retmen]

team ekip
(sporting) takım [takuhm]

teaspoon çay kaşığı [chī kashuh-uh]

tea towel kurulama bezi

teenager (male/female)
delikanlı [deleekanluh], genç
kız [gench kuhz]

telegram telgraf

telephone telefon
see phone

television televizyon

tell: could you tell him/her ...?
ona ...-i söyler misiniz?
[suh-iler]

temperature (weather) sıcaklık
[suhjakluhk]
(fever) ateş [atesh]

temple tapınak [tapuhnak]

tennis tenis

tennis ball tenis topu

tennis court tenis kortu

tennis racket tenis raketi

tent çadır [chaduhr]

term (at university, school)
dönem [durnem]

terminus (rail) son istasyon

terrible berbat

terrific müthiş [mewt-heesh]

than* –den
smaller than –den küçük
[kewchewk]

thank: thank you teşekkür
ederim [teshekkewr]
thanks teşekkürler

[teshekkewrler]

thank you very much çok
teşekkür ederim [chok]

thanks for the lift arabanıza
aldığınız için teşekkür
ederim [–nuhza alduh-uhnuhz]

no thanks hayır, teşekkür
ederim [hī-uhr]

dialogue

thanks teşekkürler
don't mention it bir şey
değil [shay deh-eel]

that*: that rug (nearby) şu
kilim [shoo]
(further away) o kilim

that one (nearby) şu
(further away) o

I hope that ... umarım ki ...
[oomaruhm]

that's nice o iyi

is that ...? şu ... mı? [muh]

that's it (that's right) tamam
işte [eeshteh]

the*

theatre tiyatro

their* onların -leri [onlaruhn]

theirs* onlarınki

them* onları [onlaruh]
for them onlar için
[eecheen]
with them onlarla
to them onlara
who? – them kim? – onlar

then (at that time) o zaman
(after that) sonra

there orada

over there şurada [sh**oo**rada], orada

up there yukarıda [yook**a**ruhda]

is there/are there ...? ... var mı? [muh]

there is/there are ... ... var

there you are (giving something) buyrun [b**oo**-iroon]

thermal spring kaplıca [kapl**uh**ja]

thermometer termometre [termom**e**treh]

thermos flask termos

these*: these men/women bu adamlar/kadınlar

I'd like these bunları istiyorum [boonlar**uh**]

they* onlar

thick kalın [kal**uh**n]
 (stupid) kalın kafalı [kafal**uh**]

thief hırsız [huhrs**uh**z]

thigh but [boot]

thin ince [eenj**eh**]

thing şey [shay]

my things benim eşyam [esh-yam]

think düşünmek [dewshewnm**e**k]

I think so bence öyle [b**o**njoh uh•**ee**leh]

I don't think so bence öyle değil [deh-**ee**l]

I'll think about it düşüneceğim [dewshewnej**eh**-eem]

third party insurance mecburi trafik sigortası [mejboor**ee** – seegortas**uh**]

thirsty: I'm thirsty susadım [soosad**uh**m]

this: this rug bu kilim

this one bu

this is my wife bu eşim [esh**ee**m]

is this ...? bu ... mi?

those*: those men (nearby) şu adamlar [sh**oo**]
 (further away) o adamlar

which ones? – those hangileri? – şunlar [sh**oo**nlar]

thread (noun) iplik

throat boğaz [bo-**az**]

throat pastilles boğaz pastilleri

through içinden [eech**ee**nden]

does it go through ...? (train, bus) ...-den geçiyor mu? [gechee-y**or**]

throw (verb) atmak, fırlatmak [fuhrlatm**a**k]

throw away (verb) atmak

thumb başparmak [bashparm**a**k]

thunderstorm gök gürültülü fırtına [gurk gewr**e**wltowl**ow** fuhrt**uh**na]

Thursday perşembe [persh**e**mbeh]

ticket bilet

dialogue

a return to İzmir İzmir'e bir gidiş-dönüş [**ee**zmeer-eh beer geed**ee**sh-durn**ew**sh]
coming back when?

dönüş ne zaman?
today/next Tuesday
bugün/gelecek salı
that will be 8,000,000 lira
sekiz milyon lira ediyor

ticket office (bus, rail) bilet
gişesi [geeshesee]
tide gel-git olayı [olī-uh]
tie (necktie) kravat
tight (clothes etc) dar
 it's too tight fazla dar
tights külotlu çorap [kewlotloo
chorap]
till (cash desk) kasa
time* zaman
 what's the time? saat kaç?
 [sa-at kach]
 this time bu sefer
 last time geçen sefer [gechen]
 next time gelecek sefer
 [gelejek]
 three times üç kez
timetable tarife [tareefeh]
tin (can) konserve kutusu
 [konserveh]
tinfoil alüminyum folyo
 [alewmeen-yoom]
tin-opener konserve açacağı
 [konserveh achaja-uh]
tiny minik
tip (to waiter etc) bahşiş
 [baH-sheesh]

expect tips but you can round off the
fare to a suitable amount. It is
customary to put something in the
pockets of barbers and hairdressers
(10-15%).

tired yorgun [yorgoon]
 I'm tired yorgunum
 [yorgoonoom]
tissues kâğıt mendil [ka-uht]
to: to Bursa/London
 Bursa'ya/Londra'ya [londrī-a]
 to Turkey/England
 Türkiye'ye/Ingiltere'ye
 [tewrkee-yeh-yeh/eengheeltereh-
yeh]
 to the post office postaneye
 [postanayeh]
toast (bread) kızarmış ekmek
 [kuhzarmuhsh]
today bugün [boogewn]
toe ayak parmağı [ī-ak
 parma-uh]
together beraber
 we're together (in shop etc)
 beraberiz
toilet tuvalet [toovalet]
 where is the toilet? tuvalet
 nerede? [neredeh]
 I have to go to the toilet
 tuvalete gitmem lazım
 [toovaleteh – lahzuhm]

 Restaurants usually add a
service charge to the bill,
but if it is not included in
the price it is customary to leave a
tip of 10-15%. Taxi drivers do not

 Except in the fancier
resort hotels and
restaurants, most public
toilets are of the squathole variety,
found either in public parks or (more
infallibly) next to any mosque. Keep

small coins handy for the custodian.
Keep a supply of toilet paper with
you (available in Turkey) – Turks
wash themselves off either with the
bidet-spout or the special vessel
filled from the handy floor-level tap.

toilet paper tuvalet kâğıdı
[ka-uhduh]
tomato domates
tomato juice domates suyu
tomato ketchup ketçap
[ketchap]
tomorrow yarın [yaruhn]
tomorrow morning yarın
sabah [sabaH]
the day after tomorrow öbür
gün [urbewr gewn]
toner (cosmetic) toner
tongue dil
tonic (water) tonik
tonight bu gece [gejeh]
tonsillitis bademcik iltihabı
[bademjeek eelteehabuh]
too (excessively) fazla
(also) de [deh]
too hot fazla sıcak
too much çok fazla [chok]
me too ben de [deh]
tooth diş [deesh]
toothache diş ağrısı [a-ruhsuh]
toothbrush diş fırçası
[fuhrchasuh]
toothpaste diş macunu
[majoonoo]
top: on top of ... ...-in
üstünde [ewstewndeh]
at the top en üstte [ewstteh]
at the top of ... ...-in en

üstünde
top floor üst kat [ewst]
topless göğüsleri açık [gur-
ewsleree achuhk], üstsüz
[ewstsewz]
torch el feneri
total (noun) toplam
tour (noun) tur
is there a tour of ...? ... turu
var mı? [muh]
tour guide rehber
tourist turist
tourist information office
turizm danışma bürosu
[danuhshma bewrosoo]
tour operator tur operatörü
[operaturew]
towards -e doğru [-eh
doh-roo]
towel havlu
tower kule [kooleh]
town kasaba
in town şehirde [sheheerdeh]
just out of town şehrin
hemen dışında [shehreen –
duhshuhnda]
town centre şehır merkezi
town hall belediye binası
[beledee-yeh]
toy oyuncak [o-yoonjak]
track (US) peron
tracksuit eşofman [eshofman]
traditional geleneksel
traffic trafik
traffic jam trafik tıkanıklığı
[tuhkanuhkluh-uh]
traffic lights trafik ışıkları
[uhshuhk-laruh]
trailer (for carrying tent etc)

römork [rurmork], trayler
[trīler]
(US) karavan
trailer park kamping
train tren
 by train trenle [trenleh]

Turkey's train network is
far from exhaustive and
it's best used to span the
distances between the three main
cities and the provincial centres.
Trains often follow tortuous routes
and may take as up to twice as long as
buses. They do, however, have the
advantage of additional comfort at
comparable or lower prices.
The better services, west of Ankara,
called **mavi tren** or **ekspres**, almost
match long-distance buses in speed
and frequency. Avoid any departure
labelled **posta** (mail train) or **yolcu**
(local) as they're very slow. On major
train routes it's a good idea to make
a reservation. You can do this for
any journey in the country in
İstanbul, İzmir and Ankara.
On long-haul journeys you have a
choice between a first- and second-
class seat. There are fare reductions
for students, return tickets and
groups.

dialogue

is this the train for Ankara?
bu Ankara treni mi?
sure tabi
no, you want that platform

there hayır, sizin şu öbür
perona gitmeniz lazım
[hī-**uhr** – shoo ewbewr –
laz**uh**m]

trainers (shoes) spor
ayakkabısı [ī-akkabuhs**uh**]
train station tren istasyonu
tram tramvay [tramvī]
translate tercüme etmek
[terjewm**eh**]
 could you translate that?
bunu tercüme edebilir
misiniz?
translation tercüme
translator tercüman
trash çöp [churp]
trashcan çöp tenekesi
travel seyahat [sayahat]
 we're travelling around
geziyoruz
travel agent's seyahat acentası
[sayahat ajentas**uh**]
traveller's cheque seyahat
çeki [chek**ee**]
 see **cheque**
tray tepsi
tree ağaç [a-**a**ch]
tremendous muazzam
[moo-azz**am**]
trendy (restaurant, club) şık
[shuhk], moda
(clothes) modaya uygun
[modī-a oo-ig**oon**]
(person) şık [shuhk]
trim: just a trim please (to
hairdresser) lütfen yalnız
uçlarından biraz alın [**lew**tfen
yaln**uh**z oochlaruhndan – **a**luhn]

trip (excursion) yolculuk
[yoljool**oo**k]
**I'd like to go on a trip
to ...** bir ... gezisi yapmak
istiyorum
trolley el arabası [arabas**uh**]
trolleybus troleybüs
[trolayb**ew**s]
trouble (noun) dert
I'm having trouble with ...
... ile başım dertte [eel**eh**
bash**uh**m dertt**eh**]
trousers pantolon
Troy Truva
true gerçek [gerch**ek**]
that's not true o doğru değil
[doh-r**oo** deh-**eel**]
trunk (US) bagaj [baga**J**]
trunks (swimming) mayo [mī-**o**]
try (verb) denemek
can I have a try? (at doing
something) bir deneyebilir
miyim? [denayebeel**eer**]
try on prova etmek
can I try it on? üstümde
deneyebilir miyim?
[ewstewmd**eh** denayebeel**eer**]
T-shirt tişört [tee-sh**urt**]
Tuesday salı [sal**uh**]
tuna ton balığı [bal**uh**-uh]
tunnel tunel [tewnel]
Turk Türk [tewrk]
Turkey Türkiye [t**ew**rkee-yeh]
Turkish (adj) Türk
(language) Türkçe [tewrkch**eh**]
Turkish bath hamam

Virtually all Turkish towns
of any size have at least
one **hamam** per
neighbourhood. Baths are usually
signposted, but if in doubt look for
the distinctive external profile of the
roof domes, visible from the street.
Baths are either permanently
designated for men or women, or
sexually segregated on a schedule –
look for the words **erkekler** (men)
and **kadınlar** (women), followed by
a time range written on a placard by
the door.
On entering, you will usually leave
your valuables in a small drawer, the
key of which (often on a wrist/ankle
thong) you keep with you for the
duration of your wash. Bring soap,
shampoo and a shaving mirror –
these are either not supplied or are
expensive; the basic admission
charge varies depending on the level
of luxury.
Men will be supplied with a
peştamal, a thin, wraparound
sarong; both sexes get **takunya**,
wooden clogs, and later a **havlu** or
proper drying towel.

Turkish coffee Türk kahvesi
[tewrk ka**H**vesee]
Turkish Cypriot (adj) Kıbrıs
Türk [**kuh**bruhs]
(person) Kıbrıslı Türk
[kuhbr**uh**sluh]
Turkish delight lokum
Turkish wrestling yağlı güreş
[ya-l**uh** gewr**esh**]

turn: turn left/right sola/sağa dönün [durn**ewn**]
turn off: where do I turn off? nereden sapmalıyım? [–luh-y**uhm**]
can you turn the heating off? kaloriferi kapatabilir misiniz?
turn on: can you turn the heating on? kaloriferi yakabilir misiniz?
turning (in road) sapak
TV TV [tee vee]
tweezers cımbız [juhmb**uhz**]
twice iki kez
twice as much iki misli [mees**lee**]
twin beds çift yatak [cheeft]
twin room çift yataklı oda [yatakl**uh**]
twist: I've twisted my ankle ayak bileğimi burktum [**ī-ak** beeleh-eem**ee**]
type (noun) tip [teep]
another type of ... başka tip bir ... [**bashka**]
typical tipik
tyre lastik

U

ugly çirkin [cheerk**een**]
UK Birleşik Krallık [beerlesh**eek** krall**uhk**]
ulcer ülser [ewls**er**]
umbrella şemsiye [shemsee-**yeh**]
uncle amca [**amja**]

unconscious baygın [b**ī**g**uhn**]
under: under
the ... (position) ...-in altında [altuhn**da**]
(less than) ...-den az
underdone (meat) az pişmiş [peeshm**eesh**]
underground (railway) metro
underpants külot [kewl**ot**]
understand: I understand anlıyorum [anl**uh**-yoroom]
I don't understand anlamıyorum [anlamuh-yuhroom]
do you understand? anlıyor musunuz? [anluh-y**or**]
unemployed işsiz [eesh-s**eez**]
United States Birleşik Amerika [beerlesh**eek**]
university üniversite [ewnee-verseet**eh**]
unleaded petrol kurşunsuz benzin [koorshoons**ooz**]
unlimited mileage kilometre kısıtlamasız [keelom**e**treh kuhsuhtlamas**uhz**]
unlock kilidi açmak [ach**mak**]
unpack eşyaları bavuldan çıkarmak [esh-yalar**uh** – chuhkarm**ak**]
until -e kadar [-eh]
unusual alışılmamış [aluhsh**uh**l-mamuhsh]
up yukarı [yookar**uh**]
up there yukarıda [yookaruh**da**]
he's not up yet (not out of bed) daha kalkmadı [kalkmad**uh**]

what's up? (what's wrong?) ne oldu? [neh old**oo**]

upmarket sükseli [sewks**elee**]

upset stomach mide bozukluğu [meed**eh** bozookloo-**oo**]

upside down baş aşağı [bash asha-**uh**]

upstairs üst katta [ewst]

urgent acil [aj**eel**]

us˙ bizi

with us bizimle [beez**ee**mleh]

for us bizim için [eech**een**]

USA ABD [a beh deh]

use (verb) kullanmak

may I use ...? ...-i kullanabilir miyim?

useful yararlı [yararl**uh**]

usual olağan [ola-**an**]

the usual (drink etc) her zamanki

V

vacancy: do you have any vacancies? (hotel) boş odanız var mı? [bosh odan**uhz** var muh]

see room

vacation tatil

on vacation tatilde [tateeld**eh**]

vaccination aşılama [ashuhlama]

vacuum cleaner elektrik süpürgesi [sewpewrges**ee**]

valid (ticket etc) geçerli [gecherl**ee**]

how long is it valid for? ne zamana kadar geçerli? [neh]

valley vadi

valuable (adj) değerli [deh-erl**ee**]

can I leave my valuables here? değerli eşyalarımı burada bırakabilir miyim? [esh-yalaruhm**uh** – buhraka-bee**leer**]

value (noun) değer [deh-**er**]

van kamyonet

vanilla vanilya

a vanilla ice cream vanilyalı dondurma [vaneel-yal**uh**]

vary: it varies değişir [deh-eesh**eer**]

vase vazo

veal dana eti

vegetables sebze [sebz**eh**]

vegetarian (noun) etyemez

vending machine otomat

very çok [chok]

very big çok büyük

very little for me bana azıcık [azuhj**uh**k]

I like it very much çok beğeniyorum [beh-enee-**yoroom**]

vest (under shirt) fanila

via üzerinden [ewzereend**en**]

video video

view manzara

villa villa

village köy [kuh-i]

vinegar sirke [seerk**eh**]

vineyard bağ [ba]

visa vize [**vee**zeh]

visit (verb) ziyaret etmek

I'd like to visit ... ...-i ziyaret etmek isterim

vital: it's vital that ... ...-si şart
[shart]
vodka votka
voice ses
voltage voltaj [voltaJ]

The supply is 220V. British appliances need a 3-to-2-pin plug adaptor; North American ones both an adaptor and a transformer (except for dual voltage shavers, which need only the former).

vomit kusmak

W

waist bel
waistcoat yelek
wait (verb) beklemek
  wait for me beni bekleyin
  [beklayeen]
  don't wait for me beni
  beklemeyin [beklemayeen]
  can I wait until my partner
  gets here? eşim gelinceye
  kadar bekleyebilir miyim?
  [esheem geleenjayeh –
  beklayebeeleer]
  can you do it while I wait?
  beklerken yapabilir misiniz?
  could you wait here for me?
  beni burada bekler misiniz?
waiter garson
  waiter! bakar mısınız!
  [muhsuhnuhz]
waitress garson kız [kuhz]

waitress! bakar mısınız!
[muhsuhnuhz]
wake: can you wake me up at
5.30? beni beş buçukta
uyandırır mısınız?
[oo-yanduhruhr muhsuhnuhz]
wake-up call telefonla
uyandırma [oo-yanduhrma]
Wales Galler
walk: is it a long walk?
yürüyerek uzak mıdır?
[yewrew-yerek – muhduhr]
  it's only a short walk
  yürüyerek çok yakın [chok
  yakuhn]
  I'll walk yürüyeceğim
  [yewrew-yejeh-eem]
  I'm going for a walk ben
  yürüyüşe çıkıyorum
  [yewrew-yewsheh chukkuh-
  yoroom]
Walkman® walkman®
wall duvar
wallet cüzdan [jewzdan]
wander: I like just wandering
around amaçsızca dolaşmayı
severim [amachsuhzja dolashmi-
uh]
want: I want a ... bir ...
istiyorum
  I don't want any ...
  ... istemiyorum
  I want to go home eve
  gitmek istiyorum [eveh]
  I don't want to ... ...-
  mek istemiyorum
  he wants to ... ...-mek
  istiyor
  what do you want? ne

istiyorsunuz? [neh]
ward (in hospital) koğuş
[ko-**oosh**]
warm sıcak [suhjak]
I'm so warm sıcak bastı
[bast**uh**]
was*: he/she/it was –di
wash (verb) yıkamak
[yuhkamak]
can you wash these? bunları
yıkayabilir misiniz?
[boonlar**uh** yuhkī-abee**leer**]
washer (for bolt etc) rondela
washhand basin lavabo
washing (clothes) çamaşır
[chamash**uhr**]
washing machine çamaşır
makinesi
washing powder çamaşır toz**u**
washing-up liquid deterjan
[deterJan]
wasp eşek arısı [eshek aruhs**uh**]
watch (wristwatch) saat [sa-**at**]
will you watch my things for
me? eşyalarıma göz kulak
olur musunuz? [esh-yalar**uh**ma
gurz]
watch out! dikkat!
watch strap saat kayışı [sa-at
KĪ-uhsh**uh**]
water su
may I have some water?
biraz su verir misiniz?
water pipe nargile [nargee**leh**]
waterproof (adj) su geçirmez
[gecheerm**ez**]
waterskiing su kayağı [kī-a-uh]
wave (in sea) dalga
way: it's this way bu taraftan

it's that way şu taraftan
[shoo]
is it a long way
to ...? ... buraya uzak mı?
[boorī-a – muh]
no way! katiyen olmaz!
[katee-y**en**]

dialogue

could you tell me the way
to ...? ...-e nereden gidilir
söyleyebilir misiniz? [-eh –
suh-ilayebee**leer**]
go straight on until you
reach the traffic lights
trafik ışıklarına kadar
dümdüz gidin
[uhshuhklaruhna – dewmde**wz**]
turn left sola dönün
[durne**wn**]
take the first on the right
sağdan ilk yola sapın
[sa-dan – sap**uhn**]
see where

we* biz
weak (person) zayıf [zī-**uhf**],
güçsüz [**gew**chsewz]
(drink) hafif
(tea) açık [a**chuhk**]
weather hava

dialogue

what's the weather
forecast? hava raporu
nasıl? [**na**suhl]
it's going to be fine hava

güzel olacak [gewzel olajak]
it's going to rain yağmur
yağacak [ya-moor ya-ajak]
it'll brighten up later sonra
hava açacak [achajak]

wedding düğün [dew-ewn]
wedding ring alyans
Wednesday çarşamba
  [charshamba]
week hafta
  a week (from) today haftaya
  bugün [hafti-a boogewn]
  a week (from) tomorrow
  yarından itibaren bir hafta
  sonra [yaruhndan]
weekend hafta sonu
  at the weekend hafta
  sonunda
weight ağırlık [a-uhrluhk]
weird tuhaf [toohaf]
weirdo kaçık [kachuhk]
welcome: welcome to ... ...-e
  hoş geldiniz [-eh hosh]
  you're welcome (don't mention
  it) bir şey değil [shay deh-eel]
well: I don't feel well kendimi
  iyi hissetmiyorum
  he/she's not well iyi değil
  [deh-eel]
  you speak English very well
  çok iyi İngilizce
  konuşuyorsunuz [chok –
  eengeeleezjeh konooshoo-
  yorsoonooz]
  well done! aferin!
  this one as well bu da
  well well! (surprise) hayret!
  [hiret]

dialogue

how are you? nasılsınız?
[nasuhlsuhnuhz]
very well, thanks, and you?
çok iyiyim, teşekkür
ederim, ya siz? [chok –
teshekkewr]

well-done (meat) iyi pişmiş
  [peeshmeesh]
Welsh (adj) Galler
  I'm Welsh Galliyim
were*: we were –dik
  you were –diniz
  they were –diler
west batı [batuh]
  in the west batıda
West Indian (adj) Batı Hint
  [batuh]
wet ıslak [uhslak]
what? ne? [neh]
  what's that? o nedir?
  what should I do? ne
  yapsaydım? [yapsiduhm]
  what a view! ne manzara!
  what bus do I take? hangi
  otobüse binmem lazım?
  [lazuhm]
wheel tekerlek
wheelchair tekerlekli iskemle
  [eeskemleh]
when? ne zaman?
  when we get back biz
  dönünce [dewnewnjeh]
  when's the train/ferry?
  tren/feribot kaçta? [kachta]
where? nerede? [neredeh]
  I don't know where it is

nerede olduğunu
bilmiyorum [oldoo-oonoo]

dialogue

> where is the Topkapı
> museum? Topkapı müzesi
> nerede? [topkapuh
> mewzesee]
> it's over there şurada
> [shoorada]
> could you show me where
> it is on the map? haritada
> yerini gösterir misiniz?
> [gurstereer]
> it's just here tam burada
> see way

which: which bus? hangi
otobüs?

dialogue

> which one? hangisi?
> that one şu [shoo]
> this one? bu mu?
> no, that one hayır, şu
> [hī-uhr]

while: while I'm here ben
buradayken [booradīken]
whisky viski
white beyaz [bayaz]
white wine beyaz şarap
[sharap]
who? kim?
who is it? kim o?
the man who ... ...-an adam
whole: the whole week bütün

hafta [bewtewn]
the whole lot hepsi
whose: whose is this? bu
kimin?
why? niçin? [neecheen]
why not? neden olmasın?
[olmasuhn]
wide geniş [geneesh]
wife hanım [hanuhm]
will: will you do it for me?
bunu benim için yapar
mısınız? [eecheen –
muhsuhnuhz]
wind (noun) rüzgâr [rewzgar]
window (of house, car) pencere
[penjereh]
(of shop) vitrin
near the window pencerenin
yakınında [yakuhnuhnda]
in the window (of shop)
vitrinde [veetreendeh]
window seat pencere yanı
[yanuh]
windscreen araba ön camı
[urn jamuh]
windscreen wiper silecekler
[seelejekler]
windsurfing yelkenli sörf
[yelkenlee surf]
windy rüzgârlı [rewzgarluh]
wine şarap [sharap]
can we have some more
wine? bize biraz daha şarap
verir misiniz? [beezeh]

Wine from vineyards
scattered across western
Anatolia between
Cappadocia, the Euphrates Valley,

Thrace and the Aegean, is often better than average; names to watch for include **Kavaklıdere**, **Doluca**, **Turasan**, **Narbağ** and **Kavalleros**. The best white wines come from around İzmir. Red is **kırmızı** [kuhrmuhzuh], white **beyaz** [bayaz] and rosé **pembe** [pembeh]/**roze** [rozeh].

wine list şarap listesi [sharap]
winter kış [kuhsh]
  in the winter kışın [kuhshuhn]
winter holiday kış tatili [kuhsh]
wire tel
  (electric) kablo
wish: best wishes en iyi dileklerimle [deeleklereemleh]
with ile [eeleh]
  I'm staying with ... ...-de kalıyorum [-deh kaluh-yoroom]
without –siz
witness tanık [tanuhk]
  will you be a witness for me? benim için tanıklık eder misiniz? [eecheen tanuhkluhk]
woman kadın [kaduhn]

women
Turkish society is deliberately gender-segregated, and if you want to avoid men completely, even if you're travelling alone, it's not too difficult. Simply seek the company of Turkish women at every opportunity, and you will generally be protected by them. Turkish women suffer from harassment themselves, and their methods of dealing with it can be very successfully imitated. Avoid eye contact with men, and try to look as confident and purposeful as possible. When all else fails, the best way of neutralizing harassment is to make a public scene.
see **bus**

wonderful harikulade [–ladeh]
won't*: it won't start çalışmıyor [chaluhshmuh-yor]
wood (material) tahta [taHta]
woods (forest) orman
wool yün [yewn]
word kelime [keleemeh]
work (noun) iş [eesh]
  it's not working çalışmıyor [chaluhshmuh-yor]
  I work in ... ...-'da çalışıyorum [chaluhshuh-yoroom]
world dünya [dewnya]
worry: I'm worried kaygılanıyorum [kiguhlanuh-yoroom]
worry beads tesbih [tesbeeH]
worse: it's worse daha kötü [kurtew]
worst en kötü
worth: is it worth a visit? ziyarete değer mi? [zeeyareteh deh-er]
would: would you give this to ...? bunu ...-e verir misiniz? [-eh]
wrap: could you wrap it up? paket yapar mısınız? [muhsuhnuhz]

wrapping paper ambalaj
kağıdı [ambalaJ ka-uhduh]
wrist bilek
write yazmak
  could you write it down?
  yazar mısınız? [muhsuhnuhz]
  how do you write it? nasıl
  yazılır? [nasuhl yazuhluhr]
writing paper yazı kâğıdı
[yazuh ka-uhduh]
wrong: it's the wrong key o
  yanlış anahtar [yanluhsh]
  this is the wrong train bu
  yanlış tren
  the bill's wrong hesap yanlış
  sorry, wrong number
  affedersiniz, yanlış numara
  sorry, wrong room
  affedersiniz, yanlış oda
  there's something wrong
  with ... ...-de bir sorun var
  [-deh]
  what's wrong? sorun nedir?

X
—

X-ray röntgen [rurntgen]

Y
—

yacht yat
yard* yarda
year yıl [yuhl]
yellow sarı [saruh]
yes evet
yesterday dün [dewn]
  yesterday morning dün

sabah [sabaH]
  the day before yesterday
  evvelsi gün [gewn]
yet henüz [henewz]

dialogue

> is it here yet? daha
> gelmedi mi?
> no, not yet hayır, henüz
> değil [hī-uhr – deh-**eel**]
> you'll have to wait a little
> longer yet biraz daha
> beklemeniz lazım
> [lazuhm]

yoghurt yoğurt [yo-**oort**]
you* (pl or pol) siz, sizler
  (sing, fam) sen
  this is for you bu sizin için
  [eecheen]
  with you sizinle [seezeenleh]

 Siz is the formal word for
'you' used when speaking
to one person and is also
the form to use when speaking to
more than one person in formal or
informal situations. **Sizler** is an even
more formal way of addressing
more than one person. **Sen** is the
word for 'you' used for family
members, friends and children
though in some families parents and
grandparents may prefer to be
addressed in the formal way.

young genç [gench]
your* (pl or pol) –iniz, –niz

155

(emphatic) sizin
(sing, fam) –in, –n
(emphatic) senin
your camera fotoğraf makinanız
yours (pl or pol) sizinki
(sing, fam) seninki
youth hostel gençlik yurdu [genchleek]

Z

zero sıfır [suhfuhr]
zip fermuar [fermoo-ar]
  could you put a new zip on?
  fermuarı değiştirir misiniz?
  [fermoo-aruh deh-eeshteereer]
zip code posta kodu
zoo hayvanat bahçesi [hīvanat baHchesee]
zucchini kabak

Turkish

→

English

Colloquial Turkish

The following are words you might well hear. You shouldn't be tempted to use any of the stronger ones unless you are sure of your audience.

Allah aşkına [ashkuhna] for God's sake
Allah kahretsin! damn!
Allah razı olsun! [razuh] bless you!
aslan sütü [sewtew] slang word for raki
baksana be! [beh] hey you!
bombok shitty
çek arabanı! [chek arabanuh] get lost!
dangalak wally
defol! get out!; go away!
eline sağlık! [eeleneh sa-luhk] well done!
eşşoğlu eşşek [esh-sholoo esh-shek] ass; lout
eyvah! [ayvaH] alas!
hay Allah! [hī] damn!
herif bloke, guy
inşallah [eenshallah] I hope so; hopefully; God willing
işler nasıl? [eeshler nasuhl] how are things?
kapa çeneni! [chenenee] shut up!
katiyen olmaz! no way!
kuş beyinli [koosh bayeenlee] stupid, bird-brained
maşallah! [mashallah] wonderful! (used to express admiration and wonder, and to avert the evil eye)
ne haber?, ne var ne yok? how are things?
saçma! [sachma] rubbish!, nonsense!
serseri tramp, vagabond
sudan ucuz [oojooz] dirt cheap
vay canına! [vī januhna] I'll be damned!
yapma be! [beh] really!

The Turkish Alphabet

This section is in Turkish alphabetical order:

a, b, c, ç, d, e, f, g, ğ, h, ı, i, j, k, l, m, n, o, ö, p, r, s, ş, t, u, ü, v, y, z

A

a! oh!

-a to

AB [a beh] EU

abartmak to exaggerate

ABD [a beh deh] USA

abi older brother

abide [abeedeh] monument

abla elder sister

abone kartı [aboneh kartuh] season ticket

abonman book of bus tickets

acaba [ajaba] I wonder

acayip [ajï-eep] odd, strange

acele [ajeleh] hurry; urgent

acele edin! hurry up!
 acele et! hurry up!

acele etmek to hurry

acemi [ajemee] beginner

acemi pisti nursery slope

acenta [ajenta] agency

acı [ajuh] bitter; hot, spicy; pain

acıkmak [ajuhkmak] to be hungry
 acıktım [ajuhktuhm] I'm hungry

acılı [ajuhluh] hot

acımak [ajuhmak] to feel pain; to ache; to hurt

acıyor [ajuh-yor] it hurts, it's sore

acil [ajeel] urgent

acildir: bu acildir! [ajeeldeer] this is an emergency!

acil durum emergency

acil servis casualty

department

acil vaka emergency

aç [ach] hungry; greedy

açgözlü [achgurzlew] greedy

açık [achuhk] open; clear, obvious; (switched) on; light

açık bilet open ticket

açık havada outdoors

açık hava tiyatrosu open air theatre

açıklamak [achuhk-lamak] to explain

açık yüzme havuzu [yewzmeh] open-air swimming pool

açılır tavan [achuhluhr] sun roof

açılış saatleri [achuhluhsh sa-atleree] opening times; collection times

açılış ve kapanış saatleri [veh kapanuhsh] opening times

açıp/kapama düğmesi [achuhp – dew-mesee] on/off switch

açmak [achmak] to open; to switch on

ad name; first name

ada island

adam man

adamlar men

adaptör [adaptur] adapter

adası [adasuh] island

adet number; sum; total

âdet custom; menstruation

adı [aduh] name

adım ... [aduhm] my name is ..., I am called ...

adınız nedir? [aduhnuhz] what's your name?

adil fair
adres address
adres defteri address book
aferin! well done!
affedersiniz sorry; excuse me
afiş [afeesh] poster
afiyet olsun! enjoy your meal!
aft mouth ulcer
ağ [a] net
ağa [a-a] formerly a rank of nobility, now used as a term of respect
ağabey [a-abay] elder brother
ağaç [a-ach] tree
ağır [a-uhr] heavy; rich
ağırlık [a-uhrluhk] weight
ağız [a-uhz] mouth; dialect
ağlamak [a-lamak] to cry
ağrı [a-ruh] ache, pain
ağrı giderici ilaçlar [geedereejee eelachlar] painkillers
ağustos [a-oostos] August
ahali people
ahçı [ahchuh] cook
ahize [aheezeh] receiver, handset
Aids [aydz] Aids
aile [a-eeleh] family
aile gazinosu [a-eeleh] family nightclub
ailesiz girilmez entry only for families
aileye mahsus only for family groups
ait: -e ait [-eh it] belonging to; relating to
ait olmak to belong

ajanda [ajanda] diary (business etc)
akciğerler [akjee-erler] lungs
Akdeniz Mediterranean
akıl [akuhl] intelligence
akıllı [akuhlluh] clever
akım [akuhm] current (electrical)
akıntı [akuhntuh] current (in water)
akraba relative
akrabalar relatives
akrep scorpion
aks axle
aksan accent
akşam [aksham] evening; in the evening; p.m.
akşam on 10 p.m.
bu akşam this evening
akşamleyin [akshamlayeen] in the evening
akşam yemeği [yemeh-ee] dinner, evening meal; supper
akşam yemeği yemek [yemeh-ee] to have dinner
aktarma connection
aktarmalı sefer [aktarmaluh] connecting flight
aktarma yapmak to change (trains etc)
aktör [aktur] actor
aktris actress
akü [akew] battery
alan area; field; square
alaturka Turkish-style
al bakalım [bakaluhm] here you are
alçak [alchak] low

alçı [alchuh] plaster cast
alerjik [alerJeek] allergic
alet device; tool
alıcı [aluhjuh] addressee
alımlı [aluhımluh] attractive
alın [aluhn] forehead
alınan mal değiştirilemez no refund or exchange
alınan para [aluhnan] charge
alıp götürmek [aluhp gurtewrmek] to take away
alışılmamış [aluhshuhl-mamuhsh] unusual
alışkanlık [aluhshkanluhk] habit
alış kuru [aluhsh] buying rate
alışmak: -e alışmak [-eh aluhshmak] to get used to
alışveriş [aluhshvereesh] shopping
alışverişe çıkmak [aluhshvereesheh chuhkmak] to go shopping
alışveriş merkezi shopping centre
Allah God
Allahaısmarladık [allahâ-uhsmarladuhk] goodbye (said by person leaving)
Allah aşkına [ashkuhna] for God's sake
Allah belanı versin! [belanuh] damn you!
Allah kahretsin! damn!
Allah razı olsun [razuh] bless you
allık [alluhk] blusher
almak to take, to accept; to receive; to buy; to obtain
Alman German (adj, person)

Almanca [almanja] German (language)
Almanya Germany
alo hello
alt bottom (of road etc)
altı [altuh] six
altın [altuhn] gold
altıncı [altuhnjuh] sixth
altında [altuhnda] below, under; at the bottom of
altmış [altmuhsh] sixty
altta underneath
alüminyum folyo [alewmeen-yoom] tinfoil
alyans wedding ring
ama but
...-amadım [-amaduhm] I couldn't ...
aman! goodness!; heavens!; careful!
ambalaj kağıdı [ambalaJ ka-uhduh] wrapping paper
amca [amja] (paternal) uncle
ameliyat operation
Amerikalı [amereekaluh] American
amfiteatr amphitheatre
amortisör [amorteesur] shock-absorber
amper(lik) amp
ampul light bulb
an moment
ana mother
Anadolu Anatolia, Asia Minor
anahtar [anaHtar] key
anahtarlık [anaHtarluhk] keyring
anavatan home, homeland

anayol main road
anayol ilerde main road
  ahead
anayurt home, homeland
ancak [anjak] only; hardly;
  but
anıt [anuht] monument
ani sudden
aniden suddenly
anlam meaning
anlamadım [–maduhm] I don't
  understand
anlamak to understand
anlamı yok [anlamuh] there's
  no point
anlamıyorum [anlamuh–] I
  don't understand
anlatmak to explain
anlıyorum [anluh–] I
  understand
anne [anneh] mother
anne baba parents
Anonim Şirket [sheerket] joint
  stock company, corporation
antifriz antifreeze
antik ancient
antika antique(s)
antikacı [anteekajuh] antique
  dealer
antiseptik antiseptic
antrenman training
antrenman ayakkabısı
  [ī-akkabuhsuh] trainers
apaçık [apachuhk] obvious
apandisit appendicitis
apartman block of flats,
  apartment block
apartman dairesi [da-eeresee]
  flat, apartment

aptal idiot; stupid
apteshane [aptes-haneh] toilet
ara interval; gap; space
araba car; cart
 arabamda in my car
araba ön camı [urn jamuh]
  windscreen
araba vapuru car ferry
arabesk Turkish 'art' music
araç giremez no entry
araç kurtarma [arach]
  breakdown service
ara durak stopover
aralık [araluhk] December
aramak to search for, to look
  for
Arap Arab
Arapça [arapcha] Arabic
arasında: ...-lerin arasında
  [arasuhnda] among the ...,
  between the ...
arasıra [arasuhra] now and
  then
ara sokak sidestreet
ardında [arduhnda] beyond
arı [aruh] bee
arı su [soo] distilled water
arıza [aruhza] breakdown
arızalı [aruhzaluh] faulty; out
  of order
arıza servisi faults service
arıza yapmak to break down
arka back (part)
arkada at the back; behind
 ...-in arkasında behind
  the ...
arkadan binilir entry at the
  back
arkadan göndermek

[gurndermek] to forward
arkadan inilir exit at the back
arkadaş [arkadash] friend;
partner, boyfriend,
girlfriend
arka lambalar rear lights
arkamdaki behind me
arka sinyal lambaları
[lambararuh] rear lights
Arnavut Albanian
arnavut kaldırımı cobblestone
pavement, cobblestone
sidewalk
Arnavutluk Albania
artık [artuhk] no longer;
residue; remnant
artık ... yok no more ...
arzu etmek to wish for
asansör [asansur] lift, elevator
aseton nail polish remover
asıl [asuhl] original; base;
basis; origin
asker soldier
askeri bölge military zone
askı [askuh] coathanger
nnln n uvar
aslan sütü [sewtew] slang
word for raki
aslen basically; originally
asma kilit padlock
astım [astuhm] asthma
Asya Asia
AŞ [a sheh] joint stock
company, corp.
aşağı [asha-uh] down
aşağıda [asha-uhda] down; at
the bottom; downstairs;
down there
aşçı [ash-chuh] cook

aşı [ashuh] vaccination
aşılama [ashuhlama]
vaccination
aşmak [ashmak] to cross
AT [a teh] EC
at horse
ata ancestor
ateş [atesh] fire; temperature,
fever
ateşli [ateshlee] feverish
atınız insert (coin)
Atina Athens
atkı [atkuh] scarf (for neck)
atlamak to jump
atletizm athletics
atmak to throw (away)
At Meydanı [maydanuh]
Hippodrome
avanak idiot
avcılık [avjuhluhk] hunting
avlu courtyard
Avrupa [avroopa] Europe;
European (adj)
Avrupalı [avroopaluh]
European (person)
avukat lawyer
Avustralya [avoostralya]
Australia; Australian
Avusturya [avoostoorya]
Austria; Austrian
Ay [I] month; moon
ayak [I-ak] foot
ayak bileği [beeleh-ee] ankle
ayakkabı [I-akkabuh] shoe(s)
ayakkabı bağı [ba-uh]
shoelaces
ayakkabıcı [I-akkabuhjuh]
shoeshop
ayakkabı cilası [jeelasuh]

shoe polish
ayak parmağı [ī-ak parma-**uh**] toe
ayakta durmak [ī-akta] to stand
aybaşı [**ī**bashuh] period (menstruation); beginning of the month; pay day
aydın [**ī**duhn] intellectual; well-lit
aydınlık [**ī**duhnl**uh**k] well-lit
ay hali period (menstruation)
ayı [ī-uh] bear; jerk; blockhead
ayık [ī-**uh**k] sober; conscious
ayılmak [ī-uhlmak] to come round
ayırma [ī-**uh**rma] parting
ayırmak [ī-uhrmak] to separate
ayırtmak [ī-uhrtmak] to reserve
ayin [ī-een] mass; religious ceremony; rite
aylık bilet [**ī**luhk] monthly season ticket
aylık taksitler monthly instalments
ayna [ina] mirror
aynı [**ī**nuh] (the) same
ayrı [**ī**ruh] separate
ayrı ayrı separately
ayrıldım [**ī**ruhld**uh**m] separated
ayrılmak [**ī**ruhlmak] to leave; to go away
ayrılmış [**ī**ruhlm**uh**sh] reserved
az not many; little
azami ağırlık weight limit
azami genişlik maximum width
azami hız maximum speed

azami park 1 saat parking limited to 1 hour
azami sürat speed limit
azami yükseklik maximum height

B

baba father; dad
bacak [bajak] leg
bacanak [bajanak] brother-in-law
bademcik iltihabı [bademjeek eelteehab**uh**] tonsillitis
badem şekeri [sheker**ee**] sugared almonds
bagaj [baga**J**] luggage, baggage; boot, (US) trunk
bagaj alma yeri baggage claim
bagaj fişi [feesh**ee**] baggage receipt
bagaj kaydı [kīd**uh**] check-in
bagaj kayıt [kī-**uh**t] check-in
bagaj kayıt masası [masas**uh**] check-in desk
bagaj kontrolü [kontrolew] baggage control
bağ [ba] cord; string; bond; link; vineyard
bağımsız [ba-uhms**uh**z] independent
bağırmak [ba-uhrmak] to shout
bağlantı [ba-lant**uh**] connection
bağlı: ...-a bağlı [ba-l**uh**] it depends on ...
bahçe [ba**H**ch**eh**] garden

bahsetmek [baнsetmek] to
 mention
bahşiş [baнsheesh] tip
bakabilir miyim? can I see it?
bakar mısınız! [muhsuhn**uhz**]
 excuse me!
bakım [bak**uh**m] care,
 attention
bakımından [bakuhmuhndan]
 from the point of view of
bakır [bak**uh**r] copper
bakkal grocer's, food store
bakkaliye [bakkalee-y**eh**]
 groceries
bakmak: -a bakmak to look
 at; to look after
baksana be! [b**eh**] hey you!
balayı [balī-uh] honeymoon
baldız [bald**uh**z] sister-in-law
 (wife's sister)
bale [bal**eh**] ballet
balık [bal**uh**k] fish
balık adamlık [adaml**uh**k]
 skindiving
balıkçı [bal**uh**kchuh]
 fishmonger's
balıkçı köyü [kur-yew] fishing
 village
balıkçılık [baluhkchuhl**uh**k]
 fishing
balık lokantası [bal**uh**k
 lokantas**uh**] fish restaurant
balık pazarı [pazar**uh**] fish
 market
balık tutmak yasaktır no
 fishing
balkon balcony; circle
 balkonlu with a balcony
balsam conditioner

balta axe
bambaşka [bambashka] quite
 different
bana to me
banka [banka] bank
banka hesabı [hesab**uh**] bank
 account
bankamatik cash dispenser,
 ATM, automatic teller
banket hard shoulder
banknot note, (US) bill
banliyö [banlee-yur] suburbs
banliyö tren şebekesi local
 railway system
banyo bath; bathroom
 banyolu (oda) with a private
 bathroom
banyo etmek to develop
banyo tuzları [toozlar**uh**] bath
 salts
banyo yapmak to take a bath
bardak glass
barmen kız [k**uh**z] barmaid
barsak intestine
basamağa dikkat mind the
 step
basın(ız) press
basit simple, easy
baş [bash] head
baş ağrısı [a-ruhs**uh**] headache
başarı [bashar**uh**] success
başarmak [basharmak] to
 succeed; to achieve
baş aşağı [asha-**uh**] upside
 down
başbakan [bashbakan] prime
 minister
başka [bashka] different;
 other(s)

başka bir another
başka bir şey [shay]
  something else; anything
  else
başka bir yer somewhere else
başka bir yerde [yerdeh]
  elsewhere
başkent [bashkent] capital city
başlamak [bashlamak] to start,
  to begin
başlangıç [bashlanguhch]
  beginning, start
  başlangıçta [bashlanguhchta] at
    the beginning
başlıca [bashluhja] main,
  principal
başparmak [bashparmak]
  thumb
baş üstüne [ewstewneh] with
  pleasure
batı [batuh] west
  batıda in the west
  ...-in batısında west of ...
batmak to sink
battaniye [battanee-yeh]
  blanket
bavul suitcase
Bay [bī] Mr
bayağı [bī-a-uh] ordinary;
  vulgar, common
Bayan [bī-an] Mrs; Miss; Ms
bayan lady; ladies
bayan iç çamaşırı [eech
  chamashuhruh] ladies'
  underwear
bayan konfeksiyon ladies'
  wear
bayanlar [bī-anlar] ladies
  (toilets), ladies' room

bayat [bī-at] stale
baygın [bīguhn] unconscious
bayılmak [bī-uhlmak] to faint
baylar [bīlar] gents (toilet)
baypas [bīpas] by-pass
bayrak [bīrak] flag
bazen sometimes
bazı [bazuh] some
bebek baby; doll
bebek bezi nappy, diaper
bebek iskemlesi highchair
bedava free (of charge)
beden size
bedesten covered market
  hall for valuable goods
beğendim [beh-endeem] I like
  it
beğenmek [beh-enmek] to like
bej [beJ] beige
bekar batchelor; single
  (unmarried)
bekârım [bekaruhm] I'm
  single
bekçi [bekchee] guard;
  watchman
beklemek: -i beklemek to
  wait; to expect
bekleme salonu [beklemeh]
  waiting room
beklemeyin [beklemayeen]
  don't wait
bekleyin! [beklayeen] wait!
  beni bekleyin wait for me
bekleyiniz! [beklayeeneez] wait!
bel spade; waist
belediye binası [beledee-yeh
  beenasuh] town hall
belediye sarayı [saī-uh] town
  hall

... belediyesi [beledee-yes**ee**]
municipality of ...;
municipal town hall
belge [belg**eh**] document
belki maybe, perhaps
belki de değil [deh deh-**eel**]
perhaps not
belli obvious
ben I
ben de [deh] so am I; so do
I; nor do I; me too
bence öyle [b**e**njeh ur-il**eh**] I
think so
bence öyle değil [deh-**eel**] I
don't think so
bende [bend**eh**] on/in me
benden from me
beni me
benim my; it's me; speaking
(phone)
benim için [eech**ee**n] for me
o benimdir it's mine
benim kendi ...-m my own ...
benimki mine
benzemek to look like
benzer similar
benzin petrol, (US) gas
benzin bidonu petrol can, gas
can
benzin istasyonu petrol
station, gas station
benzin pompası [pompas**uh**]
petrol pump
beraber together
berbat terrible, awful,
dreadful
berber men's hairdresser,
barber's
bereket blessing; abundance

bereket versin fortunately
beri here
...-den beri since ...
beş [besh] five
beşinci [beshe**e**njee] fifth
Bey [bay] Mr; sir; ruler; chief;
master; gentleman
beyaz [bay**az**] white
beyazlar whites
beyaz zehir drugs (narcotics)
beyefendi gentleman; sir
beyin sarsıntısı [bay**ee**n sarsuhn-
tuhs**uh**] concussion
bez cloth
bıçak [buhch**ak**] knife
bırakmak [buhrakm**ak**] to leave;
to abandon; to let, to allow;
to let off
bıyık [buh-y**uh**k] moustache
biberon baby's bottle
biçim [beech**ee**m] shape, form;
kind; manner
bijuteri [beejooter**ee**]
jewellery
bile [beel**eh**] even
...-se bile [-seh] even if ...
bile bile deliberately
bilek wrist
bilet ticket
biletçi [beeletch**ee**] conductor
bilet gişesi [geeshes**ee**] ticket
office; box office
biletsiz girilmez no entry
without a ticket
bilezik bracelet
bilgi information
bilgisayar [beelgees**ee**-**ar**]
computer
bilim science

167

bilinmeyen numaralar [beeleenmayen] directory enquiries

... biliyor musunuz? do you speak ...?

bilmek to know

bilmiyordum I didn't know

bilmiyorum I don't know

bin thousand

bina building

binicilik [beeneejeeleek] horse-riding

binilir get on here

biniş kartı [beeneesh kartuh] boarding card

binmek to get on; to get in

bir a, an; one

bir ... daha another ..., one more ...

biraz some; a little, a bit

biraz daha some more; a little bit more

birazcık [beerazjuhk] a bit, a little bit

birazdan in a minute

bir çift ... [cheeft] a couple of ...

birçok [beerchok] a lot of, many

birey [beeray] individual

bir gecesi [gejesee] per night

biricik [beereejeek] the only, sole, unique

bir iki tane ... [taneh] a couple of ..., a few ...

biriktirmek to collect

birinci [beereenjee] first

birinci kat first floor, (US) second floor

birinci sınıf [suhnuhf] first class

birisi somebody, someone

birkaç [beerkach] several, a few

birkaç tane [taneh] a few

bir kere [kereh] once

Birleşik Amerika [beerlesheek] the United States

Birleşik Devletler the States

Birleşik Krallık [kralluhk] the United Kingdom

birlikte [beerleekteh] together

bir parça [parcha] a little bit

bir sonraki next

bir şey [shay] something; anything

bir şey değil [deh-eel] you're welcome, don't mention it, not at all

başka bir şey? [bashka] anything else?

bir yerde [yerdeh] somewhere

bisiklet bicycle

bisikletçi [beeseekletchee] cyclist

bisiklete binmek [beeseekleteh] cycling

bisiklet sporu cycling

bitirmek: -i bitirmek to finish, to end

bitişiğinde [beeteeshee-eendeh] next to

bitişik [beeteesheek] next to

bitki plant

bitkin exhausted, tired

bitmek to end, to come to an end; to grow

bitti over

biz we

Bizans [**beez**ans] Byzantine
bizde [beezd**eh**] on/in us
bizden from us
bize [beez**eh**] (to) us
bizi us
bizim our
bizim için [eech**een**] for us
bizimki ours
bizimle [beez**eem**leh] with us
bizler we
bizzat personally, in person
blucin [bloo**jeen**] jeans
bluz blouse
bodrum basement
bodrum kat basement
boğa [bo-**a**] bull
boğaz [bo-**az**] throat; straits
boğaz ağrısı [a-ruhs**uh**] sore
 throat
Boğaziçi [bo **az**eechee] the
 Bosphorus
boğaz pastil(ler)i throat
 pastille(s)
bol wide; loose; plentiful
bol bol ... plenty of ...
bol şanslar! good luck!
bomba bomb
bombok shitty
bone [bon**eh**] bathing cap
boru pipe (for water)
boş [bosh] vacant; empty
boşanmış [boshanm**uhsh**]
 divorced
boş oda vacancy
boşta (gezer) unemployed
boş yer vacancy
boy size; height
boya paint
boyamak to paint

boyar not colourfast
boyun neck
boyunca [boyoon**ja**] along;
 throughout; during
bozmak to change
bozuk damaged; broken; out
 of order
bozuk para coins; small
 change
böbrekler [**bur**brekler] kidneys
 (in body)
böcek [bur**jek**] insect
böcek ilacı [eelaj**uh**] insect
 repellent; insecticide
böceklere karşı ilaç [burjekler**eh**
 karsh**uh** eelach] insect
 repellent
böcek sokması [sokmas**uh**]
 insect bite
Boğaz [b**oh**-az] the
 Bosphorus
bölge [burlg**eh**] region;
 district; zone
bölüm [burl**ewm**] department
böyle [buh-il**eh**] so, this way,
 like this; such
 böyle tamam that'll do
 nicely
böyle iken anyhow; while
 this is so
Britanya Britain
bronşit [bron**sheet**] bronchitis
bronzlaşmak [bronz**lashmak**] to
 get a tan
bronzlaşmış [bronzlashm**uhsh**]
 suntanned
bronzluk suntan
bronz ten suntan
broş [brosh] brooch

broşür [broshewr] brochure; leaflet

bu this (one); these; this is
 bu ... mi? is this ...?
 bu ne? what's this?

buçuk [boochook] half; and a half
 ... buçuk half past ...

budala idiot

bu gece [gejeh] tonight

bugün [boogewn] today

buji [booJee] spark plug

buji telleri jump leads

bukle [bookleh] curl

Bul. Blvd, Boulevard

bu ...-lar these ...

bulaşıcı [boolashuhjuh] infectious

bulaşık [boolashuhk] washing-up

bulaşık bezi dishcloth

bulaşık deterjanı [deterJanuh] washing-up liquid

bulaşık lavabosu sink

bulaşık yıkamak [yuhkamak] to do the washing-up

Bulgar Bulgarian

Bulgaristan Bulgaria

bulmak to find, to discover; to reach

buluşmak [boolooshmak] to meet

buluşma yeri [boolooshma] meeting place

bulut cloud

bulutlu cloudy

bulvar boulevard
 ... Bulvarı [boolvaruh] ... Boulevard

bunlar these

bunları [boonlaruh] these

bunun fiyatı ne kadar? [fee-yatuh neh] how much is it?, how much is this?

burada [boorada] here; over here
 burada aşağıda [asha-uhda] down here

burda here; over here

burası [boorasuh] here

burun nose

but [boot] thigh

buyrun [boo-iroon], buyurun [boo-yooroon] can I help you?; yes?; this way; please; there you are; go ahead

buz [booz] ice

buzdolabı [boozdolabuh] fridge

buzluk freezer

büfe [bewfeh] kiosk selling sandwiches

büro [bewro] office

büro malzemeleri office supplies

bütün [bewtewn] whole; all

büyük [bew-yewk] large, big; great

büyükanne [bew-yewkanneh] grandmother

büyükbaba grandfather

Büyük Britanya Great Britain

büyükelçilik [bew-yewkelcheeleek] embassy

büyük jeton [Jeton] large token

büyüklük [bew-yewlewk] size

büyük mağaza [bew-yewk ma-aza] department store

büyültme [bew-yewltmeh] enlargement

C

Cad. [jad] St; Ave
cadde [jaddeh] street; avenue
... Caddesi ... Street, ... Avenue
cam [jam] glass
cami [jamee] mosque
... Camii/Camisi ... Mosque
cam sileceği [seelejeh-ee] windscreen wiper
canım sıkılıyor [jahnuhm suh-kuhluh-yor] I'm bored
-a canim sıkılıyor I'm worried, I'm concerned
cankurtaran [jankoortaran] ambulance; lifeguard
canlı [janluh] alive; lively; bright
can sıkıcı [jan suhkuhjuh] annoying
can simidi lifebelt
can yeleği [yeleh-ee] life jacket
can yelekleri life jackets
can yelekleri tavandadır life jackets up above
caz [jaz] jazz
cazibeli [jazeebelee] sexy
ceket [jeket] jacket
cemiyet [jemee-yet] society
cenaze [jenazeh] funeral
cep [jep] pocket
cereyanlı [jerayanluh] draughty
cesur [jesoor] brave

cevap [jevap] answer
cevap vermek to answer
ceza [jeza] fine (punishment)
check-in yaptırmak [yaptuhrmak] to check in
cımbız [juhmbuhz] tweezers
ciddi [jeeddee] serious
cila [jeela] polish
cilt [jeelt] skin
cilt temizleyici [temeezlayeejee] skin cleanser
cins(i) [jeens(ee)] type; kind
cinsiyet(i) [jeensee-yet(ee)] sex, gender
civarında [jeevaruhnda] about
coğrafya [joh-rafya] geography
cuma [jooma] Friday
cumartesi [joomartesee] Saturday
cumhurbaşkanı [joomHoor-bashkanuh] president
cumhuriyet [joomHooree-yet] republic
cüzdan [jewzdan] wallet

Ç

çabuk [chabook] quick
çabuk ol! hurry up!
çadır [chaduhr] tent
çadır bezi tarpaulin
çadır direği [deereh-ee] tent pole
çadır kazığı [kazuh-uh] tent peg
çağ [cha] time; date; age, era
çağdaş sanat [cha-dash] modern art

çağdaş sanat galerisi modern art gallery

çağırmak [cha-uhrmak] to call; to invite

çağlayan [cha-lī-an] waterfall

çakı [chakuh] penknife

çakmak [chakmak] cigarette lighter

çalar saat [chalar sa-at] alarm clock

çalınız ring

çalışkan [chaluhshkan] hardworking

çalışmak [chaluhshmak] to try; to work

çalışma saatleri [chaluhshma sa-atleree] working hours

çalışmıyor [chalushmuh-yor] it's not working

çalıştırmak [chaluhshtuhrmak] to switch on

çalkalamak [chalkalamak] to shake; to stir; to wash out; to rinse

çalmak [chalmak] to steal; to play; to ring

çamaşır [chamashuhr] laundry, washing

çamaşırhane [–haneh] laundry (place)

çamaşır ipi clothes line

çamaşır makinesi washing machine

çamaşır mandalı [mandaluh] clothes peg

çamaşır suyu bleach

çamaşır tozu washing powder

çamaşır yıkamak [yuhkamak] to

do the washing

çamur [chamoor] mud

çan [chan] bell

çanak çömlek [chanak churmlek] pottery

Çanakkale Boğazı [chanakkaleh bo-azuh] the Dardanelles

çanta [chanta] bag

çapa [chapa] anchor

çarpışma [charpuhshma] crash

çarşaf [charshaf] sheet; long, baggy dress with a hood worn by religious Turkish women

çarşamba [charshamba] Wednesday

çarşı [charshuh] market, bazaar

... Çarşısı [charshuhsuh] ... Market

çartır (seferi) [chartuhr] charter flight

çatal [chatal] fork

çatal bıçak [buhchak] cutlery

çay [chī] tea; stream

çay bahçesi [baнchesee] tea garden

çaydanlık [chīdanluhk] kettle

çayevi [chī-evee] tea shop, tea house

çayhane [chī-наneh] café (for families)

çay kaşığı [chī kashuh-uh] teaspoon

çek [chek] cheque, (US) check

çek arabanı! [arabanuh] get lost!

çek defteri cheque book

çeker [cheker] will shrink
çekici [chekeejee] attractive
çekiç [chekeech] hammer
çekil! [chekeel] go away!
çekilip gitmek [chekeeleep] to go away
çek-in [chek] check-in
çekin pull
çekingen [chekeengen] shy
çekiniz pull
çek kabul edilir cheques accepted
çek kartı [kartuh] cheque card, (US) check card
çekmece [chekmejeh] drawer
çekmek [chekmek] to pull, to draw; to suffer
çekmez unshrinkable
çene [cheneh] chin; jaw
çengelli iğne [chengellee cc nch] safety pin
çeşit [chesheet] variety, sort, kind
çeşme [cheshmeh] fountain
... Çeşmesi [cheshmesee] ... Fountain
çeviriniz [cheveereeneez] dial
çevirmek [cheveermek] to turn; to translate; to dial
çevri sesi [chevee] dialling tone
çevir sinyali dialling tone
çevir tonu dialling tone
çevre yolu [chevreh] by-pass; ringroad
çeyizlik [chayeezleek] trousseau goods
çeyrek [chayrek] quarter (fraction)

çığlık atmak [chuh-luhk] to scream
çık dışarı! [chuk dusharuh] get out!
çıkılmaz no exit
çıkış [chuhkuhsh] exit, way out
çıkış kapısı [kapuhsuh] gate
çıkmak [chuhkmak] to go out; to go up
çıkmaz [chuhkmaz] dead-end alley
... Çıkmazı [chuhkmazuh] ... Cul-de-sac
çıkmaz sokak cul-de-sac; no through road
çıkmaz yol dead end
çıplak [chuhplak] bare, naked
çiçek [cheechek] flower
çiçekçi [cheechekchee] florist
çiçekevi [cheechekevee] florist
çift [cheeft] pair; couple; double
çiftçi [cheeftchee] farmer
çiftlik [cheeftleek] farm
çift yataklı oda [yatakluh] twin room
çiğ [chee] raw
çiğnemek için chew
çiklet [cheeklet] chewing gum
çikolata [cheekolata] chocolate
çimen [cheemen] grass; lawn
çimenlere basmayınız keep off the grass
çingene [cheegeneh] gypsy
çini [cheenee] tiles
çips [cheeps] crisps, (US) potato chips
çirkin [cheerkeen] ugly; offensive

çivi [cheevee] nail (metal)
çizgi [cheezgee] line
çizik [cheezeek] scratch
çizim [cheezeem] drawing
çizme [cheezmeh] boot
 (footwear)
çizmek [cheezmek] to draw
çocuk [chojook] child
çocuk arabası [arabasuh]
 pram
çocuk bahçesi [baнchesee]
 playground
çocuk bakıcısı [bakuhjuhsuh]
 baby-sitter, childminder
çocuk bezi nappy-liners,
 diaper-liners
çocuk doktoru pediatrician
çocuk havuzu children's pool
çocuk konfeksiyon children's
 wear
çocuklar [chojooklar] children
çocuk yatağı [yata-uh] cot
çoğu [choh-oo] many; most
 (of)
çoğunlukla [choh-oonlookla]
 mostly; most of the time
çok [chok] many; much; a lot,
 lots; very; very much
 çok daha fazla a lot more
 çok daha iyi/daha kötü
 [kurtew] much better/worse
 çok değil [deh-eel] not much
 çok fazla too much
 o kadar çok değil not a lot;
 not so much
 çok çok very much; at the
 most
 çok doğru! [doh-roo] exactly!
 çok yaşa! [yasha] bless you!

çorap(lar) [chorap(lar)] sock(s);
 stocking(s)
çöp [churp] rubbish, garbage;
 litter
çöp atmayınız no litter
 please
çöp kutusu bin
çöp tenekesi dustbin,
 trashcan
çöp torbası [torbasuh] bin
 liners
çünkü [chewnkew] because
çürük [chewrewk] bruise;
 rotten

D

D shared taxi stop
da too, also
-da at (the); in (the); on
 (the)
 İstanbul'da in Istanbul
dağ [da] mountain
 dağlarda [da-larda] in the
 mountains
 ... Dağı [da-uh] ... Mountain
 ... Dağları [da-laruh] ...
 Mountains
dağcılık [da-juhluhk] climbing;
 mountaineering
dağ köyü [kur-yew] mountain
 village
daha more; extra; still; yet
 ... daha fazla more than ...
 çok daha fazla [chok] a lot
 more
daha az less
daha iyi better

daha iyi olmak to improve
daha kötü [kurt**ew**] worse
dahi also, too; even
dahil [da**heel**] included
dahilen (alınır) to be taken internally
dahil etmek to include
dahili extension
dahiliye [da**H**eelee-y**eh**] internal
dahiliyeci [da**H**eelee-yej**ee**] specialist in internal diseases
dahiliye mütehassısı [mewtehassuhs**uh**] specialist in internal diseases
daima [da-eema] always
daire [da-**ee**reh] circle; flat, apartment; office; department
dakika minute
  beş dakikaya kadar [besh dakeekee-**a**] in five minutes
  bir dakika just a minute
dalga wave
dalmak to dive
dalma techizatı [tejhee**z**at**uh**] skin-diving equipment
dam roof
damat son-in-law
damla drop
damsız girilmez no entry without women
-dan from
  İstanbul'dan Bodrum'a from Istanbul to Bodrum
-dan biraz a little bit (of)
-dan daha iyi better than
-dan beri since
dangalak wally

danışma [dan**uh**shma] information
danışma masası [masas**uh**] information desk
Danimarka Danish (adj); Denmark
dans dance
dans etmek to dance
dar narrow; tight
darüşşifa [darewshsheef**a**] old hospital
dava trial
davet invitation; reception
davet etmek to invite
dayı [dī-**uh**] (maternal) uncle
de [deh] too, also; and; but
-de at (the); in (the); on (the)
debriyaj [debree-ya**J**] clutch
dede [ded**ch**] grandfather
dedi he/she said
defa time; turn
defol! get out!; go away!
defter notebook; exercise book
değer [deh-**er**] value
değerli [deh-**er**lee] valuable
değil [deh-**eel**] not; he/she/it is not
  değil mi? isn't it?
değiller [deh-**eel**ler] they are not
değilim [deh-**eel**eem] I am not
değiliz [deh-**eel**eez] we are not
değilsin [deh-**eel**seen] you are not
değilsiniz [deh-eelseen**eez**] you are not

175

değişir [deh-eesheer] it varies
değişken [deh-eeshken] changeable
değişmek [deh-eeshmek] to change; to alter
değiştirilmez goods cannot be exchanged
değiştirmek [deh-eeshteermek] to change; to exchange
değmek [deh-mek] to be worth; to touch
deli mad, crazy
delik hole
delikanlı [deleekanluh] teenager (male)
demek to mean; to pronounce; to say
demek istemek to mean
demir iron
demiryolu railway
demiryolu geçidi [gecheedee] level crossing
demlik teapot
-den from; than; of
-den az under, less than
-den başka [bashka] apart from

den beri since (time)
-den daha az less than
denemek to try
denetçi [denetchee] inspector
deniz sea
  deniz kenarında [kenaruhnda] at the seaside
  deniz kıyısı [kuh-yuhsuh] seashore; by the sea
  deniz kıyısında [kuh-yuh-suhnda] on the seashore, by the sea

denizanası [deneezanasuh] jellyfish
deniz gezisi cruise
deniz kabuğu [kaboo-oo] seashell
deniz kestanesi sea urchin
deniz motoru motorboat
deniz yosunu seaweed
depo tank (of car)
depozito deposit
deprem earthquake
dere [dereh] stream
derece [derejeh] degree; step
dergi magazine
derhal at once, immediately
deri skin; hide; leather
deri mamulleri leather goods
derin deep
dernek society
ders lesson; class; lecture
dert pain; suffering; disease; illness; sorrow; trouble
deterjan [deterjan] washing powder
dev enormous, giant
devam etmek to continue
devamlı virajlar series of bends
deve [deveh] camel
dev gibi enormous
devirmek to knock over, to knock down
devlet state
devre [devreh] period, term
dezenfektan disinfectant
-dir: o ...-dir it is ...
dırlar: onlar ... dırlar [duhrlar] they are ...
dış [duhsh] exterior, outside

dışarda [duhsharda] out;
outside; he/she's out

dışarı [duhsharuh] outside; out

dışarı sarkmayınız do not
lean out

dış hatlar international
flights

dışında [duhshuhnda] except

-di he/she/it was

dibinde [deebeendeh] at the
bottom of

Dicle [deejleh] the Tigris

Didim Didyma

diğer [dee-er] other

dik steep

-dik we were

dikiz aynası [inasuh] rearview
mirror

dikkat! look out!; caution!

dikkat ediniz! take care!

dikkat et! be careful!

dikkatli careful

dikkatli olun! be careful!

dikmek to sew; to plant

dil language; tongue

dilok: on iyi diloklorimlo
[deeleklereemleh] best wishes

-diler they were

dilim slice

dil kursu language course

dil okulu language school

din [deen] religion

-diniz you were

dinle! [deenleh] listen!

dinlemek to listen (to)

dinlenme [deenlenmeh] rest

dinlenmek to rest

dip bottom

diploma degree

-dir is

direk pole; column

direksiyon steering wheel

direksiyon sistemi steering

direkt direct

dirsek elbow

disket disk, diskette

dispanser out-patients'
clinic

diş [deesh] tooth

diş ağrısı [a-ruhsuh] toothache

dişçi [deesh-chee] dentist

dişeti [deeshetee] gum

diş fırçası [fuhrchasuh]
toothbrush

diş floşu [floshoo] dental floss

diş hekimi dentist

diş ipi dental floss

diş macunu [majoonoo]
toothpaste

diş tabibi dentist

diya [dee-ya], diyapozitif [dee-
yapozeeteef] slide

diz knee

doğa [doh-a] nature

doğal [doh al] natural

doğmak [doh-mak] to be
born; to rise

doğru [doh-roo] correct, right;
accurate; straight

-e doğru [-eh] towards

doğrulamak [doh-roolamak] to
confirm

doğu [doh-oo] east

doğuda [doh-ooda] in the east

...-nın doğusu [-nuhn doh-
oosoo] east of ...

doğum günü [doh-oom gewnew]
birthday

doğum gününüz kutlu olsun! [gewnewnewz] happy birthday!

doğum tarihi [tareeHee] date of birth

doğum yeri place of birth

doksan ninety

dokumak to weave

dokunmak to touch

dokunmayınız do not touch

dokuz nine

dokuzuncu [dokoozoonjoo] ninth

doküman [dokewman] document

dolap cupboard

dolayı: -den dolayı [dolĭ-uh] because of

doldurmak to fill; to fill in; to fill up

doldurunuz fill in; fill up

dolgu filling

dolmak to be filled; to become full

dolma kalem pen

dolmuş [dolmoosh] shared taxi

dolmuş durağı [doora-uh] shared taxi stand

dolmuş indirme-bindirme yeri [eendeermeh-beendeermeh] shared taxi pick-up/set-down point

dolu full, no vacancies; engaged; occupied; hail

doluyuz we're full

domuz pig

don underpants, panties; knickers; frost

donatım [donatuhm] equipment

dondurma külahı [kewl-ahuh] ice-cream cone

dondurulmuş yiyecekler [dondoorool-moosh yee-yejekler] frozen food

donmuş [donmoosh] frozen

donuk dull

dosdoğru [dosdoh-roo] straight ahead

dost friend

dökmek [durkmek] to pour (out); to spill

döndürmek [durndewrmek] to turn

dönel kavşak [durnel kavshak] roundabout

dönmek [durnmek] to come/go back, to return; to get back; to turn

... dönün [durnewn] turn ...

dönüş [durnewsh] return

dördüncü [durdewnjew] fourth

dört [durt] four

dört yol (ağzı) [a-zuh] crossroads, intersection

döşeme [durshemeh] furniture; upholstery; floor; floor covering

döviz [durveez] foreign currency

döviz alım belgesi [aluhm] document for purchase of foreign currency

döviz kuru exchange rate

draje [draJeh] coated pill

dudak lips

dudak merhemi lip salve

dul widow; widower

duman smoke

dur! stop!

duracak the bus is going to stop

duracak yer standing room

durak stop

durgun calm, still

durmak to stop; to stand; to lie; to remain

durmak yasaktır no stopping

duru clear

durulmaz no stopping

durum situation

duruma göre [gur**eh**] it depends

duş [doosh] shower

duş jeli [**J**el**ee**] shower gel

duşlu with shower

duvar wall

duygu [doo-ig**oo**] feeling

duymak [doo-im**ak**] to hear; to feel

düğme [dewm**eh**] button; switch

düğün [dew-**ewn**] wedding

dükkân [dewkkan] shop

dümdüz devam edin [dewmd**ewz**] go straight on

dümdüz ilerde [**ee**lerd**eh**] straight ahead

dün [dewn] yesterday

dün gece [gej**eh**] last night

dün sabah [saba**H**] yesterday morning

dünya [dewn-y**a**] world

dürüst [dewr**ewst**] honest

düş kırıcı [dewsh kuhruhj**uh**] disappointing

düşmek [dewshm**ek**] to fall

düşünmek [dewshewnm**ek**] to think; to think about

düşürmek [dewshewrm**ek**] to drop

düz [dewz] flat; plain (not patterned)

düzenlemek [dewzenlem**ek**] to organize

düz gidin straight on

düzine [dewz**ee**neh] dozen

yarım düzine [yar**uhm**] half a dozen

düz vitesli manual, with manual gears

E

-e [-**eh**] to; towards

...-ebilir misiniz? can you ...?, could you ...?

...-ebilir miyim? can I ...?, may I ...?

eczane [ejzan**eh**] chemist's, pharmacy

edebilir: ... edebilir miyim? can I ...?

edebiyat literature

efendi 'gentleman', 'master' – formerly respectful way of addressing social superiors; now used in a derogatory way

efendim sir; madam

efendim? pardon (me)?, sorry?

Efes Ephesus

eflatun purple

Ege [eg**eh**] the Aegean

egzos exhaust (pipe)

eğer [eh-**er**] if

eğlenmek [eh-lenm**ek**] to enjoy oneself, to have fun

eğlendik [eh-lend**eek**] it was fun

eh [eH] enough; come on; well; all right

ehliyet [ehlee-y**et**] licence

ekim October

ekip team

ekonomi sınıfı [suhnuhf**uh**] economy class

eksik missing; lacking

ekspres express (train)

ekspresyol motorway, freeway, highway

ekspresyol kavşağı [kavsha-**uh**] motorway junction

ekspresyolun sonu end of motorway/freeway/ highway

ekşi [eksh**ee**] sour

ek ücret [ewjr**et**] supplement, extra charge

el hand

el arabası [arabas**uh**] trolley; wheelbarrow

el bagajı [bagaJ**uh**] hand luggage, hand baggage

elbette [elbetteh] of course, certainly

elbezi dishcloth

elbise [elbees**eh**] clothes

elbiseler clothes

el çantası [chantas**uh**] handbag, (US) purse

elçilik [elcheele**ek**] embassy

elden düşme [dewshm**eh**] second-hand

elde yıkanabilir can be handwashed

eldiven gloves

elektrik electricity

elektrikçi [elektreekch**ee**] electrician

elektrik düğmesi [dewmes**ee**] switch

elektrik kesilmesi power cut

elektrikli electric

elektrikli aletler electrical appliances

elektrikli tıraş makinesi [tuhr**ash**] electric shaver

elektrik sobası [sobas**uh**] electric fire

elektrik süpürgesi [sewpewrges**ee**] vacuum cleaner

el feneri torch

el freni handbrake

eline sağlık! [eleen**eh** sa-l**uhk**] well done!

elle yıkayınız wash by hand

elli fifty

elmas diamond

el sanatları [sanatlar**uh**] crafts

el sanatları dükkanı [dewk-kan**uh**] craft shop

elverişsiz [elvereesh-s**eez**] inconvenient

emanet left luggage office, baggage check

emanet kasası [kasas**uh**] left luggage locker

emek work

emekli retired; pensioner

-emem I can't

emin safe; sure

emin misiniz? are you sure?

emniyet kemeri seatbelt

emniyet kemerlerinizi bağlayınız fasten seat belts

emniyetli safe (not dangerous)

emniyette [emnee-yetteh] safe (not in danger)

emzik dummy

en most; width

enayi [enī-ee] idiot, fool

en azından [azuhndan] at least

en çok [chok] mostly; at the most

ender rare

endişe etmek [endeesheh] to worry about

enfeksiyon infection

enformasyon information

enişte [eneeshteh] brother-in-law (sister's husband); aunt's husband

en iyi best

enjeksiyon [enJeksee-yon] injection

en kötü [kurtew] worst

en son latest

en sonunda eventually

epey [epay] rather; pretty well

erkek arkadaş [arkadash] boyfriend

erkek çocuk [chojook] boy

erkek giyim eşyası [esh-yasuh] menswear

erkek gömleği [gurmleh-ee] men's shirts

erkek iç çamaşırı [eech chamashuhruh] men's underwear

erkek kardeş [kardesh] brother

erkek konfeksiyon(u) menswear

erkekler men

erkekler tuvaleti gents' toilets, men's room

erkeklik organı [organuh] penis

erkek tuvaleti gents' toilet

erken(den) early

Ermeni Armenian

Ermenistan Armenia

ertelemek to postpone

ertesi next; following

ertesi gün [gewn] the following day, the next day

esas main; basic

eski ancient; old; former

eskimo® ice lolly

eski moda old-fashioned

eski şehir [sheh-heer] old town

esnasında [esnashunda] during

esnek elastic

estağfurullah [esta-fooroollaн] don't mention it; don't say so

eş [esh] wife; husband

eşarp [esharp] scarf (for head)

eşek [eshek] donkey

eşek arısı [aruhsuh] wasp

eşlik etmek [eshleek] to accompany

eşofman [eshofman] tracksuit

eşşoğlu eşek [eshsholoo eshek] ass; lout

eşya [esh-ya] furniture; things

eşya arabası [arabasuh] luggage trolley, baggage trolley

eteğinde [eteh-eendeh] bottom (of hill)

etek skirt

etiket label

etkileyici [etkeelay-eejee] impressive

etmek to do (used in compounds)

et pazarı [pazaruh] meat market

etyemez vegetarian

ev house; home

  evde [evdeh] at home

  evde mi? is he/she in?

eve gitmek [eveh] to go home

evet yes

evlenmek to get married

evlenme yıldönümü [evlenmeh yuhl-durnewm-ew] wedding anniversary

evli married

evrak çantası [chantasuh] briefcase

evvel first; before

  -den evvel before

evvelki the previous; the ... before last

  evvelki gün [gewn] the day before; the day before yesterday

evvelsi the previous; the ... before

  evvelsi gün [gewn] the day before yesterday

evye [ev-yeh] sink

eyer [ay-er] saddle

eylemek [aylemek] to do; to make (used in compounds)

eylül [aylewl] September

eyvah! [ayvaн] alas!

eyvallah! [ayvallaн] cheerio!; thanks!

ezan Muslim call to prayer

F

fabrika factory

Fahrenheit Fahrenheit

faiz [fa-eez] interest

fakat but

fakir poor

faks çekmek [chekmek] to send a fax

fakslamak to fax

falan and so on; about

fanila vest (under shirt)

far (head)light; eye shadow

fare [fareh] mouse; rat

fark difference

farlar headlights

fatura invoice

favori favourite

fayda [fida] use; advantage

fazla too (excessively); more than

fazla bagaj [bagaɹ] excess baggage

fazla pişmiş [peeshmeesh] overdone

felaket disaster

fen science

fena nasty, bad

fener lamp

fenni scientific
feribot ferry
fermuar [fermoo-**ar**] zip
fes fez
fevkalade [**fev**kaladeh]
extraordinary, unusual;
super
Fırat [Fuhrat] the Euphrates
fırça [fuhrcha] brush
fırın [fuhr**uh**n] oven; bakery
fırtına [fuhrtuhna] storm
fikir idea
film banyo etmek to develop
film banyosu film processing
film yıldızı [yuhlduhz**uh**] film
star, movie star
filtre kağıdı [feeltr**eh** ka-uhd**uh**]
filter papers
fincan [feenjan] cup
fincan tabağı [taba-**uh**] saucer
fiş [feesh] slip of paper; card;
plug (electrical)
fiyat price
flaş [flash] flash
flaster plaster
fondöten [fondurt**e**n]
foundation cream
formda fit
formüler [formewler] form
fotoğraf [fotu-raf] photo
fotoğraf çekmek [chekmek] to
photograph
fotoğrafçı [foto-rafch**uh**]
photographer; camera shop
fotoğraf makinesi camera
fön [furn] blow-dry
fönle kurutma [furnleh] blow
dry
Fransa [fransa] France

Fransız [frans**uh**z] French
(adj)
Fransızca [frans**uh**zja] French
(language)
fren brakes
fren yapmak to brake
fuar [fwar] trade fair
fuaye [fwı-eh] foyer
futbol football, soccer
futbol maçı [mach**uh**] football
match

G

galeri upper circle
galiba presumably
Galler Wales
Galli Welsh
gar terminus
garaj [gara**ı**] garage
garip strange; peculiar; poor;
lonely; stranger
garson waiter
garson kız [k**uh**z] waitress
gayet [gı-et] very
gaz gas
gazete [gaz**e**teh] newspaper
gazete bayii [bı-ee-**ee**]
newsagent's
gazete satıcısı [satuhjuhs**uh**]
newspaper kiosk; news
vendor
gaz geçirgen lensler
[gecheerg**e**n] gas permeable
lenses
gazi war veteran
gazino open-air restaurant,
nightclub

gaz pedalı [pedal**uh**] accelerator

gaz tüpü [tewp**ew**] gas cylinder

gaz vermek to accelerate

gebe [geb**eh**] pregnant

gebeliği önleyici [gebelee-**ee** urnleh-yee**jee**] contraceptive

gece [gej**eh**] night; a.m. (from midnight to 4 a.m.); overnight

geceleyin [gej**e**lay-een] at night

gece bekçisi [bekchees**ee**] night porter

gecekondu [gejekond**oo**] shanty

gecekondu bölgesi [burlges**ee**] shanty town

gece kulübü [koolewb**ew**] nightclub

gecelik [gejel**eek**] nightdress

gece yarısı [yaruhs**uh**] midnight

gecikme [gejeekm**eh**] delay

gecikmeli [gejeekmel**ee**] delayed

geç [gech] late; cross

geçe [gech**eh**] past

geçen [gech**en**] past; last

geçen hafta last week

geçen yıl [yuhl] last year

geçerli [gecherl**ee**] valid

geçici güzergah [gecheej**ee** gewzerg**ah**] diversion, detour

geçin: ...-i geçin [gech**een**] go past the ...

geçiş [gech**eesh**] crossing

geçit [gech**eet**] pass (in mountains)

geç kalmak to arrive late, to be late

geçmek [gech**mek**] to pass; to overtake; to go through; to cross

geçme yasağı no overtaking

geçmiş olsun! [gechm**eesh**] get well soon!

geçmişte [gechmeesht**eh**] in the past

geldiği ülke country of departure

gelecek [gelej**ek**] future

gelecekte [gelejekt**eh**] in future

gelecek hafta next week

gelecek yıl [yuhl] next year

gelen bagaj [baga**J**] baggage claim

gelenek custom; tradition

geleneksel traditional

gel-git tide

gel-git olayı [olÏ-**uh**] tide

Gelibolu Gallipoli

gelin daughter-in-law; bride

geliş [gel**eesh**] arrival

geliş nedeni reason for arrival

geliştirmek [geleeshteerm**ek**] to improve

gelmek to come; to arrive

gemi boat; ship

gemiyle [gemee-il**eh**] by ship

genç [gench] young; young person

genç kız [kuhz] teenager (female)

gençler [gench**ler**] young people

gençlik hosteli [genchl**eek**] youth hostel

gene [gen**eh**] again; still

genel general (adj)

genellikle [genelleekl**eh**] usually, generally

genel olarak generally

geniş [gen**eesh**] wide

gerçek [gerch**ek**] real, genuine; true

gerçekten [g**e**rchekten] really

gerçekten üzgünüm [gerchekt**e**n ewzgewn**ewm**] I'm really sorry

gerçi [gerch**ee**] although

gerek(li) necessary

gerekmek to be necessary

geri back, rear; backwards; reverse

geride [ger**ee**d**eh**] at the back

geri aramak (telefonla) to ring back

geri dönülmez no U-turns

geri gelmek to come back

geri geri gitmek to reverse

geri gidin go back

gerinmek to stretch

geri ödeme [urdem**eh**] refund

geri vites reverse gear

germek to stretch

getirmek to get, to fetch; to bring

gevşek malzeme loose chippings

gevşek şev falling rock

gevşemiş [gevshem**eesh**] loose

gezi trip

gezinti trip; outing

gezmek to walk

about/around; to stroll; to go out; to tour; to look round

gıda zehirlenmesi [guhd**a**] food poisoning

gibi as; like

gideceği yer [geedejeh-**ee**] destination

giden yolcular salonu [yoljool**ar**] departure lounge

gidermek to remove

gidilecek yer [geedeelej**ek**] destination

gidip getirmek: -i gidip getirmek to fetch

gidiş [geed**eesh**] single, one-way

gidiş bileti single ticket, one-way ticket

gidiş dönüş bileti [durn**ewsh**] return ticket, round trip ticket

girilmez no entry

girin enter, come in

giriniz enter, come in

giriş [geer**eesh**] way in, entrance; admission charge

giriş holü [hol**ew**] foyer

giriş ücreti [ewjret**ee**] admission fee

giriş ücretledir admission fee charged

giriş ücretsizdir free entrance

Girit Crete

girmek to go in, to enter, to come in

girmek yasaktır no entry, keep out

girmeyiniz do not enter

gişe [geesh**eh**] counter; ticket window

git! [geet] go away!

gitar guitar

gitmek to go

gitti he/she's gone

gittikçe [geetteekch**eh**] gradually

giydirmek [gee-id**eer**mek] to dress

giyim eşyası [esh-yas**uh**] clothing

giyinmek to get dressed

giyip denemek to try on

giymek [gee-im**ek**] to wear

gizli secret

golf sahası [s**ah**asuh] golf course

göğüs [gur-**ews**] chest; breast; bust

göğüsleri açık [gur-ewsler**ee** ach**uhk**] topless

gök [gurk] sky

gök gürültüsü [gewrewltews**ew**] thunder

göl [gurl] lake

... Gölü [gurl**ew**] Lake ...

gölge [gurlg**eh**] shade; shadow

gölgede [gurlged**eh**] in the shade

gölgede kurutunuz dry away from direct sunlight

gömlek [gurmlek] shirt

gönderen [gurnderen] sender

gönderilecek adres [gurndereelejek] forwarding address

göndermek [gurndermek] to send

göre: -e göre [-eh gur**eh**] according to

görevli [gurevl**ee**] official; officer

görmek [gurmek] to see

gör(ül)meye değer yerler [gur(ewl)may**eh** deh-**er**] (the) sights

görümce [gurewmj**eh**] sister-in-law (husband's sister)

görünmek [gurewnmek] to seem; to look

görüşmek üzere [gurewshmek ewzer**eh**] see you later

görüşürüz! [g**u**rewshewrewz] see you!

gösteri [gurster**ee**] show (in theatre)

göstermek [gurstermek] to show

götürmek [gurtewrmek] to take (away); to carry

göz [gurz] eye; drawer

göz boyası [boyas**uh**] eye shadow

göz damlası [damlas**uh**] eye drops

gözde [gurzd**eh**] favourite

göz doktoru optician

gözlük [gurzl**ewk**] glasses, spectacles, (US) eyeglasses

gözlükçü [gurzlewkchew] optician

göz makyajı çıkarıcısı [makyaJ**uh** chuhkaruh-juhs**uh**] eye make-up remover

gramer grammar

gri grey

grip [greep] flu

grup group; party
gururlu proud
gücendirmek [gewjendeermek] to offend
güçlü [gewchlew] strong
güçsüz [gewchsewz] weak, feeble
gül [gewl] rose
güle güle [gewleh] goodbye (said to person leaving)
güle güle giy! [gee-i] literally: 'wear it happily!' – said to someone who has bought new clothes
güle güle kullan! literally: 'use it happily!' – said to someone who has bought something new
gülmek [gewlmek] to laugh
gülümsemek [gewlewm-semek] to smile
gülünç [gewlewnch] ridiculous
Gümrük [gewmrewk] Customs
gümrük beyannamesi Customs declaration
gümrüksüz [gewmrewksewz] duty-free
gümüş [gewmewsh] silver; silverware
gümüş yaprak silver foil
gün [gewn] day
  gün ağarırken [a-aruhrken] at dawn
günaydın [gewniduhn] good morning
günbatımı [gewn-batuhmuh] sunset
günce [gewnjeh] diary

günde bir/iki/üç defa once/twice/three times a day
günde üç defa ikişer tablet alınız take two tablets three times a day
gündüz [gewndewz] daytime; by day
güneş [gewnesh] sun
  güneşte [gewneshteh] in the sun
güneş banyosu yapmak to sunbathe
güneş çarpması [charpmasuh] sunstroke
güneş gözlüğü [gurzlew-ew] sunglasses
güneş ışığı [uhshuh-uh] sunshine
güneşli [gewneshlee] sunny
güneşlik [gewneshleek] sunshade
güneş losyonu suntan lotion
güneş merhemi sunblock
güneşte yanmak [gewneshteh] to get a tan
güneşte yanmış [yanmuhsh] sunburnt, tanned
güneş yağı [ya-uh] suntan oil
güneş yanığı [yanuh-uh] sunburn
güney [gewnay] south
  güneyde [gewnaydeh] in the south
  ...-in güneyi [gewnay-ee] south of ...
güney batı [batuh] southwest
güney doğu [doh-oo] southeast

GÜ:

187

günlük [gewnl**ewk**] day; daily
günlük bilet day ticket
günlük gezi day trip
günü [gewn**ew**] on
Gürcistan [gewrjeestan]
  Georgia
Gürcü [gewrj**ew**] Georgian
gürültü [gewrewl-t**ew**] noise
gürültülü [gewrewl-tewl**ew**]
  loud; noisy
gürültü yapmayın! [yapmī-uhn]
  quiet!
güverte [g**ew**verteh] deck
güzel [gewz**el**] beautiful; nice;
  pretty; fine; attractive
güzergah [gewzerga**H**] route

H

haber news (on radio, TV etc)
ne haber? how are things?
hacı [haj**uh**] literally: 'pilgrim'
  – respectful way of
  addressing someone who
  has made the pilgrimage to
  Mecca
hafif light (not heavy); mild
hafif koşu [kosh**oo**] jogging
hafif müzik [mewz**eek**] light
  music
hafif rüzgar [rewzg**ar**] breeze
hafta week
  haftaya bugün [haftī-**a**
  boog**ewn**] a week (from)
  today
  haftaya yarın [yar**uhn**] a week
  (from) tomorrow
  haftada per week

haftalık bilet [haftaluhk]
  weekly ticket
hafta sonu weekend
  hafta sonunda at the
  weekend
hakikaten really, truly
hakiki true; real, genuine
hakkında [hakk**uh**nda]
  concerning
hakkıyla [hakk**uh**-ila] properly
haklı [hak**luh**] right, justified
hala aunt (paternal)
hâlâ still
halat rope
halı [hal**uh**] carpet
halıcı [haluhj**uh**] carpet seller
halı kaplama fitted carpet
halılar [haluh**lar**] carpets
Haliç [hal**eech**] the Golden
  Horn
haliç inlet; bay
halk people
halka açık [ach**uh**k] public;
  open to the public
halk dansları [danslar**uh**] folk
  dancing
halk müziği [mewz**ee**-ee] folk
  music
halk oyunları [oyoonlar**uh**] folk
  dances
halletmek: -i halletmek to fix,
  to arrange
hamal porter
hamam Turkish bath
hamamböceği [–burj**eh**-ee]
  cockroach
hamile [h**a**meeleh] pregnant
han tradesmen's hall; inn;
  caravanserai; office block

... Hanı [hanuh] ...
tradesmen's hall; ... inn;
... office block

hangi? which?

hangisi? which one?

hanım [hanuhm] lady; wife

... hanım Mrs ...

hap pill(s); contraceptive
pill(s)

hapis(hane) [hapees(haneh)]
prison

hapşırık [hapshuhruhk] sneeze

hapşırmak [hapshuhrmak] to
sneeze

harabe [harabeh] ruin

harabeler ruins

harcamak [harjamak] to spend

hareket etmek to move

hareket saati [sa-atee] time of
departure

hariç [hareech] except;
external; abroad

harika! great!

harikulade [hareekooladeh]
wonderful

harita [hareeta] map

hasar görmüş [gurmewsh]
damaged

hassas sensitive

hasta sick, ill

hastabakıcı [–bakuhjuh] nurse

hastalık [hastaluhk] illness;
disease

hastalık sigortası [seegortasuh]
health insurance

hastane [hastaneh] hospital

... Hastanesi ... Hospital

hat route; line

hata mistake; fault

hatıra [hatuhra] souvenir

hatırlamak [hatuhrlamak] to
remember

hatırlıyorum [hatuhrluh-yoroom] I
remember

hatta even

hava air; weather

hava soğuk [soh-ook] it's cold

havaalanı [hava-alanuh] airport

hava basıncı [basuhnjuh] air
pressure

hava cereyanı [jereh-yanuh]
draught

havai fişek [feeshek] fireworks

havale [havaleh] money order

havalimanı [havaleemanuh]
airport

havalimanı otobüsü
[otobewsew] airport bus

hava tahmini weather
forecast

havayolu [havī-oloo] airline

havlu bath towel

havuz pond; pool

hay Allah! [hī] damn!

hayat [hī-at] life

haydi! [hīdee] come on!

haydi gidelim! [hīdee] let's go!

hayhay! [hī-hī] certainly!, by
all means!

hayır [hī-uhr] no; goodness

hayran [hīran] fan; admirer

hayret! [hīret] well well!

hayvan [hīvan] animal

hayvanat bahçesi [hīvanat
baHchesee] zoo

hayvanlara yiyecek
vermeyiniz do not feed the
animals

hazımsızlık [hazuhm-suhzl**uh**k] indigestion

hazır [haz**uhr**] ready

hazırlamak [hazuhrlam**ak**] to prepare

haziran June

hediye [hedee-y**eh**] present, gift

hediyelik eşya dükkanı [esh-y**a** dewkkan**uh**] gift shop

hekim doctor

hela WC, toilet, restroom

hem moreover, besides; both ... and ...

hemen immediately; almost

hemen hemen almost

hemen hemen hiç [heech] hardly ever

hemen şimdi [sh**ee**mdee] straight away

hemşire [hemsheer**eh**] nurse; sister

hemzemin geçit [gech**ee**t] level crossing

henüz [hen**ewz**] yet; just now; a minute ago

henüz değil [deh-**eel**] not yet

hep always; the whole

hep birden altogether

hepimiz all of us

hepsi all of it/them, the whole lot

 hepsi bu kadar that's all

hepsi o kadar nothing else

her each; every

 her gün [gewn] every day; daily

 her defasında [defasuhnd**a**] every time

herif bloke, guy

her iki ... de [d**eh**] both ...

her ikisi de both of them

herkes everyone

her neyse [nays**eh**] anyway

her şey [shay] everything

her şey dahil all-inclusive

her şeyden önce [shayd**en** **ur**njeh] first of all

her yer everywhere

her yerde [yerd**eh**] everywhere

her zaman always

hesap bill, (US) check; account

hesap makinesi calculator

heyecan verici [hayej**an** veree**jee**] exciting

Heyelan! landslides!

heykel [hayk**el**] statue

hırdavatçı [huhrdavatch**uh**] hardware store

Hıristiyan [huhreestee-y**an**] Christian

hırka [huhrk**a**] cardigan

hırsız [huhrs**uhz**] thief

hırsızlık [huhrsuhzl**uh**k] burglary; theft

hıyar [huh-y**ar**] lout; cucumber

hız [huhz] speed

hız kısıtlaması sonu end of speed restriction

hızla [huhzl**a**] quickly

hızlı [huhzl**uh**] fast; quickly

hicri [heejr**ee**] Muslim system of dates

hiç [heech] none; nothing; never; ever

hiç de değil [deh deh-**eel**] not in the least

hiç ... iz mi? have you ever ...?

hiç ... yok I don't have any ...; there isn't any ...

hiç bir ... no ... at all

hiç biri neither of them

hiç kalmadı [kalmad**uh**] there's none left

hiçbir şey [heechb**eer** shay] nothing

hiçbir yerde [yerd**eh**] nowhere

hiçbir zaman never

hiç kimse [keems**eh**] nobody, no-one

hidrofil pamuk cotton wool, absorbent cotton

hikâye [heekī-**eh**] story

his feeling

hisar fortress, castle

hissetmek to feel

hitap ekmek to call

Hititler the Hittites

hizmet etmek to serve

hoca [ho**ja**] teacher; teacher in charge of religious instruction

hol entrance hall, lobby

... holü [hol**ew**] ... hall

horlamak to snore

hostes stewardess

hoş [hosh] nice, pleasant; fine

hoş bulduk! it's nice to be here! – usual response to 'hoş, geldiniz'

hoşça kal [hosh-cha] bye (said by person leaving)

hoşça kalın [kal**uh**n] goodbye

hoş geldiniz! welcome!

hoşlanmak [hoshlanm**ak**] to like

hükümet [hewkewm**et**] government

hür [hewr] free

hürriyet [hewr-ree-y**et**] freedom

I

-ı [-uh] his; her; its; accusative noun ending

ılıca [uhl**uh**ja] hot spring

ılık [uhl**uhk**] lukewarm

ılık ütü warm iron

ılımlı [uhluhml**uh**] mild; moderate

-ım [-uhm] my; I am

-ımız [-uhm**uh**z] our

-ın [-uhn] of; your

-ınız [-uhn**uh**z] your

...-ınız var mı? [muh] have you got ...?

Iraklı [uhrakl**uh**] Iraqi

ırmak [uhrm**ak**] river

ırza geçme [uhr**za** gechm**eh**] rape

ısırık [uhsuhr**uhk**] bite, sting

ısırma [uhs**uh**rma] bite

ısırmak [uhsuhrm**ak**] to bite

ısıtma [uhsuhtm**a**] heating

ıslak [uhsl**ak**] wet

ısmarlamak [uhsmarlam**ak**] to order

ışık [uhsh**uhk**] light

-ız [-uhz] we are

ızdıraplı [uhzduhrapl**uh**] painful

i

-i his; her; its; the
iade [ee-adeh] refund
iade etmek to give back
iç [eech] interior, inside
iç çamaşırı [chamashuhruh]
  underwear
içerde [eecherdeh] indoors,
  inside
içeri [eecheree] inside
içeride [eecheredeh] indoors,
  inside
içeri kilitlemek [eecheree] to
  lock in
içerisi [eechereesee] inside
içermek [eechermek] to
  contain
iç hastalıkları mütehassısı
  [hastaluhklaruh mewteHassuhsuh]
  specialist in internal
  diseases
iç hatlar [eech] domestic
  flights
iç hat seferi domestic flight
içilmez [eecheelmez] not for
  drinking
için [eecheen] for; as
içinde [eecheendeh] in;
  included
  iki gün içinde [gewn] in two
  days from now
içinden [eecheenden] through
içine [eecheeneh] into
iç kale [kaleh] citadel
içki [eechkee] alcoholic
  drinks
içkili olarak araba sürmek

[sewrmek] drunken driving
içkisiz no drinks allowed
iç lastik inner tube
içmek [eechmek] to drink
içme suyu [eechmeh] drinking
  water
içten [eechten] sincere
idi it was
iğne [ee-neh] needle;
  injection
iğrenç [ee-rench] disgusting,
  revolting; obnoxious
... ihtiyacında [eeHtee-yajuhnda]
  in need of ...
ihtiyaç [eeHtee-yach] need
ihtiyaç duymak [doo-imak] to
  need
ihtiyar [eeHtee-yar] old; old
  person
ikamet stay
ikamet adresi domicile
iken while
iki two
iki hafta fortnight
iki kere [kereh] twice
iki kişilik oda [keesheeleek]
  double room
iki kişilik yatak double bed
iki misli twice as much
ikinci [eekeenjee] second (adj)
ikinci kat second floor, (US)
  third floor
ikinci sınıf [suhnuhf] second
  class
ikisi: ikisi de [deh] both
  ikisinden biri either of them
iki tane tek kişilik yatak
  [taneh tek keesheeleek] twin
  beds

iki yol ağzı [a-zuh] fork (in road)

iki yönlü trafik two-way traffic

ikizler twins

iklim climate

il province; county

... İli Province of ..., County of ...

ilaç [eelach] medicine

ilan yapıştırmak yasaktır stick no bills

ilçe [eelcheh] administrative district

ile [eeleh] with; and; by

otobüs ile [otobews] by bus

ileri front part; forward

-ileri the

ileride [ilereedeh] further (on); ın future

ilerleyelim lütfen! please move forward!

iletmek to forward; to pass on

ilgilenmek to be interested in; to show interest in; to take care of

ilginç [eelgeench] interesting

ilim science

ilişki kurmak [eeleeshkee] to contact

ilişkin: -e ilişkin [eeleeshkeen] relating to

ilk first

ilk önce [urnjeh] at first

ilk kez the first time

ilkbahar spring (season)

ilk hareket first departure

ilk olarak first

ilk yardım [yarduhm] first aid

ilk yardım çantası [chantasuh] first aid kit

iltihap inflammation

-im my; I am

imam prayer leader in a Mosque

imaret soup kitchen and hostel

imdat emergency

imdat! help!

imdat freni emergency brake

-imiz our

imkansız [eemkansuhz] impossible

imza signature

imza etmek to sign

-in of; your

inanılmaz [eenanuhlmaz] incredible, amazing

inanmak to believe

ince [eenjeh] thin

incitmek [eenjeetmek] to hurt

inç [eench] inch

indirimli satış [satuhsh] sale

inek cow

İngiliz [eengeeleez] English; British; Englishman

İngiliz anahtarı [anaHtaruh] wrench

İngilizce [eengeeleezjeh] English (language); in English

İngiliz kadın [kaduhn] English woman

İngilizler the English

İngiliz sterlini pound sterling

İngiltere [eengeeltereh] England; the UK

inik lastik flat tyre
inilir get off here
-iniz your
inmek to get off; to get out; to go down; to land; to fly in
insan person; man
insanlar people
inşallah [eenshal-lah] I hope so; hopefully; God willing
inşallah öyle değildir [urleh deh-eeldeer] I hope not; God forbid
ip string; rope
ipek silk
iple çekmek [eepleh chekmek] to look forward to
iplik thread
iptal edildi cancelled
iptal etmek to cancel
İranlı [eeranluh] Iranian
iri big
İrlanda [eerlanda] Ireland; Irish
İrlandalı [eerlandaluh] Irishman; Irishwoman
İsa [eesha] Jesus
ishal [ees-hal] diarrhoea
isilik rash (on skin)
isim name
iskele [eeskeleh] jetty; quay; ferry terminal
... İskelesi ... Jetty; ... Docks; ... Terminal
iskemle [eeskemleh] chair
İskoç [eeskoch] Scottish
İskoçya [eeskochya] Scotland
iskonto discount
İslami [eeslamee] Islamic

İspanya [eespanya] Spain
İspanyol [eespanyol] Spanish (adj)
İspanyolca [eespanyolja] Spanish (language)
israr ediyorum I insist
israr etmek: -de israr etmek to insist on
İstanbul Boğazı [eestanbool bo-azuh] the Bosphorus
istasyon station
istasyonda at the station
istemek to want; to wish; to ask for
istemiyorum I don't want
isterim I want
... ister misiniz? do you want ...?
istiyor he/she wants
... istiyor musunuz? do you want ...?
istiyor(d)um I would like
istiyorsunuz: ne istiyorsunuz? [neh] what do you want?
istiyorum I want
İsveç [eesvech] Sweden; Swedish (adj)
İsveççe [eesvech-cheh] Swedish (language)
İsviçre [eesveechreh] Switzerland
iş [eesh] work; job; business; deal
işaret levhası [eesharet levhasuh] signpost
işe: bu işe yaramaz [eesheh] it's no good
iş günü [eesh gewnew] weekdays

işitme cihazı [eesheetmeh jeehazuh] hearing aid
işitmek [eesheetmek] to hear
işkembeci [eeshkembejee] tripe restaurant
işkembe salonu [eeshkembeh] tripe shop
işlek [eeshlek] busy
işleme günleri ferry timetable
iş seyahati [eesh sayahatee] business trip
işsiz [eeshseez] unemployed
iştah [eeshtaH] appetite
işte [eeshteh] here is/are; there is/are; here it is; her; him
İtalya [etalya] Italy
İtalyan [eetalyan] Italian (adj)
itfaiye [eetfa-ee-yeh] fire brigade
itiniz push
itmek to push; push
iyi good; well; kind
iyi misin? are you OK?
iyi akşamlar [akshamlar] good evening
iyice [ee-yeejeh] properly
iyi geceler [gejeler] good night
iyi günler [gewnler] hello (literally: good day); have a nice day
iyilik sağlık [sa-luhk] I'm fine
iyimser optimistic
iyi şanslar! [shanslar] good luck!
iyiyim I'm all right, I'm fine
iyi yolculuklar! [yoljoolooklar] have a good journey!

-iz we are
izin holiday, vacation; permit
izin belgesi licence
izin vermek to let, to allow
izlemek to follow

J

jaluzi [Jaloozee] blinds
jant [Jant] rim; spoke
jarse [Jarseh] jersey (cloth)
jel [Jel] jelly; hair gel
jeton [Jeton] telephone token
jikle [Jeekleh] choke
jilet [Jeelet] razor blade
jinekolog [Jeenekolog] gynaecologist
jogging yapmak to go jogging
jöle [Jurleh] hair gel

K

kaba rude; rough; vulgar
kabaca [kabaja] roughly, approximately
kabadayı [kabadi-uh] macho
kabak bald; pumpkin; marrow; courgette, zucchini
kabakulak mumps
kabarcık [kabarjuhk] blister
kabız [kabuhz] constipated
kabızlık [kabuhzluhk] constipation
kabin cabin; changing cubicle

kabin memuru steward
kablo lead; wire
kabul etmek to accept
kaburga rib
kaç? [kach] how many?; how much?
kaç kişilik [keesheeleek] for how many people?
kaç tane? [taneh] how many?
kaç yaşındasınız? [yashuhnda-suhnuhz] how old are you?
kaç gecelik? [kach gejeleek] for how many nights?
kaçak [kachak] leak; fugitive; contraband
kaçık [kachuhk] weirdo
kaçırmak [kachuhrmak] to miss (bus etc)
kadar until; about; as much as; as many as
kadar ...-e kadar [-eh] as ... as; until; as much as; as far as
ne kadar? [neh] how much?
ne kadar iyi! how nice!; it's so good!
kadın [kaduhn] woman; lady
kadın bağı [ba-uh] sanitary towel
kadın giyim eşyası [esh-yasuh] ladies' wear
kadınlar [kaduhnlar] women
kadın polis policewoman
kadran dial
kafa head
kafatası [kafatasuh] skull
kafeterya cafeteria
kâğıt [ka-uht] paper

kâğıt çocuk bezi [chojook] disposable nappies/diapers
kâğıt mendil tissues, Kleenex®
kâğıt para banknote, (US) bill
kahvaltı [kaHvaltuh] breakfast
kahvaltı dahil breakfast included
kahve [kaHveh] coffee; coffee shop (usually for men only)
kahvehane [kaHveh-Haneh] café (usually for men only)
kahverengi [kaHverengee] brown
kala: -e ... kala [-eh] to; remaining
beşe on kala [besheh] ten to five
kalabalık [kalabaluhk] crowd; crowded, busy
kalabalık saatler [sa-atler] rush hour
kalacak yer [kalajak] accommodation
kalan the rest (of)
kalça [kalcha] hip
kaldırım [kalduhruhm] pavement, sidewalk
kaldırınız lift (the receiver)
kaldırmak [kalduhrmak] to raise; to lift; to remove
kale [kaleh] castle, fort
... Kalesi ... Castle, Fort ...
kalem pencil
kalın [kaluhn] thick
kalın kafa thickhead
kalite [kaleeteh] quality
kaliteli high quality

kalkış [kalk**uh**sh] departure
kalkmak to stand up; to get up; to take off; to leave
kalmak to stay, to remain
kalorifer (central) heating; heater
kalp heart
kalp krizi heart attack
kamara cabin
kambiyo bureau de change
kamp ateşi [atesh**ee**] campfire
kamping campsite; caravan site, trailer park
kamp yapmak to camp
kamp yapmak yasaktır no camping
kamp yeri campsite
kamu the public
kamyon lorry
kamyonet van
kan blood
Kanada Canada; Canadian (adj)
Kanadalı [kanadal**uh**] Canadian (person)
kanamak to bleed
kanat wing
kan grubu blood group
kano canoe
kano kullanmak canoeing
kanun law
kapa çeneni! [chenen**ee**] shut up!
Kapadokya Cappadocia
kapak cap; lid
kapalı [kapal**uh**] closed; off; covered
kapalı çarşı [charsh**uh**] covered bazaar

kapalı havuz indoor pool
kapalı yüzme havuzu [yewzm**eh**] indoor swimming pool
kapamak to switch off; to close; to shut
kapatmak to close, to shut
kapı [kap**uh**] door; gate
kapıcı [kapuhj**uh**] caretaker; doorman; porter
kapı kolu [kap**uh**] door handle
kap kacak [kajak] cooking utensils, pots and pans
kaplıca [kapluhja] thermal spring
kaporta bonnet, (US) hood
kapsamak to include
kaptan captain
kaput bonnet, (US) hood
kar snow
kâr profit, benefit
kara black
karabasan nightmare
karaciğer [karajee-**er**] liver (in body)
Karadeniz the Black Sea
karakol police station
karanlık [karanl**uh**k] dark; darkness
karantina quarantine
karar decision
(-e) karar vermek [-eh] to decide (on)
karayolu [karĩ-ol**oo**] highway
karayolu haritası [hareetas**uh**] road map
karbüratör [karbewrat**ur**] carburettor

kardeş [kardesh] brother; sister

karı [karuh] wife

karın ağrısı [karuhn a-ruhsuh] stomachache

karınca [karuhnja] ant

karışıklık [karuhshuhkluhk] mess

karıştırmak [karuhshtuhrmak] to mix

karmaşık [karmashuhk] complicated

karşı: -e karşı [-eh karshuh] across; against; towards; contrary

karşıda [karshuhda] opposite

karşıdan gelen taşıtlara öncelik oncoming traffic has right of way

karşılaşmak [karshuhlashmak] to meet

karşın: -e karşın [-eh karshuhn] in spite of

karşısında [karshuhsuhnda] opposite

karşıt [karshuht] opposite; contrary; anti–; counter–

kart card

kartlı telefon [kartluh] cardphone

karton cardboard; box

kartpostal postcard

kartvizit business card

kas muscle

kasa till, cash desk; cashier

kasaba small town

kasadan fiş alınız please obtain ticket from the till

kasap butcher's

kasap dükkanı [dewkkanuh] butcher's shop

kase [kaseh] bowl

kasetli teyp [tayp] cassette recorder

kasım [kasuhm] November

kasis uneven road surface

kasiyer cashier

kask helmet

kasket cap

kasten deliberately

kaş [kash] eyebrow

kaşık [kashuhk] spoon

kaşıntı [kashuhntuh] itch

kaş kalemi [kash] eyebrow pencil

kat floor, storey

katakomp catacomb

katedral cathedral

katiyen olmaz! no way!

Katma Değer Vergisi [deh-er] VAT

Katolik Catholic

kavanoz jar

kavga fight

kavga etmek to fight

kavim people; tribe

kavşak [kavshak] crossroads, intersection; junction

kaya [kī-a] rock

kayak skiing

kayak pisti ski slope

kayak yapmak to ski

kaybetmek [kībetmek] to lose

kaybolmak [kībolmak] to disappear

kaygan [kīgan] slippery

kaygan yol slippery road

kaygı [kīguh] worry

Ka

kaygılanmak [kīguhlanmak] to worry about

kayık [kī-**uhk**] small boat; rowing boat

kayınbirader [kī-uhn-beerader] brother-in-law (husband's/wife's brother)

kayınpeder [kī-**uhn**peder] father-in-law

kayınvalide [kī-uhnvaleedeh] mother-in-law

kayıp eşya [kī-**uhp** esh-ya] lost property

kayıp eşya bürosu [bewros**oo**] lost property office

kayış [kī-**uhsh**] strap

kayıt numarası [kī-**uht** noomaras**uh**] registration number

kaymak [kīmak] to skid; cream

kaynak [kīnak] spring, source

kaynana [kīnana] mother-in-law

kaza accident

kazak jumper, sweater

kazan boiler

kazanmak to earn; to win

kazık [kazuhk] rip-off; tent peg

KDV [ka dell veh] VAT

kebapçı [kebapch**uh**] meat restaurant

keçe uçlu kalem [kech**eh** oochl**oo**] felt-tip pen

keçi [kech**ee**] goat

kederli depressed

kedi cat

kel bald

kelebek butterfly

kelime [keleem**eh**] word

kemençe [kemench**eh**] small violin with three strings

kemer belt

kemik bone

-ken while

kenar edge

deniz kenarında [kenar**uh**nda] by the sea

kenar mahalle poor quarters near the edge of the town, slum

kenar şeridi [shereed**ee**] hard shoulder

kendi himself; herself; itself; oneself; his/her/its own

kendileri themselves

kendim myself

kendimiz ourselves

kendin yourself

kendiniz yourselves

kent town

kepenk shutter

kere [ker**eh**] time; occasion

kerpeten pliers

kervansaray [kervansar**ī**] inn, caravanserai

kes (artık)! [art**uhk**] stop it!

kesici platinler [keseej**ee**] points

kesik cut

kesinlikle [keseenl**ee**kleh] definitely; certainly

kesinlikle! absolutely!

kesinlikle (öyle) değil [(url**eh**) deh-**eel**] definitely not, certainly not

keskin sharp

kesmece [kesmejeh] word used by street vendors meaning that melons can be cut open and examined before you buy

kesmek to cut

kestirme [kesteermeh] shortcut

keten cotton

keyif [kayeef] pleasure; disposition

kez time

Kıbrıs [kuhbruhs] Cyprus; Cypriot (adj)

Kıbrıslı [kuhbruhsluh] Cypriot (person)

Kıbrıslı Rum Greek Cypriot (person)

Kıbrıs Rum Greek Cypriot (adj)

Kıbrıs Türk [tewrk] Turkish Cypriot (adj)

kılavuz [kuhlavooz] guide; leader

kılık [kuhluhk] appearance; costume

kına [kuhna] henna

kır [kuhr] countryside

kırık [kuhruhk] broken; fracture

kırk [kuhrk] forty

kırmak [kuhrmak] to break; to offend

kırmızı [kuhrmuhzuh] red

kırsal alanlar [kuhrsal] countryside

kırtasiye [kuhrtasee-yeh] stationery

kırtasiyeci [kuhrtasee-yejee] stationer's

kısa [kuhsa] short; brief

en kısa zamanda [kuhsa] as soon as possible

kısa yolculuk [yoljoolook] short journey

kısım [kuhsuhm] part, portion

kıskanç [kuhskanch] jealous

kış [kuhsh] winter

kışın [kuhshuhn] in the winter

kış tatili winter holiday, winter vacation

kıvırcık [kuhvuhrjuhk] curly; lettuce

kıyafet [kuh-yafet] dress, attire; general appearance and dress

kıyı [kuh-yuh] coast

kıymık [kuh-imuhk] splinter

kız [kuhz] girl; daughter

kızaklı tekne [kuhzakluh tekneh] hydrofoil

kızamık [kuhzamuhk] measles

kızamıkçık [kuhzamuhkchuhk] German measles

kız arkadaş [arkadash] girlfriend

kızarmak [kuhzarmak] to be fried; to be roasted; to be toasted; to blush

kızartmak [kuhzartmak] to fry; to roast; to toast

kız(evlat) [kuhz(evlat)] daughter

kızgın [kuhzguhn] angry; furious

Kızılay [kuhzuhlī] Red Crescent – Turkish Red Cross

Kızılhaç [kuhzuhlhach] Red Cross

kızıl saçlı [kuhzuhl sachluh] red-headed

kız kardeş [kardesh] sister

kızlık adı [kuhzluhk aduh] maiden name

kızmak [kuhzmak] to get angry

ki that; who; which; so that; seeing that

kibrit matches

kilidi açmak [achmak] to unlock

kilim rug

kilise [keeleeseh] church
... Kilisesi Church of ...

kilit lock

kilitlemek to lock

kilitli locked

kilometre kısıtlaması yok [keelometreh kuhsuhtlamasuh] unlimited mileage

kim? who?

kimi some

kimin? whose?

kimlik identification

kimlik kartı [kartuh] ID card

kimse [keemseh] anybody; nobody

kira rent; rental

kiralamak to rent, to hire

kiralık [keeraluhk] for rent, for hire

kiralık bisiklet bicycle hire

kiralık kayık [kī-uhk] boat hire

kiralık otomobil [keeraluhk] car rental; rented car

kira ücreti [ewjretee] hire charge

kirli dirty; polluted

kişi [keeshee] person

kitabevi bookshop, bookstore

kitap book

kitapçı [keetap-chuh] bookshop, bookstore

kitaplık [keetapluhk] library

KKTC Turkish Republic of Northern Cyprus

klakson horn

Klasik Batı müziği [batuh mewzee-ee] Western classical music

klima air-conditioning

klimalı [kleemaluh] air-conditioned

koca [koja] husband; large; great; old; huge

kod numarası [noomarasuh] dialling code

koğuş [ko-oosh] ward

koklamak to smell

kokmak to smell; to stink

koku smell

kol arm; handle

kolay [ko-lī] easy

kolej [koleJ] college

koleksiyon collection

koli [kolee] parcel(s)

koli gişesi [geeshesee] parcels counter

kolonya eau de cologne

kol saati [sa-atee] watch

koltuk armchair; seat; stalls

kolye [kol-yeh] necklace

kombinezon slip (garment)

komik funny
kompartıman [kompartuhman] compartment
kompartıman sigara içmeyenlere mahsus [eechmayenler**eh** ma**н**s**oos**] nonsmoking compartment
komple kahvaltı [komple**h** kahvalt**uh**] full breakfast
komşu [komsh**oo**] neighbour
konak large private residence
konaklamak to stay the night
konfeksiyon off-the-peg clothes
konferans conference
konser concert
konserve açacağı [kons**e**rve**h** achaja**-uh**] can-opener
konserve kutusu tin, can
konsolosluk consulate
kontak ignition
kontak lensleri contact lenses
kontrol check, inspection
kontrol etmek to check
konu subject, topic
konuk guest
konukseverlik [kon**oo**kseverl**ee**k] hospitality
konuşma [kon**oo**shma] speech, talk; conversation; call
konuşmak [kon**oo**shmak] to talk; to speak
konut residence; house
koridor yanı [yan**uh**] aisle seat
korkmak: ...-den korkmak to be afraid (of) ...
korku fear
korkunç [kork**oo**nch] appalling; shocking; horrible

korna horn
koruma faktörü [fakt**u**rew] protection factor
korumak to protect
koruma kremi aftersun cream
koruyucu gözlük [koroo-yooj**oo** gurzl**ewk**] goggles
koruyucu sıvı [suhv**uh**] soaking solution
kostüm [kost**ewm**] dress; costume
koşmak [kosh**mak**] to run
koşu [kosh**oo**] race; jogging
koşu yapmak to race; to go jogging
kova bucket
koy bay
koymak to put
koyu dark
koyun sheep
köpek [k**u**rpek] dog
köpek var beware of the dog
köprü [k**u**rpr**ew**] bridge
kör [k**u**r] blind
körfez [k**u**rfez] gulf; bay
köşe [k**u**rsheh] corner
köşede [k**u**rshedeh] on the corner; in the corner
köşk [k**u**rshk] lodge; pavilion, gazebo; villa
kötü [k**u**rtew] bad; nasty; badly
kötü kalite [kaleet**eh**] poor quality
köy [k**u**h-i] village
köylü [k**u**rlew] villager; peasant
köy yolu country road

kral king
kraliçe [kraleecheh] queen
krank mili crankshaft
kravat tie, necktie
kredi kartı [kartuh] credit card
kredi kartı kabul edilmez
 credit cards not accepted
krem cream, lotion
krema cream
krem rengi cream (colour)
kreş [kresh] creche
kriko jack
kuaför [kwafur] hairdresser's
 (women's)
kubbe [koobbeh] dome
kuduz rabies; rabid
kulak ear
kulak, burun ve boğaz [veh
 boh-az] ear, nose and throat
kulaklıklar [koolakluhklar]
 headphones
kule [kooleh] tower
kullanım [koollanuhm] use
kullanmak to use
kulübe [koolewbeh] kiosk; hut;
 booth
kulüp [koolewp] club
kum sand
kumanda tablosu dashboard
kumanya packed lunch
kumaş [koomash] cloth,
 fabric, material
kumullar sand dunes
kundura shoes
kunduracı [koondoorajuh] shoe
 shop
kundura tamircisi
 [tameerjeesee] shoe repairer's
kupa mug; cup (sporting)

kupür bilet [koopewr] book of
 bus tickets
kur rate
kuron crown
kurşun kalem [koorshoon]
 pencil
kurşunsuz benzin
 [koorshoonsooz] unleaded
 petrol
kuru dry
kurukahveci [koorookahvejee]
 coffee seller
kurulama bezi tea towel
kurum society; institution
kurumak to dry oneself
kuru temizleme [temeezlemeh]
 dry clean
kuru temizleyici
 [temeezlayeejee] dry-cleaner's
kurutmak to dry
kuru yemişçi [yemeeshchee]
 seller of dried fruit and
 nuts
kurye [koor-yeh] courier
kusmak to vomit
kusura bakmayın [bakmi-uhn]
 pardon me
kuş [koosh] bird
kuş beyinli [bayeenlee] stupid,
 bird-brained
kuşet [kooshet] couchette
kutu box; carton
kuyruk [koo-irook] queue; tail
kuyruk olmak to queue
kuytu [koo-itoo] secluded
kuyu well
kuyumcu [koo-yoomjoo]
 jeweller's
kuzen cousin (male)

kuzey [koozay] north;
  northern
kuzeyi north of
kuzey yönünde [yurnewndeh]
  to the north
kuzeyde [koozaydeh] in the
  north
kuzeybatı [batuh] northwest
kuzeydoğu [koozaydoh-oo]
  northeast
Kuzey İrlanda [eerlanda]
  Northern Ireland
Kuzey Kıbrıs Türk Cumhuriyeti
  [kuhbruhs tewrk joomHooree-yetee]
  Turkish Republic of
  Northern Cyrprus
kuzin cousin (female)
küçük [kewchewk] little; small
küçük jeton [Jeton] small
  token
küçük paket small packet
küfür [kewfewr] swearword
külliye [kewllee-yeh] complex
  of buildings attached to a
  mosque
külot [kewlot] pants, briefs,
  panties
külotlu çorap [kewlotloo chorap]
  tights, pantyhose
kül tablası [kewl tablasuh]
  ashtray
kültür [kewltewr] culture
kültür merkezi cultural centre
küpe [kewpeh] earring(s)
kürek çekmek [kewrek chekmek]
  to row (boat)
kürk [kewrk] fur
Kürt [kewrt] Kurdish; Kurd
küsmek: -e küsmek [-eh

kewsmek] to be in a huff
  with
kütüphane [kewtewp-haneh]
  library
küvet [kewvet] bathtub

L

lacivert [lajeevert] navy blue
lağım [la-uhm] drain; sewer
lamba lamp
-lar they are; -s, -es (plural
  endings)
-ları [-laruh] their
lastik rubber; elastic; tyre
lastik bant rubber band
lastik basıncı [basuhnjuh] tyre
  pressure
lastik patlaması [patlamasuh]
  puncture
lavabo washhand basin
lazım [lazuhm] necessary;
  must; should
  bana ... lazım I need ...
-le [-leh] by; with
Lefkoşa [lefkosha] Nicosia
lehçe [leHcheh] dialect
leke [lekeh] spot
-ler they are; -s, -es (plural
  endings)
-leri their
libre [leebreh] pound (weight)
liman harbour; port
lira lira, Turkish unit of
  currency
lisan okulu language school
lise [leeseh] high school
...-'liyim I am from ...

lokanta restaurant
lokum Turkish delight
Londra London
  Londra'da in London
losyon lotion
-lu with
Lübnan [lewbnan] Lebanon
lügat [lewgat] dictionary;
  word
lüks [lewks] luxury;
  luxurious; posh
lütfen [lewtfen] please
lütfen ayakkabılarınızı çıkarınız
  please take off your shoes
lütfen bozuk para veriniz small
  change please

M
—

-m my
maalesef [ma-alesef]
  unfortunately
maç [mach] game, match
madem since, seeing that
madeni para coin
Magosa Famagusta
mağara [ma-ara] cave
  ... Mağarası [ma-arasuh] ...
  Cave
mağaza [ma-aza] store
mahalle [mahalleh] quarter;
  area of city
mahallesi district;
  neighbourhood
mahsus deliberately
mahzen cellar
makas scissors
makbuz receipt

makina/makine [makeeneh]
  machine
makinist mechanic; engine
  driver
makul reasonable
makyaj [makyaJ] make-up
makyaj malzemesi cosmetics
Malazgirt Manzikert
...-malı [-maluh] he/she has
  to ...
...-malıyım [maluh-yuhm] I have
  to ...
mallar goods
mal olmak to cost
mal sahibi owner
manastır [manastuhr]
  monastery
manav greengrocer's
mandal hook; clothes peg
manifatura drapery; textiles
manivela lever
mankafa thick, stupid
mantar mushroom(s); cork
manto coat (woman's)
manzara view; scenery
marka make, brand name
Marmara Denizi the Sea of
  Marmara
marş [marsh] starter
mart March
martı [martuh] seagull
masa table
masaj [masaJ] massage
masa örtüsü [urtewsew]
  tablecloth
masatopu table tennis
masum innocent
maşallah! [mashallah]
  wonderful! – used to

express admiration and wonder, and to avert the evil eye

matbua printed matter

matine [mateen**eh**] matinée

mavi blue

Mavi Tren blue train – Ankara-Istanbul train

mayıs [mī-**uhs**] May

mayo [mī-**o**] swimming costume; swimming trunks

mazot diesel

mecburi [mejboor**ee**] compulsory

mecburi iniş emergency landing

mecburi trafik sigortası [seegortas**uh**] third party insurance

meç [mech] highlights

medeni hali marital status

medrese [medres**eh**] theological school

... Medresesi ...Theological School

mefruşat [mefroosh**at**] fabrics and furnishings

mektup letter

mektup arkadaşı [arkadash**uh**] penfriend

mektup kutusu letterbox

...-meli he/she must ...

...-meliyim I must ...

...-mem I won't ...; I don't ...

meme vermek [mem**eh**] to breastfeed

memleket (home) country

memnun glad, pleased

memnun oldum I am pleased; pleased to meet you

memur official

memur bey [bay] officer

mendil handkerchief

mensup: -e mensup [-eh] belonging to, connected with

merak hobby

mercek [merjek] lens

merdiven ladder; stairs

merhaba! hello!, hi!

merhem ointment

merkez centre

merkezi central

merkez postanesi main post office

mersi thank you

Meryemana Virgin Mary

mesai saatleri [mesa-**ee** sa-**at**leree] opening hours

mesaj [mesa**J**] message

mescit [mesj**eet**] small mosque

mesela for example

mesele [mesel**eh**] question, problem

mesleği [mesleh-**ee**] (applicant's) occupation

meslek profession; occupation

meşgul [meshg**ool**] busy; engaged, occupied

meteliksiz broke, penniless

meteliksizim I'm broke

metro underground (railway), (US) subway

mevsim season

meydan [maydan] square

meyhane [mayhan**eh**] tavern serving alcohol and food, usually frequented by men only

mezar grave, tomb

... mezarı [mezar**uh**] ... grave, ... tomb

mezarlık [mezarl**uhk**] cemetery

mı? [muh] question particle

... mı? is it ...?, is that ...?

-mız [-muhz] our

mi? question particle

... mi? is it ...?, is that ...?

mide [meed**eh**] stomach

midem bulanıyor [boolanuh-**yor**] I feel sick

mide ağrısı [a-ruhs**uh**] stomachache

mide bozukluğu [bozookloo-**oo**] upset stomach

mide bulantısı [boolantuhs**uh**] nausea

midilli pony

mihrap [meeн**rap**] niche in a mosque indicating the direction of Mecca

mikro dalga microwave (oven)

mikroplu septic

mıktar amount

mil mile

milâdi Christian year-numbering system

millet nation

milletlerarası [meelletleraras**uh**] international

milli national

milli park national park

milliyet nationality

milyar one thousand million, (US) one billion

milyon million

minare [meenar**eh**] minaret

minibüs [meeneeb**ews**] minibus

minik tiny

minnettar grateful

misafir [meesa**feer**] guest

misiniz: bana ... verebilir misiniz? can I have ...?

miyim: ...-ebilir miyim? can I ....?, may I ...?

miyop shortsighted

-miz our

mizah humour

mizanpli set

mobilya furniture

mocamp caravan site, trailer park

moda fashion; fashionable, trendy

modaya uygun [mod**ı**-a oo-ig**oon**] trendy, fashionable

mola pause; rest

mor purple

motor motorboat, engine

motor kapak contası [jontas**uh**] cylinder head gasket

motosiklet motorbike

mozaik [moza **cek**] mosaic

M.Ö. BC

M.S. AD

mu? question particle

... mu? is it ...?, is that ...?

muavin assistant; driver's assistant on intercity coaches

muayene [moo-ı̇-en**eh**] examination

Mu

muayenehane [moo-ī-enehan**eh**] surgery
muazzam [moo-azz**am**] tremendous
muhafaza etmek to keep
muhallebici [mooHallebee**jee**] pudding shop
muhtar [mooH**tar**] village headman
muhtemelen [mooH**t**emelen] probably
mum [moom] candle
musluk tap, faucet
muslukçu [mooslookch**oo**] plumber
mutfak kitchen
mutfak eşyası [esh-yas**uh**] pots and pans
mutlu happy
-muz our
mü? [mew] question particle
   ... mü? is it ...?, is that ...?
mücevherat [mew-jevher**at**] jewellery
müddet [mewdd**et**] period (of time)
müdür [mewd**ewr**] manager; director
müdür muavini assistant director
müezzin [mew-ezz**een**] muezzin – man who pronounces call to prayer from the minaret of a mosque
mükemmel [mewkemm**el**] excellent; perfect
   mükemmel! that's great!

mümkün [mewmk**ewn**] possible
mümkün olduğu kadar çabuk [oldoo-**oo** – chab**ook**] as soon as possible
mürekkepli kalem [mewrek-kepl**ee**] pen
mürettebat [mewretteb**at**] crew
müsaade etmek [mewsa-ad**eh**] to allow
müshil [**mew**s-heel] laxative
Müslüman [mewslew**man**] Muslim
müteakip boşaltma [mewteh-ak**eep** boshaltma] next collection
mütehassıs [mewtehass**uhs**] specialist
mütevazı [mewtev**a**zuh] downmarket; modest, humble
müthiş [mewt-h**eesh**] terrific
-müz [-mewz] our
müze [mewz**eh**] museum
müzik [mewz**eek**] music
müzik aleti musical instrument
müzisyen [mewzees-y**en**] musician

N

-n your
nadide [nadeed**eh**] rare
nadiren not often
nahoş [nah**osh**] unpleasant
nakil transfer; transmission; transport

nakit: nakit ödemek [urdemek] to pay cash

nakit para cash

nalbur hardware shop

namaz Muslim prayer performed five times a day

nane şekeri [naneh shekeree] peppermints

nargile [nargeeleh] hookah, water pipe

nasıl? [nasuhl] how?

nasılsın? [nasuhlsuhn] how are you?

nasılsınız? [nasuhl-suhnuhz] how are you?; how do you do?

naylon torba [nilon] plastic bag; carrier bag

naylon yağmurluk [ya-moorlook] cagoule

nazik polite; nice; kind, generous

ne? [neh] what?
  ne ...! what a ...!
  ne var? what is it?; what's the matter?
  ne kadar? how much?

neden cause

neden? why?

nedeniyle [nedenee-ileh] because of

nedir: o nedir? what's that?

nefes almak to breathe

nefis delicious; lovely

nefret etmek to hate

nehir [neh-Heer] river
  ... Nehri [neHree] River ...

nemlendirici (krem) [–deereejee] moisturizer

nemli damp; humid

ne ... ne ... [neh] neither ... nor ...

ne oldu? what's up?, what's wrong?; what's happened?

ne oluyor? what's happening?

nerede? [neredeh] where?; where is it?

neredeyse [neredayseh] nearly; almost; soon

ne var ki but; only; however

ney [nay] reed flute

ne yazık ki unfortunately

ne zaman? when?

-nın [-nuhn] of

-nız [-nuhz] your

niçin? [neecheen] why?; why not?

nihayet [nee-Hı-et] end; at last

-nin of

nisan April

nişanlı [neeshanluh] engaged (to be married); fiancé; fiancée

niye? [nee yeh] why?

-niz your

Noel Christmas

Noel Gecesi [gejesee] Christmas Eve

Noeliniz kutlu olsun! Merry Christmas!

normal [normahl] normal; 2/3 star petrol, regular gas

Norveç [norvech] Norway; Norwegian (adj)

not defteri notebook

nöbet [nurbet] fit (attack); turn of duty, watch

nöbetçi doktor [nurbetchee] duty doctor

nöbetçi eczane [ejzaneh] duty chemist's

numara number

-nun of

-nuz your

nüfus [newfoos] population

-nün [-newn] of

-nüz [-newz] your

O

o that; those; he; she; it; it is

o işte [eeshteh] that's him/her/it

o ...-dir it is ...

o nedir? what's that?

obdüratör [obdewratur] shutter

objektif [obJekteef] lens

ocak [ojak] January; home; cooker; fireplace

oda room

oda hizmetçisi [heezmetcheesee] maid, chambermaid

oda numarası [noomarasuh] room number

oda servisi room service

o dö tuvalet [dur] eau de toilette

ofis office

oğlan [oh-lahn] boy

oğul [oh-ool] son

oje [oJeh] nail varnish

okul school

okumak to read; to study

olağan [ola-an] ordinary; usual

olamaz impossible; impractical

olay event

oldu OK; alright

ne oldu? [neh] what's up?, what's wrong?; what's happened?

olduğunca ... [oldoo-oonja] as ... as possible

oldukça [oldookcha] fairly, quite, rather

oldukça çok [chok] quite a lot

oldu mu? OK?; is it OK?

olgun ripe; mature

olmak to be; to happen; to become

olmaz it won't do; it's not possible

olur all right; I agree

oluyor: ne oluyor? [neh] what's happening?

omuz shoulder

on ten

ona him; her; it; to him/her/it

on altı [altuh] sixteen

on beş [besh] fifteen

on beş gün [gewn] fortnight

on bir eleven

onda on/in him; on/in her; on/in it

ondan from him/her/it

ondan sonra then, after that

on dokuz nineteen

on dört [durt] fourteen

on iki twelve

onlar they; those; them

onlara them; to them

onlarda on/in them
onlardan from them
onları [onlaruh] them
onların [onlaruhn] their; theirs
onlarınki [onlaruhnkee] theirs
onlarla with them
on sekiz eighteen
onu him; her; it
onun his; her; hers; its
onuncu [onoonjoo] tenth
onun için [eecheen] for
   him/her/it; therefore
onunki his; hers
on üç [ewch] thirteen
on yedi seventeen
ora that place
orada over there
orası [orasuh] there
oraya [orī-a] there
orda over there
ordu army
orijinal [oreeJeenal] original;
   unusual; original
   soundtrack
orman woods, forest
orta middle; medium; mean;
   average
   ortada in the middle
orta büyüklükte
   [bowyowklowktoh] medium
   sized
orta jeton [Jeton] medium
   token
ortalama olarak on average
ortopedi uzmanı [oozmanuh]
   orthopaedist
Osmanlı [osmanluh] Ottoman
ot grass
otel hotel

otel odası [odasuh] hotel
   room
otobüs [otobews] bus, coach
   otobüs ile [eeleh] by bus
otobüs bileti bus ticket
otobüs durağı [doora-uh] bus
   stop
otobüs garajı [garaJuh] bus
   station
otobüsle gezi [otobewsleh]
   coach trip
otobüs terminali bus station
otogar bus terminal, bus
   station
otomat vending machine
otomatik automatic
otomatik arama direct
   dialling
otomatik para çekme makinesi
   [chekmeh] cash dispenser,
   automatic teller
otomatik vitesli automatic
   (car)
otomatlı çamaşırhane
   [otomatluh chamashuhr-haneh]
   launderette
otomobil car
   otomobil ile [eeleh] by car
otomobil kiralama (servisi) car
   rental (service)
otomobil yıkama yeri
   [yuhkama] carwash
otopark car park, parking lot
otostop hitch-hiking
otostop yapmak to hitch-
   hike
otoyol motorway, freeway,
   highway
oturacak yer [otoorajak] seat

oturmak to live; to sit down
oturma odası [odasuh] living room
oturun! sit down!
otuz thirty
ova plain; plateau
... Ovası [ovasuh] ... Plain
oynamak to play; to folkdance
oynatmak to move
oysa but; yet; whereas
oyun play; folkdancing; game
oyuncak [oyoonjak] toy
oyuncu [oyoonjoo] actor; actress
o zaman then, at that time

Ö

öbür [urbewr] the other
öbür gün [gewn] the day after tomorrow
öbür türlü [tewrlew] otherwise
öbürü [urbewrew] the other one
ödemek [urdemek] to pay
ödemeli [urdemelee] reverse charge call, collect call
ödemeli konuşma [konooshma] reverse charge call, collect call
ödeyiniz [urdayeeneez] pay
ödünç almak [urdewnch] to borrow
ödünç vermek to lend
öfkeli [urfkelee] angry
öğle [ur-leh] midday, noon

öğleden sonra [urleden] afternoon; p.m.
öğle yemeği [urleh yemeh-ee] lunch
öğleyin [ur-layeen] midday, noon
öğrenci [ur-renjee] student
öğrenci kartı [kartuh] student card
öğrenci yurdu student hostel
öğrenmek [ur-renmek] to learn
öğretmek [ur-retmek] to teach
öğretmen [ur-retmen] teacher
öksürük [urksew-rewk] cough
öksürük şurubu [shoorooboo] cough medicine
ölçek [urlchek] scale
öldürmek [urldewrmek] to kill
ölmek [urlmek] to die
ölü [urlew] dead
Ölü Deniz the Dead Sea
ölüm [urlewm] death
ön [urn] front
ön tarafta at the front
ön cam [jam] windscreen, windshield
önce [urnjeh] before; ago; first; at first
-den önce before
önceden [urnjeden] in advance
öncelik [urnjeleek] priority
öncelikle [urnjeleekleh] first of all
önce siz (buyrun) [urnjeh – (booiroon)] after you
önde [urndeh] in front
önden [urnden] at the front

önden binilir entry at front
önem [urnem] importance
  önemi yok it doesn't matter
önemli [urnemlee] important
önermek [urnermek] to advise;
  to suggest
önünde: ...-in önünde
  [urnewndeh] in front of ...
öpmek [urpmek] to kiss
öpücük [urpewjewk] kiss
ören [uren] ruin
  ören yeri ruins
örgü [urgew] knitwear
örnek [urnek] example;
  pattern
  örneğin [urneh-een] for
  example
örümcek [urewmjek] spider
övgü [urvgew] compliment
öyle [ur-ileh] so, thus
  öyle yapmayın! [yapmī-uhn]
  stop it!
öyleyse [ur-ilayseh] then, in
  that case
özel [urzel] private; special
özel bakım ünitesi [bakuhm
  ewneetesee] special care unit
özel fiyat special price
özel hasta private patient
özel indirim special offer
özellikle [urzelleekleh]
  especially
özel ulak special delivery;
  express mail
özür [urzewr] apology;
  excuse; defect
özür dilemek to apologize
özür dilerim I'm sorry;
  excuse me

özürlü [urzewrlew] disabled;
  defective
özürlü kişiler handicapped
  people, the disabled

P

padişah [padeeshaн] Sultan;
  ruler
pahalı [paнaluh] expensive
paket packet, package
paketlemek to pack
paket tur package holiday
paletler flippers
palto coat
pamuk cotton
pamukçuk [pamookchook]
  mouth ulcer
panayır [panī-uhr] fair,
  funfair
pansiyon guesthouse
pansuman dressing
pantolon trousers, (US) pants
para money
para almak to charge
para cüzdanı [jewzdanuh]
  wallet
para çantası [chantasuh]
  purse
paraya çevirmek [parī-a
  cheveermek] to cash
parayı geri vermek [parī-uh] to
  refund
parça [parcha] part; piece
  bir parça ... a piece of ...
  büyük bir parça [bew-yewk] a
  big bit
pardon pardon; excuse me

parfüm [parfe**wm**] perfume
parfümeri [parfewmer**ee**]
 perfumes
park edilir parking
park edilmez no parking
park etmek to park
park lambaları [lambalar**uh**]
 sidelights
park yapılmaz no parking
parlak brilliant
parmak finger
parmaklık [parmakl**uhk**] fence
parti party
pasaport passport
pasaport kontrolü [kontrol**ew**]
 passport control
Paskalya Easter
pastane [past**a**neh] cake shop;
 café
pasta ve şekerlemeler [veh
 shekerlemel**er**] confectionery
pastil pastilles; lozenges
patika path
patiska cambric
patlak burst; punctured
patlak lastik puncture
patron boss
pavyon cheap nightclub,
 joint; pavilion; stand
paylaşmak [p**ī**lashmak] to
 share
pazar Sunday; market
pazar çantası [chantas**uh**]
 shopping bag
pazar günleri dışında except
 Sundays
pazarlık [pazarl**uhk**] bargaining
pazarlık edilmez no
 bargaining

pazarlık etmek to bargain
pazartesi Monday
pazen brushed cotton
peçete [pech**e**teh] napkin
pek very; extremely; a great
 deal; firm; strong
 pek (fazla) değil [deh-**eel**] not
 too much
pekâlâ all right; very well
pek az few
peki all right
pembe [pemb**eh**] pink
pencere [penjer**eh**] window
pencere yanı [yan**uh**] window
 seat
perçem [perch**em**] fringe; tuft
 of hair
perde [perd**eh**] curtain; act
perdeler curtains
perhiz diet
peron platform, (US) track
perşembe [pershemb**eh**]
 Thursday
peşin [pesh**een**] in advance
pezevenk pimp
piç [peech] bastard
pijama [pee**J**ama] pyjamas
pikap record player
piknik yemeği [yemeh-**ee**]
 packed lunch
pil battery
pipo pipe (for smoking)
pire [peer**eh**] flea
pis [pees] filthy
pislik dirt
pişirmek [peesheerm**ek**] to
 cook
piyes play
PK PO box

plaj [plaJ] beach
  plajda on the beach
plaj şemsiyesi [shemsee-yesee]
  beach umbrella
plaj yaygısı [yïguhsuh] beach
  mat
plak record
plaka number plate
plaster plaster(s), (US)
  Bandaid®
poliklinik out patients clinic
polis police; policeman
polis karakolu police station
polis memuru policeman,
  officer
pompa pump
pop müzik [mewzeek] pop
  music
popo bottom (of person)
pop şarkıcısı [sharkuhjuhsuh]
  pop singer
porselen china
porsiyon portion
portatif yatak campbed
portbebe [portbeheh] carry-cot
portre [portreh] portrait
posta post, mail
postacı [postajuh] postman
posta kartı [kartuh] postcard
posta kodu postcode, zip
  code
posta kutusu postbox,
  mailbox
postalamak to post, to mail
postane [postaneh] post office
Posta Telgraf Telefon post and
  telephone office
pozometre [pozometreh] light
  meter

pratik practical
prens prince
prenses princess
prezervatif condom
priz socket, power point
protez dentures
prova etmek to try on
PTT [peh teh teh] post and
  telephone office
pul stamp(s)
puro cigar
puset pushchair, buggy
pusula compass

R

radyatör [radyatur] radiator;
  heater
radyo radio
  radyoda on the radio
raf shelf
rahat comfortable
rahatsız etmek [rahatsuhz] to
  disturb
rahip priest
Ramazan Ramadan – the
  Muslim month of fasting
  and prayer
randevu appointment
ranza bunk; berth; couchette
ray [rï] track; rail
razıyım [razuh-yuhm] I agree; I
  accept
rebap three-stringed violin
reçete [recheteh] prescription
reçete ile satılır prescription
  only
reçete yazmak to prescribe

rehber [reHber] guide;
guidebook

rehberli tur [reHberlee] guided
tour

renk colour

renkli colour

renkliler colours

resepsiyon reception

resepsiyonda at reception

resepsiyoncu [resepsee-yonjoo]
receptionist

resepsiyon masası [masasuh]
reception desk

resepsiyon memuru
receptionist

resim picture; painting

resmi formal

resmi tatil public holiday

restoran restaurant

reyon [rayon] department

rezervasyon reservation

rıhtım [ruhHtuhm] quay

rıhtımda on the quayside

rica ederim [reeja] my
pleasure, don't mention it

rica etmek to request

rimel mascara

rizikolu risky

robdöşambr [robdurshambr]
man's dressing gown

rock müziği [mewzee-ee] rock
(music)

Rodos Rhodes

roman novel

Romanya Rumania

romatizma rheumatism

rondela washer

rota route

römork [rurmork] trailer

röntgen [rurntgen] X-ray

ruh durumu mood

ruj [rooJ] lipstick

Rum [room] ethnic Greek

Rumca [roomja] Greek
(language)

Rum kadını [kaduhnuh] ethnic
Greek (woman)

Rum Ortodoks Greek
Orthodox

Rus Russian

rüya [rew-ya] dream

rüzgâr [rewzgar] wind

rüzgârlı [rewzgarluh] windy

S

saat [sa-at] hour; o'clock;
clock; wristwatch

saat kaç? [kach] what time
is it?

saat kayışı [kı-uhshuh] watch
strap

sabah [sabaH] morning; a.m.
(from 4 a.m. to noon)

bu sabah this morning

sabahleyin [sabaHlayeen] in the
morning

sabahlık [sabaHluhk] woman's
dressing gown

sabun soap

sabun tozu soap powder

saç [sach] hair

saç fırçası [fuhrchasuh]
hairbrush

saç kesme [kesmeh] haircut

saç kurutma makinesi
hairdryer

saçma [sachma] silly
  saçma! rubbish!, nonsense!
saç spreyi [sach spray-ee]
  hairspray
saç tıraşı [tuhrashuh] haircut
saç tokası [tokasuh]
  hairgrip(s)
sade [sa-deh] plain, simple
sadece [sa-dejeh] only, just
sağ [sa] alive; right (not left)
sağa dön [sa-a durn] turn
  right
sağa dönülmez no right turn
sağa dönün [durnewn] turn
  right
sağanak [sa-anak] shower
sağa sapın [sapuhn] turn
  right
sağa viraj bend to right
sağda [sa-da] on the right
sağdan direksiyonlu [sa-dan]
  right-hand drive
sağdan gidiniz keep to the
  right
sağında [sa-uhnda] on the
  right
sağır [sa-uhr] deaf
sağlığınıza! [sa-luh-uhnuhza]
  your health!
sağlıklı [sa-luhkluh] healthy
sağol [sa-ol] bless you; thanks
saha field; area
sahil coast; shore, seafront
  sahilde [saHeeldeh] on the
  coast
sahil yolu coast road
sahi mi? really?
sahip owner
sahip olmak to have; to own

sahne [saHneh] stage
sahte [saHteh] false;
  counterfeit
sakal beard
sakal tıraşı [tuhrashuh] shave
sakın! [sakuhn] beware!;
  don't!
sakin quiet; peaceful
sakız [sakuhz] chewing gum
saklamak to hide
saklanmak to hide
saldırgan [salduhrgan]
  aggressive
saldırı [salduhruh] attack
salı [saluh] Tuesday
salık vermek [saluhk] to
  recommend
salon lounge; hall
saman nezlesi hay fever
sana you; to you
sanat art
sanatçı [sanatchuh] artist
sanat galerisi art gallery
sanayi [sanī-ee] industry
sandal sandal(s); dinghy
sandık [sanduhk] box; chest;
  coffer
saniye [sanee yeh] second (in
  time)
  bir saniye! just a second!
sanki as if
sanmak to suppose; to
  think
santigrat centigrate
santimetre [santeemetreh]
  centimetre
santral memuru operator
santrifüjlü kurutma makinesi
  [santreefewJlew] spindryer

sap stem; stalk; handle

sapak turning

saray [sarī] palace

... Sarayı [sarī-uh] ... Palace

sargı [sarguh] bandage

sarhoş [sarhosh] drunk

sarı [saruh] yellow

sarışın [saruh-shuhn] blond

sarmak to wrap

satılan mal geri alınmaz goods cannot be exchanged

satılık [satuhluhk] for sale

satın alma [satuhn] purchase

satın almak to buy

satış [satuhsh] sale; selling

satış kuru selling rate

satışlarımız peşindir no credit allowed

satmak to sell

satranç [satranch] chess

savaş [savash] war

sayfa [sīfa] page

sayı [sī-uh] number

sayın ... [sī-uhn] esteemed ... – formal way of addressing people followed by surname

saymak [sīmak] to count; to value; to consider

saz oriental music; reed; Turkish string instrument

seans [seh-ans] performance

sebep cause

sebil public drinking fountain

seçmek [sechmek] to choose

sefer journey; flight; voyage; time; occasion

bu sefer this time

geçen sefer [gechen] last time

gelecek sefer [gelejek] next time

seferden kaldırıldı [kalduhruhlduh] flight/departure cancelled

sefer numarası [noomarasuh] flight number

sefer sayısı [sī-uhsuh] flight number

sekiz eight

sekizinci [sekeezeenjee] eighth

seks sex

seksen eighty

sel flood

Selçuklular [selchookloolar] Selchuks

sele [seleh] saddle

seloteyp [selotayp] Sellotape®, Scotch tape®

sema dervish ceremony

sempatik nice

semt area, district, neighbourhood

sen you

sende [sendeh] you; on/in you

senden (from) you

sene [seneh] year

seni you

senin your; yours

seninki yours

sepet basket

serbest vacant; free, independent; allowed

sergi exhibition; trade fair

serin cool; fresh

sersem silly; fool

serseri tramp, vagabond

sert hard; strong; stern

sert dönüş sharp turn

sert lensler hard lenses

sert viraj sharp bend

servis dahildir service charge included

servis istasyonu service station

servis otobüsü [otobewsew] shuttle bus

servis ücreti [ewjretee] service charge

ses voice

sessizlik silence

sever:... sever misiniz? do you like ...?

sevgi love

sevici [seveejee] lesbian

sevilen popular

sevişmek [seveeshmek] to make love

sevmek to love

seyahat [sayahat] travel; journey

seyahat acentası [ajentasuh] travel agency

seyahat çeki [chekee] traveller's cheque

seyahat çekleri [chekleree] traveller's cheques

seyahat etmek to travel

seyirci [sayeerjee] audience

seyretmek [sayretmek] to watch

-sı [-suh] his; her; its

sıcak [suhjak] hot; warm

  hava sıcak it's hot

sıcaklık [suhjakluhk] heat; temperature

sıcak su [suhjak] hot water

sıçan [suhchan] rat

sıfır [suhfuhr] zero

sığ [suh] shallow

sıhhat [suh-hat] health

sık [suhk] frequent; dense; thick

sıkıcı [suhkuh-juh] boring

sıkıntılı [suhkuhn-tuhluh] dull

sıkışmış [suhkuhsh-muhsh] stuck

sıkmayınız do not wring

sık sık [suhk] often

-sın [-suhn] you are

sınav [suhnav] exam

sınıf [suhnuhf] class; sort, kind

sınır [suhnuhr] border

-sınız [suhnuhz] you are

sırasında [suhra-suhnda] during

sırf [suhrf] only

sırf gidiş [geedeesh] single ticket, one-way ticket

sırt [suhrt] back (of body)

sırt ağrısı [a-ruhsuh] backache

sırt çantası [chantasuh] rucksack

sıska [suhska] skinny

sızıntı [suhzuhntuh] leak

-si his; her; its

sigara cigarette

sigara içenler [eechenler] smokers

sigara içilen [eecheelen] smoking

sigara içilmez no smoking

sigara içmek [eechmek] to smoke

sigara içmek yasaktır no smoking

sigara içmeyenler [eechmayenler] nonsmokers

sigara içmeyenlere mahsus bölüm/kısım [eechmayenlereh maHsoos burlewm/kuhsuhm] nonsmoking section

sigara içmeyenlere mahsus (kompartıman) [kompartuhman] nonsmoking (compartment)

sigara içmeyiniz do not smoke

sigorta insurance; fuse

sigorta kutusu fuse box

sigorta teli fuse wire

silah weapon

silecekler [seelejekler] windscreen wipers

silgi rubber, eraser

-sin you are

sinek fly

sinema cinema, movie theatre

sinir hastası [hastasuh] neurotic

sinirli nervous

-siniz you are

sinyal indicator

sipariş [seepareesh] order

sis fog; mist

sisli foggy

site [seeteh] estate

sivil civilian

sivilce [seeveeljeh] pimple

sivrisinek mosquito

sivrisinek ilacı [eelajuh] mosquito repellent

siyah black

siyah beyaz [bayaz] black and white

siz you; one

-siz without

sizde [seezdeh] on/in you

sizde kalsın [kalsuhn] please keep it

sizden from you

size [seezeh] to you

sizi you

sizin your; yours

sizinki yours

sizinle [seezeenleh] with you

sizlerin your

ski yapmak skiing

slayt [slit] slide

sofa hall

soğuk [so-ook] cold

soğuk aldım [alduhm] I have a cold

soğuk algınlığı [alguhnluh-uh] cold

soğuk su cold water

Sok. St

sokak street; road

sokma insect bite

sokmak to sting; to bite; to thrust into; to insert

sokulgan friendly

sol left

sola to the left

sola dön [durn] turn left

sola dönülmez no left turn

sola dönün [durnewn] turn left

solak left-handed

sola sapın [sapuhn] turn left

sola viraj bend to left

solda on the left

solgun pale

solunda on the left of

somun nut (for bolt); loaf

somun anahtarı [anaHtaruh] spanner

son end; last; final

yolun sonunda at the end of the street

sona erdi it's over

sonbahar autumn, (US) fall

sonbaharda in the autumn, in the fall

son derece [derejeh] extremely

son durak terminus

son hareket last train; last bus

son istasyon rail terminus

son kullanma tarihi ... use before ...

son moda trendy

sonra next; after; afterwards; later

-den sonra after

daha sonra later; later on

sonradan afterwards

sormak to ask

soru question

sorumlu responsible

sorun problem

hiç sorun değil! [heech – deh-eel] no problem!

sorun nedir? what's wrong?

sorup öğrenmek [ur-renmek] to find out

soyadı [soyaduh] surname

soyunma odası [odasuh] fitting room; changing room

sömestr [surmestr] term

söndürmek [surndewrmek] to put out, to extinguish

sönük [surnewk] off; dim; lacklustre; extinguished

sörf [surf] surf

sörf tahtası [taHtasuh] surfboard

sörf yapmak to surf

söylemek [sur-ilemek] to say; to tell

sözcük [surzjewk] word

sözlük [surzlewk] dictionary

söz vermek [surz] to promise

spiral [spee-ral] IUD; spiral

spor sport

spor malzemeleri sports goods

spor salonu gym

spor tesisleri sporting facilities

stabilize yol macadam road

su water; river; stream

-su his; her; its

suçiçeği [soochecheh-ee] chickenpox

sufi dervish; mystic

su geçirmez [gecheermez] waterproof

su kayağı [kī-a-uh] waterski; water-skiing

Sultan Ahmet Camii [aHmet jamee-ee] Blue Mosque

-sun you are

suni artificial; false; affected

-sunuz you are

Suriye [**soo**ree-yeh] Syria
Suriyeli Syrian
sus! shut up!
susadım [soosad**uh**m] I'm
  thirsty
susamak to be thirsty
su sporları [sporlar**uh**] water
  sports
suyla [soo-ila] with water
-suz without
-sü [-sew] his; her; its
süet [sew-**et**] suede
sükseli [sewkse**lee**] fashionable
-sün [-sewn] you are
sünger [sewng**er**] sponge
sünnet [sew**nnet**] circumcision
-sünüz [-sewn**ewz**] you are
süper [sew**per**] 4-star petrol,
  premium gas
süpürge [sewpewrg**eh**] broom
sürahi [sewra**hee**] jug; carafe
sürat tahdidi speed limit
süre [sewr**eh**] period (of time)
sürgülemek [sewrgewle**mek**] to
  bolt
sürmek [sewrm**ek**] to drive; to
  rub on; to smear; to
  continue
sürpriz [sewrpr**eez**] surprise
sürücü [sewrewj**ew**] driver
sütlü çikolata [sewt**lew**
  cheekolata] milk chocolate
sütsüz çikolata [sewts**ewz**]
  plain chocolate
sütun [sew**toon**] column
sütyen [sewt-yen] bra
svetşört [svet-sh**urt**] sweatshirt

Ş

şadırvan [shaduhr**van**] fountain
  attached to mosque for
  ritual ablutions
şafak [sha**fak**] dawn
şahane [shaHa**neh**] wonderful,
  amazing, very good
şair [sha-**eer**] poet
şaka [sha**ka**] joke
şal [shal] shawl
şalter [shal**ter**] mains switch
şamandıra buoy
şampuan [shampoo-**an**]
  shampoo
şampuan ve mizanpli [veh]
  shampoo and set
şans [shans] luck
şapka [shap**ka**] hat
şarkı [shark**uh**] song
şarkıcı [sharkuhj**uh**] singer
şarkı söylemek [shark**uh** sur-
  ile**mek**] to sing
şarküteri [sharkewter**ee**]
  delicatessen
şart [shart] essential
... şarttır [shart**tuhr**] it is
  essential that ...
şaşılacak [shashuhla**jak**]
  amazing, surprising
şaşırtıcı [shashuhr-tuhj**uh**]
  surprising, astonishing
şato [shat**oh**] castle
şayet [shi-**et**] if
şebeke planı [shebek**eh** plan**uh**]
  network map
şef [shef] boss
şehir [sheh-**heer**] city

şehirde [sheh-heerdeh] in town

şehiriçi [sheh-heereechee] local; local mail

şehir kodu area code

şehirlerarası konuşma [sheh-heerler-arasuh konooshma] long-distance call

şehirlerarası otobüs işletmesi [otobews eeshletmesee] long-distance coach service

şehir merkezi city centre

şehir planı [planuh] streetmap

şehir turu city tour

şehzade [sheHzadeh] prince; heir apparent

şeker [sheker] sugar; sweet, candy

şeker hastası [hastasuh] diabetic

şemsiye [shemsee-yeh] umbrella

şenlik [shenleek] carnival; amusement

şerefe [sherefeh] balcony of minaret

şerefe! cheers!

şerit [shereet] motorway lane

şerit metre [metreh] tape measure

şey [shay] thing

şeyh [shayH] sheikh – head of a religious order

şezlong [shezlong] deckchair; sun lounger

şık [shuhk] trendy

şiddetli [sheeddetlee] sharp

şikayet [sheekī-et] complaint

şikayet etmek to complain

şilebezi [sheelebezee] cheesecloth

şilte [sheelteh] mattress

şimdi [sheemdee] now

şimdi değil [deh-eel] not just now

şimdi anladım [anladuhm] I see, I understand now

şimdiden [sheemdeeden] already

şimşek [sheemshek] lightning

şirket [sheerket] company, firm

şişe [sheesheh] bottle

şişe açacağı [achaja-uh] bottle-opener

şişlik [sheeshleek] swelling

şişman [sheeshman] fat

şişmiş [sheeshmeesh] swollen

şofben [shofben] water heater

şoför [shofur] driver

şoför ehliyeti driver's licence

şok [shok] shock

şort [short] shorts

şöyle [shuh-ileh] thus, such

şöyle böyle [buh-iloh] so so

şu [shoo] this; that

şubat [shoobat] February

şube [shoobeh] branch

şu ...-lar those ...

şunlar [shoonlar] those

şura [shoora] that place

şurada [shoorada] over there

şurda [shoorda] there

şurup [shooroop] cough syrup

T

-ta in

taahhütlü [ta-ah-hewtl**ew**] by registered mail

taahhütlü mektup registered mail

tabak plate; dish

taban floor; base; sole

tabanca [tab**a**nja] gun, pistol

tabii! [tab**ee-ee**] sure!; of course!

  tabii değil [deh-**eel**] of course not

tabla ashtray

tablet çikolata [cheekol**a**ta] bar of chocolate

tahta [ta**H**ta] wood (material)

takıldı [takuhld**uh**] jammed

takım [tak**uh**m] set; team

takım elbise [elbees**eh**] suit (man's)

takıp denemek [tak**uh**p] to try on

takip etmek to follow

taklit imitation, fake

takma ad nickname

takma diş [deesh] dentures

taksi taxi

taksi durağı [door**a**-uh] taxi rank

taksimetre [takseemetr**eh**] taximeter

taksi şoförü [shofur**ew**] taxi-driver

taksitler instalments

takunya pattens, clogs – worn in Turkish baths

takvim calendar

talep etmek to demand

tali secondary

talihin açık olsun! [ach**uh**k] good luck!

tali yol kavşağı secondary junction

talk pudrası [tah**l**k poodras**uh**] talcum powder

tam quite; exact; complete, entire; perfect

tamam OK, all right; complete, finished; perfect

tamam! right!

  (böyle) tamam [b**uh**-ileh] that'll do nicely

...-in tamamı [tamam**uh**] the whole of ...

tamamen completely

tamamlamak to finish

tam bilet full-price ticket

tamirci [tameerj**ee**] mechanic

tamir etmek to mend, to repair

tamirhane [tameerh**a**neh] garage (for repairs)

tam pansiyon full board

tampon bumper, fender; tampon

tam ücret [ewjr**e**t] exact fare

tam zamanında [zaman**uh**nda] on time

tanbur long-necked stringed instrument like a lute

tane [tan**eh**] item; piece

tanık [tan**uh**k] witness

tanım [tan**uh**m] description

tanımak [tan**uh**mak] to know; to recognize

tanıştığımıza memnun oldum!
[tanuhshtuh-uhmuhza] pleased
to meet you!

tanıştırmak [tanuhshtuhrmak] to
introduce

tanıtmak [tanuhtmak] to
introduce

Tanrı [tanruh] God

tanrıça [tanruhcha] goddess

tanrılar [tanruhlar] gods

tansiyon blood pressure

tapınak [tapuhnak] temple

taraf side; part

... tarafından yazılan
[tarafuhndan yazuhlan] written
by ...

tarafta: bu tarafta this way
o tarafta that way

taraftar fan (sports etc)

tarak comb

taramak to comb

tarife [tareefeh] charges, price
list; timetable, (US)
schedule

tarifeli sefer scheduled flight

tarih [tareeH] date (time);
history

tarihi yerler [tareeHee]
historical places

tarla field

tas bowl

taş [tash] stone, rock

taşımak [tashuhmak] to carry

taşıma ücreti [tashuhma ewj-
retee] fare

taşıt [tashuht] vehicle

taşıt giremez no entry for
vehicles

taşıt trafiğine kapalı yol closed
to all vehicles

tat taste; flavour

tatil holiday, vacation
tatilde [tateeldeh] on holiday,
on vacation

tatil köyü [kur-yew] holiday
village

tatil sitesi holiday village

tatmak to taste

tava frying pan

tavan ceiling

tavla backgammon

tavsiye etmek [tavsee-yeh] to
recommend

tayyör [tī-ur] suit (woman's)

taze [tazeh] fresh

taze boya wet paint

TC [teh jeh] Republic of
Turkey

TCDD [teh jeh deh deh] Turkish
State Railways

-te [teh] in

tebrikler! congratulations!

tecrübeli [tejrewbelee]
experienced

tedavi treatment

tedavi etmek to cure

tedricen [tedreejen] gradually

tehlike [tehleekeh] danger

tehlike çıkışı [chuhkuhshuh]
emergency exit

tehlikeli dangerous

tehlikeli akıntı dangerous
current

tehlikeli eğim steep gradient

tek one, sole, single

tekel government
monopoly on alcohol and
tobacco

Tekel bayii [bī-ee-**ee**] off-
licence, liquor store
tekerlek wheel
tekerlekli araba trolley
tekerlekli sandalye [sand**a**lyeh]
wheelchair
tek gidiş bilet [geed**ee**sh]
single ticket, one-way
ticket
tekke [tekk**eh**] dervish
convent; lodge
tek kişilik (bir) oda
[keesheel**ee**k] single room
tek kişilik yatak single bed
teklif etmek to offer; to
propose
tekrar again
tekrar gelmek to come back
tekrarlamak to repeat
tek yön [yurn] one-way street
tek yönlü yol [yurnl**ew**] one-
way street
tel wire
teleferik cable car
telefon phone
telefon etmek to phone, to
call
telefon kabini telephone
box/cubicle
telefon kartı [kart**uh**]
phonecard
telefon kodu dialling code
telefon konuşması
[konooshmas**uh**] phone call;
phone conversation
telefon kulübesi [koolewbes**ee**]
phone box
telefonla uyandırma [oo-
yanduhrm**a**] wake-up call

telefon numarası [noomaras**uh**]
phone number
telefon rehberi [reнber**ee**]
phone book
teleks telex
telesiyej [telesee-ye**J**] chairlift
televizyon television
telgraf telegram
tembel lazy
temiz clean
temizlemek to clean
temizleme kremi [temeezlem**eh**]
cleansing lotion
temizleme losyonu cleansing
lotion
temizleme sıvısı [suhvuhs**uh**]
cleaning solution
temizleyici krem
[temeezl**a**yeejee] cleansing
lotion
temmuz July
temsilci [temseelj**ee**] agent;
representative
tencere [tenjer**eh**] pan,
saucepan
teneke kutu [tenek**eh**] can, tin
tenis kortu tennis court
tepe [tep**eh**] hill
tepsi tray
terbiyesiz rude, ill-mannered
tercih etmek to prefer
tercüman [terjewma**n**]
translator; interpreter
tercüme [terjewm**eh**]
translation
tercüme etmek to translate;
to interpret
terlemek to sweat
terlik slipper(s)

termometre [termom**e**treh] thermometer

termos vacuum flask

tersane [tersan**eh**] shipyard

... Tersanesi ... Shipyard

terzi tailor's

tesadüfen [tesadewf**en**] by chance

tesisatçı [teseesatch**uh**] plumber

teslim delivery

teslim etmek to deliver

teşekkür (ederim) [teshekk**ewr**] thanks, thank you

çok teşekkür ederim [chok] thank you very much

teşekkür etmek to thank

teyp [tayp] tape, cassette; tape recorder

teyze [tayz**eh**] aunt (maternal)

THT [teh ha teh] domestic air service

THY [teh ha yeh] Turkish Airlines

tıkaç [t**uh**kach] plug (in sink)

tıkalı [t**uh**kal**uh**] blocked

TIR [t**uh**r] international road haulage

tıraş fırçası [t**uh**rash f**uh**rchas**uh**] shaving brush

tıraş köpüğü [k**uh**rp**ew-ew**] shaving foam

tıraş losyonu aftershave

tıraş makinesi electric shaver

tıraş makinesi prizi shaving point

tıraş olmak to shave

tıraş sabunu shaving soap

tırnak [t**uh**rn**a**k] fingernail

tırnak cilası [jeelas**uh**] nail polish

tırnak fırçası [f**uh**rchas**uh**] nailbrush

tırnak makası [makas**uh**] nail clippers

tırnak törpüsü [turpews**ew**] nailfile

tiksindirici [–reej**ee**] disgusting

tip [teep] sort, type

tipi blizzard

tipik typical

tirbuşon [teerboosh**on**] corkscrew

tişört [tee-sh**u**rt] T-shirt

tiyatro theatre

TL [teh leh] Turkish Lira

tok full; thick

ton vermek tint

top ball

toplam total

toplamak to collect

toplantı [toplant**uh**] meeting

toplu iğne [ee-n**eh**] pin

toprak earth

toprak eşya [esh-y**a**] pottery

tıpık tool

tornavida screwdriver

Toros Taurus

torun grandchild

toz dust; powder

tozlu dusty

trafik ışıkları [**uh**sh**uh**k-lar**uh**] traffic lights

trafik kanunu traffic laws

trafik kazası [kazas**uh**] road accident

Trafik Kuralları Highway Code

trafik lambaları [–lar**uh**] traffic
lights

trafik tıkanıklığı [tuhkanuhkl**uh**-
uh] traffic jam

Trakya Thrace

tramplen diving board

tramvay [tramv**ı**] tram

tren train

trenle [tr**en**leh] by train

tren bileti train ticket

tren istasyonu railway station

tren yolu geçidi [gecheed**ee**]
level crossing

triko knitwear

troleybüs [trolayb**ew**s]
trolleybus

TRT [teh reh teh] Turkish
Radio and Television

Truva Troy

tuğla [too-l**a**] brick

tuhaf weird

tuhafiyeci [toohafee-yej**ee**]
haberdasher's

tur tour

turist tourist

turistik otel tourist hotel

turizm tourism

turizm bürosu [bewros**oo**]
tourist office

turnike [toorneek**eh**] turnstile

tur operatörü [operatur**ew**] tour
operator

turuncu [tooroonj**oo**] orange
(colour)

tutar amount

tutmak to take, to accept; to
hold; to hire, to rent; to
support

tutuklamak to arrest

tutuşmak [tootoosh**mak**] to
catch fire

tutuşturmak [tootooshtoorm**ak**]
to set on fire, to ignite

tuvalet toilet

tuvalet kağıdı [ka-uhd**uh**] toilet
paper

tuvalet temizleyicisi [temeezlay-
eejees**ee**] bleach

tuzlu salty

tüfek [tew**fek**] rifle

tüh! [tewH] oh no!

tükendi [tewken**dee**] sold out

tükenmez (kalem) [tewken**mez**]
ballpoint (pen)

tüm [tewm] whole

tümüyle [tewm**ew**leh]
altogether

Tünel [tew**nel**] Istanbul
underground/subway

tünel tunnel

tüpgaz [tew**p**gaz] camping
gas

tür [tewr] kind, sort, type

ne tür ...? [neh] what sort
of ...?

türbe [tewrb**eh**] tomb

... Türbesi [tewrbes**ee**] Tomb
of ...

Türk [tewrk] Turk; Turkish
(adj)

Türkçe [tewrkch**eh**] Turkish
(language); in Turkish

Türk Hava Yolları [yollar**uh**]
Turkish Airlines

Türkiye [tew**r**kee-yeh] Turkey

Türkiye Cumhuriyeti [tew**r**kee-
yeh joomHooree-yet**ee**] Republic
of Turkey

Türkiye Cumhuriyeti Devlet Demiryolları Turkish State Railways

Türkiye Radyo Televizyon Kurumu Turkish Radio and Television Corporation

Türkiye'ye giriş tarihi date of entry to Turkey

Türk Lirası [leerasuh] Turkish Lira

Türk sanat müziği [mewzee-ee] Turkish classical music

türkü [tewrkew] folk song

türlü [tewrlew] sort, kind, variety

tütün [tewtewn] tobacco

U

-u his; her; its; accusative noun ending

ucuz [oojooz] cheap, inexpensive

uçak [oochak] aeroplane

uçakla by air; airmail

uçak postası [postasuh] airmail

uçak postasıyla [postasuh-ila] by airmail

uçak seferi flight

uçak zarfı [zarfuh] airmail envelope

uçmak [oochmak] to fly

uçuk [oochook] pale

uğramak: -e uğramak [-eh oo-ramak] to drop by, to drop in, to stop by

ulus nation

uluslararası [oolooslararasuh] international

-um my; I am

ummak to hope

umumi general; common; public

umumi hela public convenience

umumi tatil public holiday

umumi telefon payphone

umut hope; expectation

-umuz our

-un of; your

unutmak to forget

unuttum I forget, I've forgotten

-unuz your

unvanı [oonvanuh] title

usta skilful; clever; foreman; master craftsman – often used respectfully/ironically to address master craftsman

ustura razor

utanç [ootanch] shame

utanç içinde [eecheendeh] ashamed .

utandırıcı [ootanduhruhjuh] embarrassing; disgraceful

utangaç [ootangach] shy

uyandırmak [oo-vanduhrmak] to wake

uyanık [oo-yanuhk] awake; vigilant; sharp; smart

uyanmak to wake up

uydurma şeyler [oo-idoorma shayler] rubbish

uygun [oo-igoon] convenient; appropriate; reasonable; just right

uykuda [oo-ikooda] asleep

uyku ilacı [oo-ikoo eelajuh] sleeping pill

uykulu [oo-ikooloo] sleepy

uykusu gelmiş [oo-ikoosoo gelmeesh] sleepy

uykusuzluk [oo-ikoosoozlook] insomnia

uyku tulumu [oo-ikoo] sleeping bag

uyluk [oo-ilook] thigh

uyruk [oo-irook] nationality

... uyruğu [oo-iroo-oo] ... nationality

uyudunuz: iyi uyudunuz mu? [oo-yoodoonooz] did you sleep well?

uyumak [oo-yoomak] to sleep

uyuşturucu [oo-yooshtooroojoo] drug, narcotics

-uz we are

uzak far

  uzakta in the distance

uzak dur keep out; keep away

uzaklık [oozakluhk] distance

uzanmak to lie down

uzatma kablosu extension lead

uzun long

uzun boylu tall

uzunluk length

uzun süre [sewreh] a long time

Ü

-ü [-ew] accusative noun ending

ücret [ewjret] cost; pay; fee; wage

ücretler [ewjretler] charges; wages

ücretsiz giriş admission free

üç [ewch] three

üçüncü [ewchewnjew] third

üçüncü kat third floor, (US) fourth floor

ülke [ewlkeh] country, nation

ülser [ewlser] ulcer

-üm [-ewm] my; I am

-ümüz [-ewmewz] our

-ün [-ewn] of; your

üniversite [ewnee-verseeteh] university

ünlü [ewnlew] famous

-ünüz [-ewnewz] your

üst [ewst] top

üst bagaj yeri [bagaJ] roof rack

üst kat upper floor; upstairs; top floor

üstte [ewstteh] at the top

üstünde [ewstewndeh] on; above; over

  ...-in üstünde on top of ...

üstünü değiştirmek [ewstewnew deh-eeshteermek] to get changed

üşümek [ewshewmek] to feel cold

üşütmek [ewsewtmek] to catch cold

ütü [ewtew] iron

ütülemek [ewtewlemek] to iron

üvey anne [ewvay anneh] stepmother

üvey baba stepfather

-üz [-ewz] we are
üzere [ewzereh] in order to;
just about to
üzerinden [ewzereenden] via;
from the top of
üzgün [ewzgewn] sad
üzgünüm [ewzgewnewm] I'm
sorry

V

vadi valley
vagon carriage, coach
vagon restoran dining car
vajina [vaJeena] vagina
vakıf [vakuhf] Islamic
religious foundation
vakit time
vali governor
valide sultan [valeedeh] sultan's
mother
valiz suitcase
vana valve
Van Gölü [gurlew] Lake Van
vantilatör [vanteelatur] fan
(electrical)
vantilatör kayışı [kī-uhshuh]
fanbelt
vapur steamer; passenger
ferry
vapur gezisi cruise
var there is, there are
... var mı? [muh] is there/
are there ...?; do you
have...?
ne var? [neh] what is it?;
what's the matter?
varış [varuhsh] arrival

varış istasyonu destination
varış saati [sa-atee] time of
arrival
varmak: -e varmak [-eh] to
arrive
varyete [var-yeteh] floor show,
variety show
vatan motherland
vay anasını! [vī anasuhnuh] I'll
be damned!
vay canına! [vī januhna] I'll be
damned!
vazo vase
ve [veh] and
vejetaryen [veJetar-yen]
vegetarian
veresiye verilmez no credit
allowed
vergi tax
vermek to give
vestiyer cloakroom
veteriner vet
veya [vay-a] or
vezne [vezneh] cash desk, till;
cashier
veznedar cashier
vida screw
video (aleti) video recorder
video kamera camcorder
vilayet [voolī ot] province
... Vilayeti Province of ...
vilayet konağı [kona-uh]
provincial headquarters
building
viraj [veeraJ] bend
vites gears
vites kolu gear lever
vites kutusu gearbox
vitrin shop window

vitrinde [veetreend**eh**] in the window

vize [**vee**zeh] visa

vizör [veez**ur**] viewfinder

voltaj [**vol**ta**J**] voltage

vurmak to knock; to hit; to shoot

vurunuz knock

vücut [vew**joot**] body

Y

ya or

ya! oh!; really?

-ya to

-'ya to

yabanarısı [yab**a**naruhsuh] wasp

yabancı [yaban**juh**] foreign; foreigner; stranger

yabancı dil kılavuzu [kuhlavooz**oo**] phrasebook

yabani wild

yafta placard; label; poster

yağ [ya] fat; oil

yağlı [ya-l**uh**] greasy

yağlı güreş [gewr**esh**] Turkish wrestling

yağmak [ya-m**ak**] to rain

yağmur [ya-m**oor**] rain

yağmurda in the rain

yağmur yağıyor [ya-uh-y**or**] it's raining

yağmurluk [ya-moorl**ook**] raincoat

yağ seviyesi oil level

Yahudi Jew; Jewish

yaka collar

yakalamak to catch; to arrest

yakın [yak**uh**n] near

...-e yakın [-eh] near to ...

en yakın ... the nearest ...

yakında [yakuhnd**a**] soon; nearby; recently

yakınında [yak**uh**nuhnd**a**] near

yakışıklı [yak**uh**-shuhkl**uh**] handsome

yakıt deposu [yak**uh**t] tank

yaklaşık [yaklash**uhk**] about, approximately

yaklaşmak: -e yaklaşmak [-eh yaklashm**ak**] to approach

yakmak to burn

yalanlamak to deny

yalan söylemek [suh-ilem**ek**] to lie, to tell a lie

yalı [yal**uh**] waterside residence

yalnız [yaln**uh**z] just, only; alone

yalnız biraz just a little

yalnız burada just here

yalnız başıma [bashuhm**a**] by myself

yalnız başına [bashuhn**a**] by yourself

yalnız gidiş [geed**ee**sh] single journey

yan side

yanak cheek

yangın [yang**uh**n] fire

yangın var! fire!

yangın alarmı [alarm**uh**] fire alarm

yangın çıkışı [chuhkuhsh**uh**] emergency exit; fire exit

yangın merdiveni fire escape

yangın söndürme cihazı [surndewrm**eh** jeehaz**uh**] fire extinguisher

yanık [yan**uhk**] (switched) on; burn

yanında [yan**uh**nda] beside

yanıt [yan**uht**] answer

yanıtlamak [yan**uh**tlamak] to answer

yanıyor [yanuh-**yor**] it's on fire

yani that is to say

yankesici [yankeseej**ee**] pickpocket

yanlış [yan**luh**sh] wrong; mistake

yanlış anlama misunderstanding

yanlış numara wrong number

yanmak to burn

yanmış [yan**muh**sh] burnt

yapı [yap**uh**] building

yapma artificial
  yapma! don't!
  yapma be!? [beh] really?

yapmak to do; to make

yaprak leaf

yar cliff

yara wound

yaralı [yaral**uh**] injured

yararlı [yararl**uh**] useful; helpful

yardım [yard**uh**m] help

yardım etmek to help

yarı [yar**uh**] half

yarı fiyat half-price

yarım [yar**uh**m] half
  yarım düzine [dewzeen**eh**] half a dozen

yarım saat [sa-**at**] half an hour

yarım pansiyon half board

yarım tarife [tareef**eh**] half fare

yarın [yar**uh**n] tomorrow

yarın sabah [sabaH] tomorrow morning

yarın görüşürüz [gurewshewr**ewz**] see you tomorrow

yarış [yar**uh**sh] race (competition)

yasa law

yasak forbidden

yasak bölge restricted zone

yasaktır not allowed

yastık [yast**uh**k] pillow; cushion

yastık kılıfı [kuhluhf**uh**] pillow case

yaş [yash] age

yaşamak [yashamak] to live

yaşlı [yashl**uh**] old

yaşlılar [yashluhl**ar**] old people

yat yacht

yatak bed

yatakhane [yalakhan**eh**] dormitory

yataklı vagon [yatakl**uh**] sleeping car

yatak odası [odas**uh**] bedroom

yatak takımı [takuhm**uh**] bed linen

yatmak to lie down; to go to bed

yavaş [yav**ash**] slow; quiet
  yavaş! slow down!
  çok yavaş [chok] very slowly

yavaşça [yavash-cha] slowly

yavaş git go slow

yavaş vasıta şeridi crawler lane

yay [yī] spring

ya ... ya ... either ... or ...

yaya [yī-a] pedestrian; on foot

yaya geçidi [gecheedee] pedestrian crossing

yaya giremez no entry for pedestrians

yayalar pedestrians

yayalara mahsus bölge [yī-alara – burlgeh] pedestrian precinct

yayan [yī-an] on foot

yaz summer

yazın [yazuhn] in the summer

yazık [yazuhk] pity; it's a pity
ne yazık! [neh] what a shame!

yazı kâğıdı [yazuh ka-uhduh] writing paper

yazı makinesi typewriter

yazmak to write

-ye [-yeh] to

-'ye to

yedek spare; reserve; standby

yedek depo spare tank

yedek lastik spare tyre

yedek parça [parcha] spare part

yedi seven

yedinci [yedeenjee] seventh

yeğen [yeh-en] nephew; niece

yelek waistcoat

yelken sail

yelkencilik [yelkenjeeleek] sailing

yelkenli sailing boat

yelkenli sörf [surf] windsurfing; sailboard

yelkenliyle gezmek [yelkenlee-ileh] to sail

yelpaze [yelpazeh] fan (handheld)

yemek to eat; meal; dish; food

yemeklerden önce [urnjeh] before meals

yemeklerden sonra after meals

yemekli vagon buffet car, restaurant car

yemek salonu dining room

yemek takımları [takuhmlaruh] crockery

yemek tarifi recipe

yen sleeve

yenge [yengeh] sister-in-law (brother's wife); uncle's wife

yeni new

Yeni Yıl [yuhl] New Year
Yeni Yılınız Kutlu Olsun! [yuhluhnuhz] Happy New Year!

Yeni Zelanda New Zealand

Yeni Zelandalı [zelandaluh] New Zealander

yepyeni brand new

yer place; seat; ground; floor

yerde [yerdeh] on the floor; on the ground

yeraltı şehri [shehree] underground city

yer ayırtmak [ī-uhrtmak] to book, to reserve
yerel local
yerel konuşma [konooshma] local call
yerfıstığı [yerfuhstuh-**uh**] peanuts
yerine [yereen**eh**] instead of
yerleşmek [yerleshmek] to check in; to settle
yosaltı mezarı [yesalt**uh** mezar**uh**] catacomb
yeşil [yesheel] green
yeşil kart [yesheel] green card
yeter enough, sufficient
bu kadar yeter that's enough
yeterince [yetereenj**eh**] enough; sufficiently
yetişkin [yeteesh-keen] adult
yetişkinler [yeteeshkeenler] adults
yetmez insufficient
yetmiş [yetmeesh] seventy
-yı [-yuh] accusative noun ending
yıkamak [yuhkamak] to wash
yıkama ve mizanpli [yuhkama veh] wash and set
yıkanmak [yuhkanmak] to have a wash, to get washed
yıl [yuhl] year
yılan [yuhlan] snake
Yılbaşı (Gecesi) [yuhlbash**uh** (gejes**ee**)] New Year's Eve
yıldırım telgraf [yuhlduhr**uh**m] express telegram
yıldız [yuhld**uhz**] star
yıldönümü [yuhlduhrnewm**ew**] anniversary

-yım [-yuhm] I am
-yız [-yuhz] we are
-yi accusative noun ending
-yim I am
yine [yeen**eh**] (once) again; still
yirmi twenty
yitirmek to lose
yiyecek [yee-yejek] food
-yiz we are
yoğun bakım ünitesi [yo-**oon** bak**uh**m ewneetesee] intensive care unit
yok no; there isn't; there's none (left)
... yok there isn't any ...
yok be! [beh] really!
yok canım? [jan**uh**m] really?
yoksa otherwise
yol road; route; path; way
yolcu [yolj**oo**] passenger
yolcular passengers
yolculuk [yoljool**ook**] trip; journey
yolcu otobüsü [yolj**oo** otobews**ew**] coach
yolcu salonu passenger lounge
yolda çalışma roadworks
yol hakkı right of way
yol inşaatı roadworks
yol kapalı road closed
yollamak to send
yol ver give way
yorgan duvet; quilt
yorgun tired
yorgunluktan bitmiş [beetmeesh] very tired, shattered

yosun seaweed
yön [yurn] direction
yönetici [yurneteejee] manager
yönetici bayan [bi-an] manageress
-yu accusative noun ending
yukarı [yookaruh] up
yukarıda [yookaruhda] at the top; above; upstairs; up there
-yum I am
yumuşak [yoomooshak] soft
yumuşak kontak lensleri soft lenses
Yunan Greek (adj)
Yunanistan Greece
Yunanca [yoonanja] Ancient Greek
Yunanlı [yoonanluh] Greek (man)
Yunanlı kadın [kaduhn] Greek (woman)
yurdumda at home (in my country)
yurt home; homeland; student housing; hostel
yurtdışı [yoortduhshuh] abroad
yurt dışında [duh-shuhnda] abroad
yurtdışı posta ücretleri [yoortduhshuh – ewjretleree] overseas postage rates
yurtiçi [yoorteechee] inland
yurtiçi posta ücretleri [ewjretleree] inland postal rates
yutmak to swallow
yuvarlak round
-yuz we are

-yü [-yew] accusative noun ending
yüksek [yewksek] tall, high
yükseklik [yewksekleek] height
yüksek sesle [sesleh] loud
yüksek tansiyon high blood pressure
-yüm [-yewm] I am
yün [yewn] wool
yünlü [yewnlew] woollen
yürümek [yewrewmek] to walk
yürüyüş [yewrew-yewsh] walk; walking
yürüyüşe çıkmak [yewrew-yewsheh chuhmak] to go for a walk
yüz [yewz] face; surface; hundred
-yüz [-yewz] we are
yüzde [yewzdeh] per cent
yüzde yüz 100 per cent
yüz kremi cold cream
yüz losyonu toner
yüzme [yewzmeh] swimming
yüzmeye gitmek [yewzmayeh] to go swimming
yüzme havuzu swimming pool
yüzmek [yewzmek] to swim
yüzmek yasaktır no swimming
yüz numara toilet
yüzük [yewzewk] ring
yüzyıl [yewz-yuhl] century

Z

zam increase
zaman time; when
  zaman? when?
  o zaman then, at that time
  zaman zaman from time to
  time
zamk glue
zarar damage
zararı yok [zararuh] never
  mind
zarar vermek to damage
zarf envelope
zarif elegant
zaruri essential, necessary
zaten anyway
zatürree [zatewrreh]
  pneumonia
zaviye [zavee-yeh] lodge for
  dervishes
zayıf [zī-uhf] slim; thin;
  weak
zehir poison
zehirli poisonous
zeki intelligent
zemin kat ground floor, (US)
  first floor
zengin rich
zevkli enjoyable; pleasant;
  amusing
zil bell
zincir [zeenjeer] chain
ziyan loss; damage; harm
ziyaret visit
ziyaret etmek to visit
zor hard, difficult
zorluk difficulty

zurna reed instrument like
  an oboe
zücaciye [zewjajee-yeh]
  glassware

Menu
Reader:
Food

Essential Terms

appetizers meze [mez**eh**]
cup fincan [feenjan]
dessert tatlı [tatl**uh**]
fork çatal [chat**a**l]
glass (tumbler) bardak
   (wine glass) kadeh
knife bıçak [b**uh**ch**a**k]
meat dishes et yemekleri
menu yemek listesi
pepper biber
plate tabak
salad salata
salt tuz
set menu tabldot [tabld**o**t]
soup çorba [chorb**a**]
spoon kaşık [kash**uh**k]
starter (food) ordövr [ord**u**rvr], meze [mez**eh**]
table masa

another ... başka bir ... [b**a**shka]
excuse me! (to call waiter/waitress) bakar mısınız! [muhsuhn**uh**z]
could I have the bill, please? hesap, lütfen [l**ew**tfen]

The Turkish Alphabet

This section is in Turkish alphabetical order:

a, b, c, ç, d, e, f, g, ğ, h, ı, i, j, k, l, m, n, o, ö, p, r, s, ş, t, u, ü, v, y, z

acı biber [aj**uh**] hot chillies
Adana kebabı [kebab**uh**] spicy
  meatballs
ahtapot [a**H**tapot] octopus
ahtapot salatası [salatas**uh**]
  octopus salad
ahududu [a**H**oodoodoo]
  raspberries
akıtma [akuhtma] pancake
akşam yemeği [aksham yemeh-
  ee] evening meal
alabalık [alabal**uh**k] trout
ananas pineapple
ançüez [anchew-ez]
  anchovies
armut pear
Arnavut ciğeri [jee-**er**ee] spicy
  fried liver with onions
aşure [ashoor**eh**] 'Noah's
  pudding' – a dessert made
  from wheat grains, nuts and
  dried fruit
av eti game
ayşekadın fasulyesi
  [ishekad**uh**n] French beans
ayva [**i**va] quince
ayva laabı [la-ab**uh**] quince
  jelly
ayva reçeli [rechel**ee**] quince
  jam
az pişmiş [peeshm**ee**sh] rare;
  underdone

badem almond(s)
badem kurabiyesi macaroons;
  giant almond biscuits/
  cookies
badempare [–par**eh**] almond
  cakes in syrup

badem tatlısı [tatluhs**uh**]
  almond cakes
baharat spice
baharatlı [baharatl**uh**] spicy
bakla broad beans
baklava pastry filled with
  nuts and syrup
bal honey
balık [bal**uh**k] fish
balık buğulaması [boo-
  oolamas**uh**] fish baked with
  tomatoes
balık çorbası [chorbas**uh**] fish
  and lemon soup
balık köftesi [kurftes**ee**] fish
  balls
balık pane [pan**eh**] fish
  coated in breadcrumbs and
  fried
balık plaki fish baked with
  potatoes, carrots, celery and
  onions
bamya okra, ladies' fingers
barbunya red mullet; a type
  of red bean
barbunya pilakisi beans
  cooked in olive oil and
  served hot or cold
barbunya tava fried red
  mullet
bazlama flat bread cooked
  on a hotplate
beyaz peynir [bay**a**z payn**ee**r]
  white sheep's cheese,
  similar to Greek feta
beyaz peynirli makarna
  noodles with sheep's cheese
beyin salatası [bay**ee**n salatas**uh**]
  brain salad

beyin tava brain slices in batter

beykın [**bay**kuhn] bacon

bezelye [be**ze**lyeh] peas

bıldırcın ızgara [buhlduhrj**uh**n uh**zgara**] grilled quail

bıldırcın yahni quail stew with onions

biber pepper(s), capsicum(s)

biber dolması [dolmas**uh**] stuffed green peppers/capsicums

biftek steak

bir buçuk [booch**ook**] a portion and a half

bisküvi [beeskew-**vee**] biscuits, cookies

bonfile [**bon**feeleh] fillet steak

böbrek [**bur**brek] kidneys

böbrek ızgara [uh**zgara**] grilled kidneys

böbrek sote [sot**eh**] sautéed kidneys

böğürtlen [bur-**ewrt**len] blackberries

börek [bur-**rek**] layered pastry with cheese, meat or spinach filling

börülce [burewlj**eh**] black-eyed beans

Brüksel lahanası [**brewk**sel laHanas**uh**] Brussels sprouts

buğulama [boo-oolama] steamed; poached

bulgur bulgur wheat, cracked wheat

bulgur pilavı [peelav**uh**] bulgur wheat cooked with tomatoes

Bursa kebabı [kebab**uh**] grilled lamb kebab on pitta bread with tomato sauce and yoghurt

bülbül yuvası [bewlbewl yoovas**uh**] dessert with nuts and syrup

cacık [jaj**uhk**] cucumber, garlic and yoghurt dip

caneriği [janeree-**ee**] greengage

ceviz [jev**eez**] walnuts

cezeriye [jezeree-**yeh**] carrot, honey and nut bar

ciğer [jee-**er**] liver

ciğer sarması [sarmas**uh**] minced liver wrapped in lamb's fat

ciğer tava fried liver

çam fıstığı [cham fuhst**uh**-uh] pine nuts

çavdar ekmeği [chavdar ekm**eh**-ee] rye bread

çerez [**cher**ez] pumpkin seeds, chickpeas, almonds etc served in bars

Çerkez peyniri [cherkez payn**eeree**] cheese similar to Edam

Çerkez tavuğu [tav**oo**-oo] cold chicken in walnut sauce with garlic

çeşni veren otlar [chesh**nee**] herbs

çevirme [cheveerm**eh**] spit-roasted

çılbır [chuhlb**uhr**] poached

eggs with yoghurt

çift porsiyon [cheeft] double portion

çiğ köfte [chee kurfteh] raw meatballs made from minced meat, bulgur wheat and chilli powder

çikolata [cheekolata] chocolate

çikolatalı [cheekolataluh] with chocolate

çikolatalı dondurma chocolate ice cream

çikolatalı pasta chocolate cake

çilek [cheelek] strawberry

çilekli dondurma [cheeleklee] strawberry ice cream

çilek reçeli [rechelee] strawberry jam

çips [cheeps] crisps, (US) potato chips

çipura [cheepoora] gilt-headed bream

çiroz [cheeroz] salted dried mackerel

çoban salatası [choban salatasuh] mixed tomatoes, peppers/capsicums, cucumbers and onion salad

çocuk porsiyonu [chojook] children's portion

çorba [chorba] soup

çöp kebabı [churp kebabuh] small pieces of lamb or offal grilled on wooden skewers

çörek [chur-rek] sweet or savoury bun

çulluk [choollook] woodcock

dana eti veal

dana rozbif roast veal

deniz ürünleri [ewrewnleree] seafood

dereotu [dereh-otoo] dill

dil tongue

dil balığı [baluh-uh] sole

dilber dudağı [dooda-uh] sweet pastry with nut filling

dil peyniri [payneeree] cheese similar to mozzarella

dolma stuffed vegetables

domates tomato(es)

domatesli with tomatoes

domatesli pilav rice cooked with tomatoes

domatesli pirinç çorbası [peereench chorbasuh] rice and tomato soup

domates salatası [salatasuh] tomato salad

domates salçalı patlıcan kızartması [salchaluh patluhjan kuhzartmasuh] fried aubergines/eggplants with tomato and garlic sauce

domates salçası [salchasun] tomato purée

domuz eti pork

dondurma ice cream

döner kebap [durner] lamb grilled on a spit and served in thin slices, usually served with rice and salad

dövme dondurma [durvmeh] special type of sticky ice cream

dut [doot] mulberries

düğün çorbası [dew-**ew**n chorbas**uh**] 'wedding soup' made from meat stock, yoghurt and egg

ekmek bread

ekmek kadayıfı [kadϊ-uhf**uh**] sweet pastry

ekşi [eksh**ee**] sour

elma apple(s)

elmalı tart [elmal**uh**] apple pie

elma tatlısı [tatluhs**uh**] dessert made with apples

enginar [engee**nar**] artichoke(s)

erik plum(s)

erişte [ereesht**eh**] homemade noodles

et meat

etli with meat

etli ayşekadın [ϊshehkad**uh**n] meat with green beans

etli bezelye [bezelyeh] pea and meat stew

etli biber dolması [dolmas**uh**] peppers/capsicums stuffed with rice and meat

etli börek [bur-**rek**] meat pie

etli bulgur pilavı [peelav**uh**] bulgur wheat with meat

etli domates dolması [dolmas**uh**] tomatoes stuffed with meat and rice

etli kabak dolması marrows stuffed with meat and rice

etli kapuska cabbage and meat stew

etli kuru fasulye [fas**oo**lyeh] lamb and haricot beans in tomato sauce

etli lahana dolması [la**ʜ**ana dolmas**uh**] cabbage leaves stuffed with meat and rice

etli nohut chickpea and meat stew

etli taze fasulye [taz**eh** fas**oo**lyeh] stew of meat, runner beans, tomatoes and onions

etli yaprak dolması [dolmas**uh**] vine leaves stuffed with rice and meat

et sote [sot**eh**] sautéed meat

et suyu meat stock

ezme [ezm**eh**] purée

ezo gelin çorbası [chorbas**uh**] lentil and rice soup

fasulye [fas**oo**lyeh] haricot beans

fasulye pilaki(si) haricot beans cooked in olive oil

fasulye piyazı [pee-yaz**uh**] haricot bean and onion salad

fava broad bean purée

fındık [fuhnd**uh**k] nuts; hazelnuts

fındık fıstık [fuhst**uh**k] nuts

fırın [fuhr**uh**n] baked; oven-roasted

fırında [fuhruhnda] baked; oven-roasted

fırın sütlaç [sewt**la**ch] baked rice pudding

fıstık [fuhst**uh**k] peanuts; pine nuts

fıstıklı [fuhstuhkl**uh**] with pistachio nuts

fıstıklı dondurma [fuhstuhkl**uh**] pistachio ice cream

fıstıklı muhallebi rice flour and rosewater pudding with pistachio nuts

fileto fillet

füme [fewm**eh**] smoked

garnitür salata [garneet**ewr**] side salad

gözleme [gurzlem**eh**] crêpe-like bread with various toppings; pancake

greyfrut grapefruit

güllaç [gewll**ach**] rice wafers filled with nuts, cooked in rose-flavoured milky syrup

gümüş balığı [gew-m**ew**sh baluh-**uh**] silverfish

güveç [gew-v**ech**] meat and vegetable casserole

güvercin [gew-ver**jeen**] pigeon

hamsi anchovy

hanım parmağı [han**uhm** parma-uh] 'Lady's Fingers' – finger-shaped pastry sticks in syrup

hardal mustard

has ekmek white bread

haşlama [hashlam**a**] boiled; stewed

haşlanmış yumurta [hashlanm**uh**sh] boiled egg

havuç [hav**ooch**] carrot(s)

havuç salatası [salatas**uh**] grated carrot salad

havyar caviar

haydari [h**i**dar**ee**] thick garlic dip with parsley or spinach

hazır yemek [haz**uhr**] ready-to-eat food

helva baked flour, butter, sugar and flavoured water with various fillings like tahini paste

hesap bill, (US) check

hıyar [huh-y**ar**] cucumber

hindi turkey

hindiba wild chicory

hindi dolması [dolmas**uh**] stuffed turkey

hindistan cevizi [jeveez**ee**] coconut

hoşaf [hosh**af**] stewed fruit

höşmerim [hurshmer**eem**] cheese helva

hurma dates

hünkar beğendi [hewnkar beh-end**ee**] 'Sultan's Delight' – lamb served with aubergine/eggplant purée

ıspanak [uhspan**ak**] spinach

ıspanaklı börek [uhspanakl**uh** bur-**rek**] pastry filled with spinach

ıspanaklı yumurta eggs with spinach

ıstakoz [uhstak**oz**] lobster; crayfish

ızgara [uhzgar**a**] grilled

ızgara balık [bal**uh**k] grilled fish

ızgarada grilled

ızgara köfte [kurfteh] grilled meatballs

... ızgarası [uhzgarasuh] grilled ...

ızgara tavuk [uhzgara] grilled chicken

ızgara yemek meat dishes grilled to order

iç [eech] filling

içecek [eechejek] beverage

içli köfte [eechlee kurfteh] meatballs stuffed with bulgur wheat

iç pilav [eech] rice with currants, pine nuts and onions

imam bayıldı [bī-uhlduh] 'Imam Swoons' – aubergine/eggplant with tomatoes and onions, cooked with olive oil and eaten cold

incir [eenjeer] figs

irmik helvası [helvasuh] semolina helva – sweet made from semolina, nuts, butter and sugar

islim kebabı [kebabuh] steamed kebab

istavrit horse mackerel

istiridye [eesteereed-yeh] oyster(s)

işkembe çorbası [eeshkembeh chorbasuh] tripe soup

İskender kebabı [eeshkender kebabuh] döner kebab on pitta bread with tomato sauce and yoghurt

iyi pişmiş [peeshmeesh] well-done; well-cooked

jambon [Jambon] ham

jelatin [Jelateen] gelatin

kabak courgette, zucchini; pumpkin; marrow

kabak dolması [dolmasuh] stuffed courgettes/zucchini

kabak kızartması [kuhzartmasuh] fried marrows

kabak reçeli [rechelee] marrow jam

kabak tatlısı [tatluhsuh] pumpkin with syrup and walnuts

kabuklu deniz ürünleri [ewrewnleree] shellfish

kadayıf [kada-yuhf] shredded wheat-type dessert in syrup

kadın budu köfte [kaduhn – kurfteh] 'Lady's Thighs' – meat and rice croquettes

kadın göbeği [gurbeh-ee] 'Lady's Navel' – a ring-shaped pastry with syrup

kağıt kebabı [ka-uht kebabuh] lamb and vegetables baked in paper

kağıtta barbunya [ka-uhtta] red mullet baked in paper

kağıtta pişmiş [peeshmeesh] baked in paper

kahvaltı [kahvaltuh] breakfast

kalamar squid

kalamar tava fried squid

kalkan turbot

kara biber black pepper

karadut black mulberries
kara ekmek brown bread
karagöz [karagurz] black
bream
kara turp horseradish
kara zeytin [zayteen] black
olives
karışık [karuhshuhk] mixed
karışık dondurma [karuhshuhk]
mixed ice cream
karışık ızgara [uhzgara] mixed
grill
karışık salata mixed salad
karides prawns
karides güveç [gewvech]
prawn stew
karides kokteyl [koktayl]
prawn cocktail
karides tava prawns in batter
karides tavası [tavasuh]
prawns in batter
karnabahar cauliflower
karnabahar tavası [tavasuh]
fried cauliflower
karnıyarık [karnuh-yaruhk] split
aubergine/eggplant with
meat filling
karper peyniri [payneeree]
processed cheese, cheese
spread
karpuz water melon
kaşar (peyniri) [kashar
payneeree] mild yellow
cheese
kaşar peynirli makarna
noodles with kaşar
kavun honeydew melon
kavunlu dondurma melon ice
cream

kayısı [kī-uhsuh] apricot(s)
kayısı reçeli [rechelee] apricot
jam
kaymak [kī-mak] clotted
cream
kaymaklı [kīmakluh] with
clotted cream
kaymaklı dondurma dairy ice
cream
kaynamış yumurta [kīnamuhsh]
boiled egg
kaz goose
kazan dibi pudding with a
caramel base
kebap roast meat, kebab
keçi eti [kechee] goat's meat
keçi peyniri [payneeree] goat's
cheese
kefal grey mullet
kefal pilakisi mullet cooked
in olive oil with
vegetables
kek cake
keklik partridge
Kemalpaşa [kemalpasha]
syrup-soaked dumpling
kepekli ekmek bread made
from whole bran
kerevit crayfish
kereviz celery
kestane [kestanoh] chestnut(s)
kestane şekeri [shekeree]
marrons glacés, candied
chestnuts
keş [kesh] dry curd cheese
keşkek [keshkek] lamb with
bulgur wheat
keşkül [keshkewl] almond
pudding

ketçap [ketchap] tomato ketchup

kılıç (balığı) [kuhluhch (baluh-uh)] swordfish

kılıç ızgara [uhzgara] grilled swordfish

kılıç şiş [sheesh] swordfish on skewers

kırmızı biber [kuhrmuhzuh] paprika; red pepper, capsicum

kırmızı mercimek çorbası [merjeemek chorbasuh] red lentil soup

kırmızı turp radish

kısır [kuhsuhr] bulgur wheat salad with spring onions, green pepper/capsicum and tomatoes

kış türlüsü [kuhsh tewrlewsew] stewed winter vegetables

kıvırcık salata [kuhvuhrjuhk] lettuce

kıyma [kuh-ima] minced meat

kıymalı [kuh-imaluh] with minced meat

kıymalı bamya okra with minced meat

kıymalı ıspanak [uhspanak] spinach with minced meat

kıymalı karnabahar cauliflower with minced meat

kıymalı makarna noodles with minced meat

kıymalı mercimek [merjeemek] minced meat and lentils

kıymalı pide [peedeh] flat bread with minced meat topping

kıymalı yumurta eggs with minced meat

kızarmış [kuhzarmuhsh] fried; toasted; grilled

kızarmış ekmek [kuhzarmuhsh] toast

kızartma [kuhzartma] fried; broiled

kiraz cherries

kiremitte balık [keeremeetteh baluhk] fish baked on a tile

koç yumurtası [koch yoomoortasuh] ram's testicles

kokoreç [kokorech] lamb's intestines grilled on a spit

kolyoz chub mackerel

komposto fruit compote

koyun (eti) mutton

köfte [kurfteh] meat balls or patties

köpek balığı [kurpek baluh-uh] shark

krema cream

kremalı mantar [kremaluh] mushrooms with cream

kremalı pasta cream cake

krem karamel crème caramel

krem şantiye [shantee-yeh] whipped cream

krik krak cracker

kupes type of sea bream

kurabiye [koorabee-yeh] cake with almonds or nuts

kuru dried

kuru fasulye [fasoolyeh]

haricot beans in tomato
sauce
kuru köfte [kurfteh] fried
meatballs
kuru üzüm [ewzewm] raisins
kuru yemiş [yemeesh] dried
fruit and nuts
kuskus pilavı [peelavuh]
couscous – semolina grains
with a meat stew
kuşbaşı et [koosh-bashuh] small
pieces of meat
kuşkonmaz [kooshkonmaz]
asparagus
kuzu (eti) lamb
kuzu fırında [fuhruhnda] roast
leg of lamb
kuzu kapama lamb stew with
lettuce and carrots
kuzu pirzolası [peerzolasuh]
lamb chops
külbastı grilled cutlet
**kümes hayvanları [kewmes
hïvanlaruh]** poultry

lahana [laHana] cabbage
lahana dolması [dolmasuh]
stuffed cabbage leaves
lahana turşusu [toorshoosoo]
pickled cabbage
lahmacun [laHmajoon] kind of
pizza with spicy meat
topping
lakerda pickled tuna fish
leblebi roasted chickpeas
levrek sea bass
limon lemon
limonlu dondurma lemon ice
cream

lokum Turkish Delight
lop yumurta hard-boiled
egg
lüfer [lewfer] bluefish

makarna macaroni; noodles;
pasta
mama baby food
mandalina tangerine
mantar mushroom(s)
mantarlı omlet [mantarluh]
mushroom omelette
mantı [mantuh] similar to
ravioli
**Maraş dondurması [marash
dondurmasuh]** type of ice
cream
margarin margarine
marmelat jam
marul cos lettuce
maydanoz [mïdanoz] parsley
mayonez [mï-onez]
mayonnaise
mayonezli balık [baluhk] fish
with mayonnaise
menemen omelette with
tomatoes and peppers/
capsicums
mercan [merjan] bream
mercimek [merjeemek] lentils
mercimok çorbası [chorbasuh]
lentil soup
mersin balığı [baluh-uh]
sturgeon
mevsim salatası [salatasuh]
seasonal salad
meyve [mayveh] fruit
meyveli pay [mayvelee pï] fruit
pie

meze [mezeh] hors d'œuvres, appetizers

mezgit whitebait

mısır [muhsuhr] corn

midye [meed-yeh] mussels

midye dolması [dolmasuh] stuffed mussels

midyeli pilav rice with mussels

midye pilakisi mussels cooked in oil with vegetables

midye tava/tavası [tavasuh] deep-fried mussels

misket limonu lime

muhallebi pudding made from rice flour and rosewater

musakka moussaka

muska böreği [bur-reh-ee] triangular pastries filled with cheese and parsley

Mustafakemalpaşa [–pasha] syrup-soaked dumpling

muz banana

mücver [mewjver] vegetable patties

nane [naneh] mint

nar pomegranate

nemse böreği [nemseh bur-reh-ee] meat pie made with puff pastry

nohut chickpeas

nohutlu paça [pacha] lamb's trotters with chickpeas

nohutlu yahni lamb stew with chickpeas

omlet omelette

ordövr [ordurvr] starter, hors d'œuvre

orfoz giant grouper

orman kebabı [kebabuh] veal or lamb, fried then cooked with vegetables

orta pişmiş [peeshmeesh] medium-rare

otlu peynir [payneer] herb-flavoured cheese from around Lake Van

öğle yemeği [urleh yemeh-ee] lunch

ördek [urdek] duck

paça [pacha] lamb's trotters

paça çorbası [chorbasuh] lamb's trotter soup

palamut tunny fish

pancar [panjar] beetroot

pancar turşusu [toorshoosoo] pickled beetroot

pandispanya sponge cake

pane [paneh] coated in breadcrumbs and fried

papaz eriği [eree-ee] green plum

parça [parcha] piece, slice

paskalya çöreği [chureh-ee] 'Easter bread' – slightly sweet plait-shaped bread

pasta cake

pastırma [pastuhrma] beef cured with cumin and garlic

pastırmalı yumurta [pastuhrmaluh] fried eggs

with 'pastırma'

patates potato(es)

patates kızartması [kuhzartmas**uh**] chips, French fries

patates köftesi [kurftes**ee**] potato and cheese balls

patatesli with potatoes

patates püresi [pewres**ee**] mashed potatoes

patates salatası [sal**a**tasuh] potato salad

patlıcan [patluhj**a**n] aubergine(s), eggplant(s)

patlıcan dolma turşusu [toorshoos**oo**] pickled stuffed aubergines/eggplants

patlıcan ezmesi aubergine/eggplant pâté

patlıcan kebabı [kebab**uh**] pieces of meat wrapped in aubergine/eggplant and roasted or baked

patlıcan kızartması [kuhzartmas**uh**] fried aubergines/eggplants with garlic sauce

patlıcanlı pilav [patluhjanl**uh**] rice with aubergines/ eggplants

patlıcan salatası [sal**a**tasuh] aubergine/eggplant purée

pavurya crab

pestil pressed dried fruit

peynir [payn**ee**r] cheese

peynirli with cheese

peynirli omlet cheese omelette

peynirli pide [peed**eh**] flat bread with cheese topping

peynirli tepsi böreği [bur**eh**-ee] cheese pie

peynir tatlısı [tatluhs**uh**] small cheesecakes in syrup

pırasa [puhr**a**sa] leek(s)

pide [peed**eh**] leavened flat bread

pilaki haricot bean vinaigrette

pilav cooked rice

pilavlı tavuk [peelavl**uh**] chicken and rice

pil füme [fewm**eh**] smoked tongue

piliç [peel**ee**ch] young chicken

piliç ızgara(sı) [uhzg**a**ra(suh)] grilled chicken

pirinç [peer**ee**nch] rice (uncooked)

pirzola chop

pisi plaice

pişkin [peeshk**ee**n] well-cooked, well-done

pişmemiş [p**ee**shmemeesh] underdone; not cooked

poğaça [po-**a**cha] pastries filled with meat or cheese

portakal orange(s)

portakallı ördek [portakall**uh** urd**ek**] duck with orange

portakal reçeli [rechel**ee**] marmalade, orange jam

puf böreği [bur-r**eh**-ee] cheese or meat pasties

püre [pewr**eh**] purée

rafadan (yumurta) soft-boiled egg

reçel [rechel] jam
revani sweet semolina
  pastry
roka rocket
rosto roasted
rozbif roast beef
rus salatası [salatasuh]
  Russian salad – potatoes,
  peas, salami and gherkins
  with mayonnaise

saç kavurma [sach] Anatolian
  speciality made from meat,
  vegetables, spices and oil,
  fried in a Turkish wok
sade omlet [sa-deh] plain
  omelette
sade pilav plain rice pilav
sahanda yumurta fried eggs
salam salami
salata salad
salatalık [salataluhk] cucumber
salata sosu salad dressing
salça [salcha] tomato sauce
  or paste
salçalı [salchaluh] with
  tomato sauce
salçalı köfte [kurfteh]
  meatballs in tomato sauce
salyongoz snails
sandviç [sandveech] sandwich
sandviç ekmeği [ekmeh-ee]
  roll(s)
sap kerevizi celery
saray lokması [sarî lokmasuh]
  fried batter in syrup
sardalye [sardal-yeh] sardines
sarıgöz [saruhgurz] black
  bream

sarığıburma [saruh-uh-boorma]
  'Twisted Turban' – turban-
  shaped baklava
sarmısak [sarmuhsak] garlic
sazan carp
sazan güveç [gewvech] carp
  casserole
sazan kiremit carp baked on
  a tile
sebze [sebzeh] vegetables
sebze çorbası [chorbasuh]
  vegetable soup
semizotu purslane – a herb
  used in salads and stews
semizotu salatası [salatasuh]
  purslane salad
servis course
servis ücreti service charge
sıcak [suhjak] hot; warm
sığır (eti) [suh-uhr] beef
sigara böreği [burreh-ee]
  cigarette-shaped filo pastry
  filled with cheese and
  parsley
simit ring-shaped bread
  covered with sesame seeds
sirke [seerkeh] vinegar
sivribiber long, thin hot or
  mild peppers
siyah zeytin [seeyaн zayteen]
  black olives
soğan [soh-an] onion(s)
soğan dolması [dolmasuh]
  stuffed onions
soğuk [soh-ook] cold
soğuk antreler [so-ook] cold
  hors d'œuvres
soğuk büfe [bewfeh] cold
  food

som balığı [sohm baluh-**uh**] salmon

somun loaf

sos sauce; gravy; salad dressing

sosis sausage

soslu with sauce

sote [sot**eh**] sautéed

söğüş et [so-e**w**sh] cold meat

söğüş salata salad served without dressing

su böreği [bur-r**eh**-ee] layered pastry filled with cheese, parsley and dill

sucuk [sooj**ook**] spicy Turkish sausage with garlic

sucuklu with sausage

sucuklu pide [peed**eh**] flat bread with sausage

sumak sumach – herb eaten with kebabs •

su muhallebisi rice flour pudding with rosewater

supanglez chocolate pudding

sülün [sewl**ewn**] pheasant

süt [sewt] milk

sütlaç [sewtl**ach**] rice pudding

sütlü tatlılar [sewtl**ew** latluhlar] milk puddings

süzme yoğurt [sewzmeh yoh **oo**rt] strained yoghurt

şalgam [shalg**am**] turnip

şamfıstığı [shamfuhst**uh**-uh] pistachio nuts

şam tatlısı [sham tatluhs**uh**] dessert with syrup

şeftali [sheftal**ee**] peach(es)

şeftali reçeli [rechel**ee**] peach jam

şehriye [sheHree-y**eh**] vermicelli

şehriye çorbası [chorbas**uh**] vermicelli soup with lemon

şehriyeli with vermicelli

şehriyeli pilav rice with vermicelli

şeker [shek**er**] sugar; sweets, candies

şekerpare [shekerpar**eh**] small cakes with syrup

şinitzel [sheeneetz**el**] cutlet, thin slice of meat

şiş [sheesh] cooked on a skewer

şiş kebabı [kebab**uh**] small pieces of lamb grilled on skewers

şiş köfte [kurft**eh**] grilled meatballs on skewers

şöbiyet [surbe-y**et**] sweet pastry

şurup [shoor**oop**] syrup

tabldot set menu

tahin helvası [helvas**uh**] sesame seed paste helva

talaşkebabı [talashkebab**uh**] lamb baked in pastry

tam ekmek wholemeal bread

tarama roe pâté

tarator nut and garlic sauce

taratorlu karnabahar cauliflower with nut and garlic sauce

tarhana çorbası [chorbasuh] soup made with dried yoghurt, tomato and pimento

taskebabı [taskebabuh] diced lamb with rice

tatar böreği [bur-reh-ee] ravioli

tatlı [tatluh] sweet, dessert

tatlı sucuk [soojook] fruit, nut and molasses roll

tava(da) fried

tavşan [tavshan] rabbit

tavuk chicken

tavuk çorbası [chorbasuh] chicken soup

tavuk göğsü [gur-sew] chicken breast pudding – creamy dessert made with rice flour and finely shredded chicken

tavuk ızgara(sı) [uhzgara(suh)] grilled chicken

tavuklu pilav chicken and rice

tavuk söğüş [sur-ewsh] cold chicken

tavuk suyu chicken consommé

taze [tazeh] fresh

taze beyaz peynir [bayaz payneer] fresh sheep's cheese

taze soğan [soh-an] spring onions

tekir striped mullet

tel kadayıf [kadī-uhf] shredded wheat-type dessert with nuts and syrup

terbiye [terbee-yeh] egg and lemon sauce

terbiyeli with egg and lemon sauce

terbiyeli haşlama [hashlama] boiled lamb with egg and lemon sauce

terbiyeli köfte [kurfteh] meatballs with egg and lemon sauce

tere [tereh] cress

tereyağı [tereh-ya-uh] butter

ton balığı [baluh-uh] tuna

torik large tunny fish

tost toast; toasted sandwich

tulumba tatlısı [tatluhsuh] semolina doughnut in syrup

tulum peyniri [payneeree] dry, crumbly, parmesan-like cheese made from goat's milk in a goatskin

turna pike

turp radish

turşu [toorshoo] pickled vegetables

turşu suyu juice from pickled vegetables

turta fruit pie

turunç [tooroonch] Seville oranges

tuz salt

tuzlama salted; pickled

tükenmez [tewkenmez] eggs fried with tomatoes and peppers/capsicums

türlü (sebze) [tewrlew (sebzeh)] meat and vegetable stew

un flour

un helvası [helvasuh] helva
made from flour, sugar,
milk, butter, and sometimes
with nuts
Urfa kebabı [kebabuh] very
spicy kebab
uskumru mackerel
uskumru dolması [dolmasuh]
stuffed mackerel

üzüm [ewzewm] grapes

vanilya vanilla
vanilyalı dondurma [vaneel-
yaluh] vanilla ice cream
vişne [veeshneh] black
cherries, morello cherries

yağ [ya] oil; fat
yağda yumurta [ya-da] fried
egg
yahni meat stew with onions
yalancı dolma [yalanjuh]
stuffed vine leaves
yaprak dolması [dolmasuh]
stuffed vine leaves
yayın sheatfish
yayla çorbası [yıla chorbasuh]
yoghurt soup
yaz türlüsü [tewrlewsew]
stewed summer vegetables
yemek meal; dish
yemek listesi menu
yengeç [yengech] crab
yerfıstığı [yerfuhstuh-uh]
peanuts
yeşil biber [yesheel] green
pepper, capsicum
yeşil mercimek çorbası

[merjeemek chorbasuh] green
lentil soup
yeşil salata green salad
yeşil zeytin [zayteen] green
olives
yiyecek [yee-yejek] food
yoğurt [yoh-oort] yoghurt
yoğurtlu with yoghurt
yoğurtlu kebap kebab with
pitta bread and yoghurt
yoğurtlu paça [pacha] lamb's
trotters with yoghurt and
garlic
yoğurt tatlısı [tatluhsuh]
yoghurt cake with syrup
yufka filo pastry
yufka ekmek thin sheets of
unleavened bread
yumurta egg
yumurtalı [yoomoortaluh] with
egg
yumurtalı pide [peedeh] flat
bread with egg
yürek [yewrek] heart

zerde [zerdeh] saffron rice
dessert
zeytin [zayteen] olive(s)
zeytinyağı [zayteenya-uh] olive
oil
zeytinyağlı [zayteenya-luh]
vegetable dish in olive oil,
served cold
zeytinyağlı biber dolması
[dolmasuh] stuffed peppers/
capsicums cooked with
olive oil
zeytinyağlı enginar artichokes
cooked with olive oil

Menu Reader: Food

zeytinyağlı kereviz celery
cooked with olive oil

zeytinyağlı patlıcan pilavı
[patluhjan peelavuh] rice with
aubergines/eggplants
cooked in olive oil

zeytinyağlı pırasa [puhrasa]
leeks cooked with olive oil

zeytinyağlı pilaki red haricot
beans cooked with olive oil

zeytinyağlı taze bakla [tazeh]
fresh broad beans cooked
with olive oil

zeytinyağlı taze fasulye
[fasoolyeh] runner beans
cooked with tomatoes and
olive oil

zeytinyağlı yaprak dolması
[dolmasuh] vine leaves
stuffed with rice, pine nuts
and raisins

Menu Reader: Drink

Essential Terms

beer bira
bottle şişe [sheesheh]
brandy konyak
coffee kahve [kaHveh]
cup fincan [feenjan]
alcoholic drinks içkiler [eechkeeleer]
gin cin [jeen]
glass (tumbler) bardak
  (wine glass) kadeh
milk süt [sewt]
mineral water maden suyu
red wine kırmızı şarap [kuhrmuhzuh sharap]
soda (water) maden sodası [sodasuh]
soft drinks meşrubat [meshroobat]
sugar şeker [sheker]
tea çay [chī]
tonic (water) tonik
vodka votka
water su
whisky viski
white wine beyaz şarap [bayaz sharap]
wine şarap
wine list şarap listesi

another ... başka bir ... [bashka]
a glass of tea bir bardak çay
a gin and tonic bir cintonik [jeentoneek]

acıbadem likörü [ajuhbadem leekur**ew**] almond liqueur

açık [ach**uh**k] weak

ada çayı [chī-**uh**] type of sage infusion

alkol alcohol

alkollü [alkoll**ew**] alcoholic

alkolsüz [–**sewz**] non-alcoholic

alkolsüz içki [eechk**ee**] soft drink

ananas suyu pineapple juice

ayran [ıran] yoghurt drink

az şekerli kahve [shekerl**ee** ka**h**v**eh**] slightly sweetened Turkish coffee

bardak glass

beyaz şarap [bayaz shar**a**p] white wine

bira beer; lager

bitkisel çay [chī] herbal tea

boza thick fermented grain drink

buz [b**oo**z] ice

buzlu with ice

buzlu kahve [ka**h**v**eh**] iced coffee

cin [jeen] gin

cintonik gin and tonic

Çankaya [chankī-**a**] dry, white wine from Cappadocia

çay [chī] tea

çok şekerli kahve [chok shekerl**ee** ka**h**v**eh**] very sweet Turkish coffee

demli steeped

domates suyu tomato juice

dömi sek [durm**ee**] medium-dry

Efes Pilsen® type of lager

elma çayı [chī-**uh**] apple tea

elma suyu apple juice

elma şırası [shuhras**uh**] cider

fıçı birası [fuhch**uh** beeras**uh**] draught beer

fincan [feenj**a**n] cup

gazlı [gazl**uh**] fizzy

gazoz fizzy drink

greyfrut suyu grapefruit juice

ıhlamur [uh-Hlam**oor**] lime blossom tea

içecek [eechej**e**k] beverage

içki [eechk**ee**] alcoholic drinks

içkiler [eechkeel**ee**r] alcoholic drinks

içkili [eechkeel**ee**] alcoholic drinks served

ithal imported

kafeinsiz kahve [kafeh-eens**eez** ka**h**v**eh**] decaffeinated coffee

kahve [ka**h**v**eh**] coffee; coffee shop (usually for men only)

kakao [kaka-o] hot chocolate; cocoa

kanyak [kanyak] French brandy

kayısı suyu [ka-yuhs**uh**] apricot juice

kırmızı şarap [kuhrmuhz**uh** sharap] red wine
konyak brandy
koyu steeped
köpüklü şarap [kurpewkl**ew** sharap] sparkling wine

Lāl dry, rosé wine from Denizli
likör [leek**ur**] liqueur
limonata still lemon drink
limonlu çay [ch**ī**] lemon tea

maden sodası [sodas**uh**] soda (water)
maden suyu mineral water
Marmara® type of lager
menba suyu spring water
meşrubat [meshroob**at**] soft drinks
meyve suyu [mayv**eh**] fruit juice
milkşeyk [meelksh**ayk**] milkshake
Mocca® almond liqueur

Narbağ [narb**a**] white, medium-dry wine from Central Anatolia
neskafe [neskaf**eh**] general word for any instant coffee

orta şekerli kahve [shekerl**ee** kaHv**eh**] medium sweet Turkish coffee

papatya çayı [ch**ī-uh**] camomile tea

pembe şarap [pemb**eh** sharap] rosé
portakal suyu orange juice
porto şarabı [sharab**uh**] port

rakı [rak**uh**] spirit distilled from grape juice and flavoured with aniseed, similar to Greek ouzo
rom rum
roze [roz**eh**] rosé

sade kahve [sad**eh** kaHv**eh**] Turkish coffee without sugar
sahlep drink made from sahlep root infused in hot milk and cinnamon
sek dry; straight (no ice)
sek şarap [shar**ap**] dry wine
sıcak süt [suhjak sewt] hot milk
su water
suyla [soo-il**a**] with water
suyu juice
süt [sewt] milk
sütlü [sewtl**ew**] with milk
sütlü kahve [kaHv**eh**] coffee with milk
süzme kahve [sewzm**eh**] filter coffee

şampanya [shamp**a**nya] champagne
şarap [shar**ap**] wine
şarap listesi wine list
şaraplar wines
şeftali suyu [sheftal**ee**] peach juice

şeker [sheker] sugar
şekerli [shekerlee] with sugar
şerbet [sherbet] sweetened
  and iced fruit juice
şeri [sheree] sherry
şıra [shuhra] grape juice
şişe [sheesheh] bottle

tatlı şarap [tatluh sharap] sweet
  wine
taze portakal suyu [tazeh]
  fresh orange juice
tonik tonic (water)
torba çay [chī] teabags
Tuborg® type of lager
Turasan® dry red or white
  wine from Central Anatolia
Türk kahvesi [tewrk kaнvesee]
  Turkish coffee

Venus® type of lager
viski whisky, scotch
vişne suyu [veeshneh] black
  cherry juice
votka vodka

Yakut dry, red wine
yarım şişe [yaruhm sheesheh]
  half-bottle
Yeni Rakı® [rakuh] brand of
  raki
yerli Turkish brand